BIBLICAL A-Z CHARACTERS

Getting Discipled for Exploits

ABIODUN A. OLAJIRE

BIBLICAL A-Z CHARACTERs

Except otherwise stated, all scriptural quotations are taken from the New Living Translation (NLT)

Contents

Introduction

This book is intended to help children and all readers identify and understand the lives of biblical characters that could serve as role models or someone they can pattern their lives after to experience the realness of God's nature, while they also apply every lesson learned to their lives for a better life, family, society, nation, and world at large.

When God completed all His work of creation, including you and me; He testified that everything He made was good[1]. God's agenda for all His creation is to have and live a good peaceable life. Due to man's carelessness, he lost out on God's original plan for him. However, because of God's unending love for us, He made lots of provisions that could reconnect us back to His original plan if we are willing to commit to the demands. Among many avenues is the gift of His only begotten Son, "Jesus," as a major and primary point of reconciliation.

"If you openly declare that Jesus is Lord and believe in your heart that God raised him from the dead, you will be saved."[1]

---

1   Romans 10:9

Anyone who is willing to be reconnected back to God's original plan for their lives must profess Jesus as their Lord and Savior by saying this simple prayer of salvation:

"Lord Jesus, I accept you as my Lord and Savior; forgive all my sins and wash me with your blood, I believe you died and rose on the third day for my sins, and to be reconciled with God. Engrace me to walk with you all the days of my life. Take away the desire for anything ungodly from my life right now. I believe all my sins are forgiven; I'm justified by your blood. Thank you, Jesus, because I am saved and born again."

Congratulations!

Now that the salvation prayer has been said, the next thing is to look into the perfect law of liberty to discover other provisions God has in store for us to live a life worthy of emulation.

"But if you look carefully into the perfect law that sets you free, and if you do what it says and don't forget what you heard, then God will bless you for doing it."[2]

One of those provisions is living a life patterned after the Word of God. Throughout the Scripture, great men who were servants of God, apostles, preachers, and lovers of

---

2 James 1:25

God, lived a life worthy of emulation. Learning, walking, and applying their principles to our lives will take us one step closer to those plans of God for us.

'This is what the Lord says: "Stop at the crossroads and look around. Ask for the old, godly way, and walk in it. Travel its path, and you will find rest for your souls. But you reply, 'No, that's not the road we want!'[3]

This book will reveal to us the lives of men and women from the pages of the Bible worthy of emulation or that we can learn from. Be blessed and inspired as you read.

---

3 Jeremiah 6:16

Chapter 1

ABRAHAM

—◆◇◇◉◇◇◆—

Abraham - The friend of God.

He was a native of Ur in Mesopotamia, and his father's name was Terah. At 75 years old, God brought him out of limitation and stagnation into the fulfilment of destiny. God has a good plan for you and me, just as He had for Abraham[4]

'For I know the plans I have for you," says the Lord. "They are plans for good and not for disaster, to give you a future and a hope'.[5]

However, it will take our prompt obedience to God's instruction to walk into the fulfillment of destiny.

---

4 See Genesis 12:1-4
5 Jeremiah 29:11

"If they listen and obey God, they will be blessed with prosperity throughout their lives. All their years will be pleasant."[6]

Abraham was a man of obedience, he never had a problem following God's instruction; as a result, God blessed him. If we can commit ourselves to obey the instructions of God to the letter without complaints or murmuring, we set ourselves on that part of being called a friend of God like Abraham.

"It was by faith that Abraham obeyed when God called him to leave home and go to another land that God would give him as his inheritance. He went without knowing where he was going."[7]

Abraham secured generational blessings and preservation just by obeying God foolishly. Every time God gave an instruction, he moved without knowing what will happen and how it will happen. Abraham brought himself to a place of trust that God who made everything will not be wicked to lead him astray. His selfless act of prompt obedience always invokes the integrity of God, and God will never allow His name or reputation to be soiled.

"And God gave a set of instructions to Abraham, though difficult; Abraham judge God faithful by carrying out those set of instructions. God had no choice but proclaim eternal blessings over Abraham"[8]

---

6   Job 36:11
7   Hebrews 11:8
8   Genesis 22:1-19 Paraphrased

Abraham's humility was a key in his quest for obedience to God. Only those who are humble can be guided or led, and Abraham used this to his own advantage.

"He leads the humble in doing right, teaching them his way."[9]

We can also commit to obeying the set of instructions God gives to us daily, either from the Bible or through the people placed over our lives with humility and trust in God. Doing so will make us enjoy the same thing Abraham enjoyed. Remember, Jesus admonishes that if we are truly the children of Abraham, then we should do his works[10]

ATTRIBUTES OF ABRAHAM

Obedience: "If you will only obey me, you will have plenty to eat." A wise man once said, "Obedience may be costly, but the result is rewarding." That is what we saw in the life of Abraham. He was committed to obeying God no matter how difficult it was. The Bible says the commandments of God are not grievous11. It is the demonstration of our love for Him, and love is a potent tool to move the hand of God in our direction.

---

9   Psalms 25:9
10 John 8:39
11 1 John 5:3

"Those who accept my commandments and obey them are the ones who love me. And because they love me, my Father will love them. And I will love them and reveal myself to each of them."[12]

From the moment God called and began to give Abraham instructions, he had no reason to doubt God or question God's authority. He simply moved in obedience and asked for guidance if and when necessary. No wonder Abraham became the friend of God, and God could even vouch for him as His friend. If we want to be the friend of God, we must be committed to being obedient. We must remember that God will only show up at the end of a completed obedience circle. Many today have failed to see or hear from God at the end of their obedience circle, not because God is not ready to uphold the end of His bargain or words but because we deviated along the way, when carrying out those instructions, to what we like before completing that which God commanded us.

"The LORD had said to Abram, "Leave your native country, your relatives, and your father's family, and go to the land that I will show you. [2] I will make you into a great nation. I will bless you and make you famous, and you will be a blessing to others. [3] I will bless those who bless you and curse those who treat you with contempt. All the families on earth will be blessed through you." [4] So Abram departed as the LORD had instructed, and Lot went with him. Abram was seventy-five years old when he left Haran. [5] He took his wife, Sarai,

---

12 John 14:21

his nephew Lot, and all his wealth—his livestock and all the people he had taken into his household at Haran—and headed for the land of Canaan. When they arrived in Canaan, ⁶ Abram traveled through the land as far as Shechem. There he set up camp beside the oak of Moreh. At that time, the area was inhabited by Canaanites. ⁷ Then the LORD appeared to Abram and said, "I will give this land to your descendants." And Abram built an altar there and dedicated it to the LORD, who had appeared to him."¹³

Abraham left immediately God told him to depart, kept following the instructions and at the end of his circle of obedience, God reappeared to uphold His end of the bargain. Only if we can be like Abraham, who refused to be distracted but was committed to carrying the instructions. Today, many of us have fallen a victim to distraction along our journey to fulfill God's purpose for our lives. It is never too late to re-align and ask God for mercy. My mentor once said, "It is never late to make a U-turn when going the wrong way." The Scripture says if we are indeed the seed of Abraham, then we should do exactly what he did to secure the hand of God in our lives¹⁴

Humble: Being in a state of humility does not make you dumb, or less of a person. It is a demonstration of strength and wisdom that enables you to submit to another authority to achieve a purpose regardless of your status.

---

13 Genesis 12:1-7
14 John 8:39

"6 Though he was God, he did not think of equality with God as something to cling to. 7 Instead, he gave up his divine privileges[b]; he took the humble position of a slave and was born as a human being. When he appeared in human form, 8 he humbled himself in obedience to God and died a criminal's death on a cross. 9 Therefore, God elevated him to the place of highest honor and gave him the name above all other names,"[15]

Abraham listened and followed God's direction without complaint. If we desire to experience the order of blessings Abraham enjoyed with God, we must be willing and ready to be mentored by the life of Abraham and do the same.

"He leads the humble in doing right, teaching them his way."[16]

Being humble is not foolishness, but the ability to recognize and submit to the authority of the one who is better and is capable of making things happen. When we live a life of humility, we bring ourselves under the tutelage of a superior authority that is able to make our life count. Note that being under a superior authority is not a function of age, but a function of the ability, knowledge, or insights possessed by the superior authority. We may decide to claim we know, but it will not harm even if we still bring ourselves to learn from others. Abraham, though a man of choice like all of us[17], he still subjected himself to the leading of God.

---

15 Philippians 2:6-9
16 Psalms 25:9
17 Deuteronomy 30:19

"Anyone who claims to know all the answers doesn't really know very much."[18]

Abraham's meek nature allowed him to yield the good and flourishing land to his cousin, Lot, while he took the patched land. Sometimes, some things are not worth fighting over because everything God made and placed in our path, regardless of its physical appearance, is meant to result in beauty.

"And we know that God causes everything to work together for the good of those who love God and are called according to his purpose for them."[19]

If we are meek enough, we will know that we were called to a life of purpose and fulfillment in God regardless of the present situation. At that point, Lot thought he had picked the best thing that could ever happen to man, but Abraham was wise enough to trust God to bring the best out of the worst situation.

"[8] Finally Abram said to Lot, "Let's not allow this conflict to come between us or our herdsmen. After all, we are close relatives! [9] The whole countryside is open to you. Take your choice of any section of the land you want, and we will separate. If you want the land to the left, then I'll take the land on the right. If you prefer the land on the right, then I'll go to the left." [10] Lot took a long look at the fertile

---

18 1 Corinthians 8:2
19 Romans 8:28

plains of the Jordan Valley in the direction of Zoar. The whole area was well watered everywhere, like the garden of the LORD or the beautiful land of Egypt. (This was before the LORD destroyed Sodom and Gomorrah.) [11] *Lot chose for himself the whole Jordan Valley to the east of them. He went there with his flocks and servants and parted company with his uncle Abram.* [12] *So Abram settled in the land of Canaan, and Lot moved his tents to a place near Sodom and settled among the cities of the plain.* [13] *But the people of this area were extremely wicked and constantly sinned against the LORD.* [14] *After Lot had gone, the LORD said to Abram, "Look as far as you can see in every direction—north and south, east and west.* [15] *I am giving all this land, as far as you can see, to you and your descendants as a permanent possession.* [16] *And I will give you so many descendants that, like the dust of the earth, they cannot be counted!* [17] *Go and walk through the land in every direction, for I am giving it to you."*[20]

Every time we exhibit our meek nature, we subscribe to the leading of God that will make us inherit the blessings of God.

"God blesses those who are humble, for they will inherit the whole earth."[21]

"The lowly will possess the land and will live in peace and prosperity."[22]

Trust: Abraham demonstrated his trust in God throughout

---

20 Genesis 13:8-17
21 Matthew 5:5
22 Psalms 37:11

his lifetime by doing exactly what he was told to do. He never had a moment to create a contingency plan for God's instruction, he trusted God without any iota of doubt that he risked everything, including his personality. His trust in God secured him a medal of righteousness[23]

"[17] That is what the Scriptures mean when God told him, "I have made you the father of many nations." This happened because Abraham believed in the God who brings the dead back to life and who creates new things out of nothing. [18] Even when there was no reason for hope, Abraham kept hoping—believing that he would become the father of many nations. For God had said to him, "That's how many descendants you will have!" [19] And Abraham's faith did not weaken, even though, at about 100 years of age, he figured his body was as good as dead—and so was Sarah's womb. [20] Abraham never wavered in believing God's promise. In fact, his faith grew stronger, and in this he brought glory to God. [21] He was fully convinced that God is able to do whatever he promises."[24]

Those who trust God are never weak in faith, their eyes are constantly on Him, and they are persuaded and certain that God will never fail.

"Those who look to him for help will be radiant with joy; no shadow of shame will darken their faces."[25]

---

23 Genesis 15:5, Romans 4:22
24 Romans 4:17-21
25 Psalms 34:5

It may look like shame is staring you and me in the face, or we risk being mocked for trusting God. We must remember that all things, whether working good or bad for us, in our favor or not; are all expected to turn out good at the end in our favor says the word of God[26]

We must learn to trust God like our father Abraham, and we will never see or experience shame. All through the scriptures, we saw men and women who trusted God even in the face of death, and they came out victorious. The three Hebrew boys, Meshach, Shadrach, and Abednego, trusted God for their rescue even when death was in their faces.

"[16] Shadrach, Meshach, and Abednego replied, "O Nebuchadnezzar, we do not need to defend ourselves before you. [17] If we are thrown into the blazing furnace, the God whom we serve is able to save us. He will rescue us from your power, Your Majesty. [18] But even if he doesn't, we want to make it clear to you, Your Majesty, that we will never serve your gods or worship the gold statue you have set up."[27]

David trusted God to deliver Goliath into his hand. "Today the LORD will conquer you, and I will kill you and cut off your head. And then I will give the dead bodies of your men to the birds and wild animals, and the whole world will know that there is a God in Israel!"[28]

---

26 Romans 8:28
27 Daniel 3:16-18
28 1 Samuel 17:46

The woman with the issue of blood after spending all her life savings on doctors still did not get the healing she wanted. She made up her mind that if only she could touch the tip of Jesus' cloth, her health will be restored. She was not even waiting to be touched by Jesus physically. Of course, her trust in God secured her healing for her.[29]

The key word in David's statement to Goliath in the scenario is "This day, the Lord will", not "David will." Likewise, the three Hebrew boys and the woman with the issue of blood. They Judged God faithful to do what only He can do.

"And it is impossible to please God without faith. Anyone who wants to come to him must believe that God exists and that he rewards those who sincerely seek him."[30]

To secure the hand of God in our situation, we must learn to cast all our care upon God responsibly and believe that He will definitely come to our rescue.

Hospitable: We have been called to a life of hospitality, of course; taking care of ourselves, while we also look out for others around us who may be in one need or the other. Hospitality rendered should go beyond those who are in need, but to others who may even be in a better place than us. It is an expression of love and care towards people around

---

29 Matthew 9:21, Mark 5:24-29, Luke 8:43-44
30 Hebrews 11:6

11

us regardless of their background or status[31]   Abraham extended his hospitality to total strangers, unbeknown to him that they were carriers of what he needed in his life. This singular act of his secured him the blessings he had longed for a while.

"And Abraham entertained strangers, and his long-awaited desire was delivered to him. And the Lord visited Sarah as he had said, and the Lord did unto Sarah as he had spoken."[32]

"For Sarah conceived, and bare Abraham a son in his old age, at the set time of which God had spoken to him."[33]

The scriptures remind us that whatever a man sows he will reap. Extending a good hand to others is simply sowing a seed that could eventually be a generational harvest. Our act of kindness should be futuristic, and not immediate only.

Let us look at this analogy: When a man pulls a bowl of water, and then throws it up into the air, the water eventually pours back on him except he tries to run away. You will agree with me that no one runs away from the good they have done. They stand by it, even when they don't look for a return, it comes looking for them because it is a law. There is always a harvest time.

---

31   Mark 12:31, Matthew 25:35-45
32   Genesis 18:2-10 Paraphrased
33   Genesis 21:1-3 Paraphrased

The scripture shared the story of Jonathan, and how he did right by tipping off David about his father's treacherous plan. As a result, he secured a blessing beyond himself that was extended to his child.

"One day David asked, "Is anyone in Saul's family still alive— anyone to whom I can show kindness for Jonathan's sake?"[34]

A good seed will always produce and outlive the planter making him a blessing to other generations after him. We must live a life of love, care, kindness, and support because they are all encapsulated in hospitality. We should not live a life driven by our possessions, but a life driven by empathy and love toward others[35]

It is important to know that we live in a world filled with people with different thoughts and dispositions. Every act of hospitality should be done with the wisdom, and guidance of the Holy Spirit[36]

BENEFITS OF ABRAHAM'S ATTRIBUTES

Obedience: It is the pathway to a life of fulfillment, as it ushers our path through the thorns of life to reach our destination in peace, and not in pieces.

---

34   2 Samuel 9:1
35   Mark 12:31, Luke 12:15
36   Psalms 74:20

"Stay on the path that the LORD your God has commanded you to follow. Then you will live long and prosperous lives in the land you are about to enter and occupy."[37]

When we live a life of obedience, we secure access to the heavenly GPS that leads and guides us to our place of glory and honor. That heavenly GPS is the voice of God.

"Your own ears will hear him. Right behind you a voice will say, "This is the way you should go, whether to the right or to the left"[38]

God will only guide those who subscribe to His instructions. Abraham was devoted to following God's instructions, no wonder God released upon him trans-generational blessings.

"God instructed Abraham to depart into purpose and fulfilment, and Abraham departed…"[39]

The key word in the verse was Abraham departed as the Lord instructed him. He did not even bother to ask questions about what the journey entailed. He moved foolishly. Of course, it is okay to ask questions for clarity when instructions are given for the purpose of understanding, but when you understand who the Giver of instructions is, and His capability; you move excitedly before remembering to even ask for a breakdown of the instructions. Most

---

37 Deuteronomy 5:33
38 Isaiah 30:21
39 Genesis 12:1-4 Paraphrased

times, when God gives instructions, we want to analyze them before making a move. And if care is not taken, that analysis may lead to disobedience which may be costly.

"This is what the LORD says: "Stop at the crossroads and look around. Ask for the old, godly way, and walk in it. Travel its path, and you will find rest for your souls. But you reply, 'No, that's not the road we want!'"[40]

Those who follow God sheepishly like a sheep will follow the shepherd, are never grounded.

"They were not thirsty when he led them through the desert. He divided the rock, and water gushed out for them to drink."[41]

We must ensure we live a life of obedience in order to enjoy the blessings of God. Sometimes, those instructions may come with difficulties, or appear irrational; remember that God will always use the foolish things of this world to confound the wise[42] Also, we must remember that the likes of fine gold and diamonds are brought out of unimaginable places. If the miners dare to consider the location of these precious ornaments, they wouldn't dig them out.

The mother of Jesus told the stewards at the marriage in Cana, "Whatever He tells you to do, do it"[43] Sheepishly,

---

40 Jeremiah 6:16
41 Isaiah 48:21
42 1 Corinthians 1:27
43 John 2:5

they did it without analyzing what the instructions were. Of course, at the instance of the instruction, their human reasoning will tell them the result of pouring water into the jar will result in drawing out water back, but they chose to align their mental state with that of Jesus at that moment, forsaking their own human reasoning and the miraculous happened. Every time we align our reasoning in obedience to God's instruction, we gain access into the mind of God that will enable us to operate beyond the normal.

"Who can know the LORD's thoughts? Who knows enough to teach him?" But we understand these things, for we have the mind of Christ."[44]

When we live a life of obedience like our father Abraham, we unlock the heavenly GPS, and the treasure room of sworn blessings.

Genesis 22:17-18 "That in blessing I will bless thee, and in multiplying I will multiply thy seed as the stars of the heaven, and as the sand which is upon the seashore; and thy seed shall possess the gate of his enemies; And in thy seed shall all the nations of the earth be blessed, because thou hast obeyed my voice.

Humility: One of the most dangerous things in life is to live life in a vacuum, not knowing what to do or how to go.

---

44 1 Corinthians 2:16

"The labor of a fool so wearies him [because he is ignorant] that he does not even know how to go to a city."[45]

He knows there is a way, but he lacks access to the things that will help him go around his business and other things around the city. Many of us are like him, some of us know our purpose, but we lack access to those things that will get us there. While some don't even have any clue. A life of humility will secure for us the necessary help that will help us discover and navigate life in order to fulfill purpose.

"The meek will he guide in judgment: and the meek will he teach his way."[46]

Those who are guided are guarded against the wolves of life as they sojourn towards fulfilling purpose.

"And the disciples went everywhere and preached, and the Lord worked through them, confirming what they said by many miraculous signs."[47]

From the above scripture, we see that those who subscribe to the guidance and leading of God secure partnership with Him, and also the fulfilment of their given assignment.

---

45   Ecclessiastes 10:15 AMP
46   Psalms 25:9 KJV
47   Mark 16:20

"Jesus sent out the disciples on an assignment with strict instructions, and they departed and returned with good news."[48]

The revelation from the above verse is that those who follow instructions in humility will always return with results to show. It is important to do away with the spirit of pride in order not to miss out of God's divine agenda for our lives. Moses was termed the meekest man because he understood the secret behind total dependence on God in a responsible way.

"(Now Moses was very humble—more humble than any other person on earth.)"[49]

"Then Moses said, "If you don't personally go with us, don't make us leave this place."[50] *In order words, Moses was saying, "without You we can do nothing"*[51]

When you are humble like Abraham, God will guide and teach you things you don't know.

Trust: It gives us access to secrets that guarantee returns on our investment with God. When we trust God, heavenly trade secrets are revealed to us, and these secrets boost and give us confidence in all that we do.

---

48   Luke 19:1-7, 10 Paraphrased
49   Numbers 12:3
50   Exodus 33:15
51   John 15:5, Proverbs 3:5-6, Zechariah 4:6

"The LORD is a friend to those who fear him. He teaches them his covenant."[52]

"But blessed are those who trust in the LORD and have made the LORD their hope and confidence."[53]

"¹ Those who trust in the LORD are as secure as Mount Zion; they will not be defeated but will endure forever. ² Just as the mountains surround Jerusalem, so the LORD surrounds his people, both now and forever."[54]

We can then say that trusting God gives us confidence regardless of the negative situations because God will always show us the template of escape from the situation. Our trust in God will also secure for us His eternal preservation, provisions, and exemption no matter what is befalling the world around us.

A songwriter said, "It is very sweet to trust in God", and why is that? It is because true lovers will always trust each other with secrets, and the only secret lovers will always share with themselves are secrets that will benefit them and also protect them from harm. No wonder, when you see true lovers; they are always excited because they share one bond which is trust that is built on true love, not deceit.

---

52 Psalms 25:14
53 Jeremiah 17:7
54 Psalms 25:1-2

"8Most important of all, continue to show deep love for each other, for love covers a multitude of sins. 9 Cheerfully share your home with those who need a meal or a place to stay. 10 God has given each of you a gift from his great variety of spiritual gifts. Use them well to serve one another."55

Prayer: Lord, grant me the grace to be humble, and obedient, even as I exercise my trust in You.

Chapter 2

BOAZ

Boaz was a native of Judea. He was Ruth's brother-in-law, and king David's great-grandfather. He was kind and generous, owned a lot of lands where people farmed, was very wealthy, and was hardworking. Boaz was a very kind man who rewarded people around him with good gestures and favor.[56]

"Do you see any truly competent workers? They will serve kings rather than working for ordinary people"[57]

God expects us to be hardworking because hard work is rewarding.

---

56 Ruth 2 & 3
57 Proverbs 22:29

ATTRIBUTES OF BOAZ

Hard work: "Lazy people are soon poor; hard workers get rich."[58] God loves those who work hard because that is His nature. When you are diligent at your work, you preserve the present, and you protect the future in case of famine (Economy downturn). God expects us to be wise like the ants who prepare themselves for future uncertainties.[59] Hard work does not kill, it elevates, promotes, beautify, honor and bless. "Lazy people want much but get little, but those who work hard will prosper."[60] All through the Bible, everyone who worked hard was honored and rewarded. Therefore, whatever God commits into our hands as work, we must do it with all our hearts because it is an avenue that ushers in God's blessings. Psalm 128: 2 "You will enjoy the fruit of your labor. How joyful and prosperous you will be!"[61]

Our hard work portrays us as responsible individuals who are not willing to just sit idle. It is said always that there is dignity in labor.

Kindness: Boaz was a kind man. He reciprocated kindness and favor to people around him, including his employees. God expects us to be kind to one another. When we are

---

58 Proverbs 10:4
59 Proverbs 6:4-11
60 Proverbs 13:4
61 Psalms 128:2

kind to others, we make them feel loved and appreciated. "Be kind to one another, tenderhearted, forgiving one another, as God in Christ forgave you."[62] Our show and expression of love and kindness to others shows that we have the nature of God in us. Doing this selflessly will draw people to us and to God because they feel loved and cared for. The world today is broken and in disarray because genuine love is missing. The genuine love of God can be restored if only we take our focus off the external make up of others around us and focus on the real person behind the make up. Ruth was not of the same tribe as her husband and family, but she chose to love them even when what brought her to the family was no longer there. Her love was beyond the physical appearance of her in-laws. As a result, she encountered favor with her in-laws. Remember, whatsoever a man sows he will always reap, either directly or indirectly.

Wealthy: Boaz was a wealthy man. His wealth did not just appear like magic, he worked very hard, and was diligent. God's plan for you is to live a good life in wealth, but you must be diligent and hard-working. "Beloved, I pray that you may prosper in all things and be in health, just as your soul prospers."[63] God's ultimate goal for us is to prosper physically, spiritually, and health-wise, however; it will take us being responsible in our work to experience and enjoy

---

62 Ephesians 4:2 ESV
63 3 John 2 NKJV

23

those wishes. We must commit ourselves to genuine labor that guarantees wealth because any wealth not worked for will diminish. Our wealth puts us in a position where we can help others. Job was a wealthy man, his wealth was a result of hard work, and God blessed him.[64] Job also used his wealth to help the poor around him. " I served as eyes for the blind and feet for the lame. I was a father to the poor and assisted strangers who needed help."[65]

BENEFITS OF BOAZ ATTRIBUTES

Hard work: Hard work does not kill, it enhances man's ingenuity, forces personal development, and makes society a better place. Not everyone seeks to work hard because such individuals lack the mentality to engage. A diligent hard worker positions himself or herself for God to prosper and bless the work of their hands with riches and wealth.

"A hard worker has plenty of food, but a person who chases fantasies ends up in poverty. Hard work enthrones and beautifies."[66]

"All hard work brings a profit, but mere talk leads only to poverty. The wealth of the wise is their crown, but the folly of fools yields folly."[67]

---

64 Job 1:1-3
65 Job 29:15-16
66 Proverbs 28:19 NLT
67 Proverbs 14:23-24

Working hard does not equal dissipating energy, but smart work with results or proofs to show successful work. It is a demonstration of responsibility, which gives man a sense of belonging, stability, and fulfillment. The scriptures talk about how the hand of the diligent will bear rule, but a lazy person remains mediocre and may die in poverty. So, hard work does not kill, it sets a man on the path of greatness and success as long as they are willing to commit to the process. It is unfortunate that today's generation is not willing to commit to the process of hard work. The reason many are frustrated, angry, and penniless is that they broke the law process that guides hard work[68]) Every successful and lasting thing in life anchors on the boat of process.

It is important to note that not all hard work ends up in success. How the work is been done with the result it commands over a period will be the determinant. So, we must endeavor to work smart, I don't mean cutting corners, but applying wisdom, seeking counsel, studying materials, and asking God for direction. These are basically what will make the hard work translate into success[69]

Kindness: Kindness is looking beyond ourselves and considering others around us that may need our support. The act of kindness defuses tension, stress, and restores hope and love among people. A life of kindness, like that

---

68   Proverbs 13:11
69   Ecclessiastes 10:15

of Boaz, makes the world a better place for everyone. It creates an atmosphere of love, peace, joy, and happiness. Remember life is like a circle, what we do to others will come back to us.

"So then, as we have opportunity, let us be kind to everyone..."[70]

Apostle Paul shared with us how the people of the church in Macedonia expressed their kindness even in their poverty. Therefore, our kindness should not be limited to when we are rich, but a lifestyle because of the beauty that comes with it[71] Every good deed always gets rewarded.

"Your kindness will reward you, but your cruelty will destroy you."[72]

Wealth: The blessings of God in our lives are not just to take care of ourselves and our families. We are expected to extend the blessings of God in our lives to others around us. There are individuals who are only wealthy to themselves and family, and they think they are rich. It is the highest level of poverty anyone can think of. Being rich or wealthy is of the heart, and not in the abundance of papers stashed in banks or deposit boxes, nor accumulation of blocks of the building. The abundance of a man's wealth is in the number of persons he or she has impacted, lifted out of poverty, and supported.

---

70 Galatians 6:10 Paraphrased
71 2 Corinthians 8:2
72 Proverbs 11:17 NLT

"There is one who makes himself rich, yet *has* nothing; *And* one who makes himself poor, yet *has* great riches."[73]

"Give to those around you out of the abundance God has given to you, don't be selfish or greedy"[74]

When you use your wealth like Boaz to take care of those who are poor around you, you give them hope and make them feel loved. Doing this secures more of God's blessings, security, and provisions. "Whoever is kind to the poor lends to the LORD, and he will reward them for what they have done."[75] There will always be people among us who need help, and as a child of God, we are expected to help them with whatever we have.

"There will always be poor people in the land. Therefore I command you to be openhanded toward your fellow Israelites who are poor and needy in your land."[76]

Prayer: God, I pray for the grace and wisdom to be hardworking, exhibit acts of kindness, and help those around me with what you have blessed me with like Boaz. Amen!

---

73 Proverbs 13:7 NKJV
74 Deuteronomy 15:7-8 Paraphrased
75 Proverbs 19:17
76 Deuteronomy 15:11

Chapter 3

CAIN

Cain was the first son of Adam and Eve. He had a brother called Abel who was a keeper of sheep. Cain took a job for himself as a tilter of the ground, he planted and harvested fruits from his tilted ground. He offered some of his fruits as a gift unto God, just as his brother Abel also offered a gift to God from his herds. God expects us to bring gifts to Him, and doing this helps us secure the hand of God in all our activities. "But remember the LORD your God, for it is he who gives you the ability to produce wealth, and so confirms his covenant..."[77] It is also important to offer our gifts with a good heart and intention, if not, the gift will not be accepted by God. Cain was a victim of an imperfect heart; his heart was not right when he offered his gift to God, so God did not accept Cain's gift but He accepted his

---

77 Deuteronomy 8:18

brother's, Abel. This got Cain jealous and angry, he hurt his brother, and he suffered the consequences of his action. "…So Cain was very angry… Then the Lord said to Cain, "Why are you angry? … If you do what is right, will you not be accepted?"[78]

ATTRIBUTES OF CAIN

God first: Cain thought about giving God part of what God has given to him as blessings from his fruits. This was a good gesture on his part; however, he gave not the very best of his fruits. Note, God never asked him, it was a decision he made. "In the course of time Cain brought some of the fruits of the soil as an offering to the Lord."[79]

God is not in need, our giving to God is to secure and keep the pipeline of blessings open continually[80] Everything we have was given to us by God, therefore we must ensure we give with the sincerity of heart, and never under pressure or show off. What God needs from us is a gift coming from a genuine heart, and not any hypocritical giving.

"…No one can receive anything unless God gives it from heaven."[81] Cain gave God a gift from the blessings of God upon his life which was a good gesture, but not with the best of intentions. Even though he

---

78   Genesis 4:5-6 Paraphrased
79   Genesis 4:3
80   Isaiah 50:8-14
81   John 3:27

thought to give to God, he reserved not the very best for God. However, his brother Abel gave God the best of his produce, and God was pleased with him.

"And Abel also brought an offering—fat portions from some of the firstborn of his flock. The Lord looked with favor on Abel and his offering, but on Cain and his offering he did not look with favor."[82]

In everything we do unto God and the people around us, God expects us to do it with a good heart, and a right motive. "…God loves a cheerful giver."[83] "And he did that which was right in the sight of the LORD, but not with a perfect heart."[84]

There are many ways we can make God the priority in our lives, and it is not limited to just physical gifts. Time is one of the great gifts God gave to man, and how we spend it determines the outcome of our lives. Some give God a portion of their time, while some give their leftover, and some don't at all. God wants to take the first place in our life, and when we make Him so, He puts us on His priority list as well[85]

Giving: This is an act of love. It is a demonstration that we have the love of God shed abroad in our hearts. The

---

82 Genesis 4:4-5
83 2 Corinthians 9:7
84 2 Chronicles 25:2 KJV
85 Matthew 6:32-33

entire universe today came into existence because God gave His time to make it happen. Subsequently, when man failed to uphold the tenets of creation which led to a lot of damage, God gave again His best to fix the problem man created. So, there is power in giving. A wise man once said you can give and not love, such giving is anchored on necessity or obligation, but you cannot love and not give. Cain decided to practice the law of giving by giving a gift back to God. Genuine lovers are givers; parting with what they own to help mankind is a lifestyle to them, not those who give because they want to be known, or secure favor from fellow men.

"If I give all my possessions to feed the poor, and if I surrender my body to be burned, but do not have love, it does me no good at all."[86]

"And do not forget to do good and to share with others, for with such sacrifices God is pleased."[87]

Giving makes the giver and the receiver happy, and when we give with a joyful heart, God blesses us in return. "Give, and it will be given to you..."[88] Giving makes the world a better and happy place.

Anger: Anger is a demonstration of displeasure about something. It is okay to be displeased about something, but

---

86   1 Corinthians 13:3 AMP
87   Hebrews 13:16
88   Luke 6:38

it is dangerous to make decisions during a state of anger. Often, decisions made in anger results in regrets because it colors our perception and shapes our behavior. Sometimes, anger could be channeled positively in cases whereby one is tired of a status quo and desires a change. In all, it is important to always take a deep breath to calm down, or perhaps take a break or a walk to clear the head before decisions are made.

Cain's display of anger got him into trouble, and his displeasure about his unaccepted sacrifice, and the accepted sacrifice of his brother got him mad. As a result, rather than ask questions about why that happened, he gave himself up to his anger hormone which led to his wrong decision. God did warn him about the sin of anger but he failed to put it under control which led to killing his brother, and he suffered the consequence.

"And the LORD said to Cain, "Why are you so angry? And why do you look annoyed? If you do well, will you not be accepted? And if you do not do well [but ignore My instruction], sin crouches at your door; its desire is for you [to overpower you], but you must master it." Cain talked with Abel his brother [about what God had said]. And when they were [alone, working] in the field, Cain attacked Abel his brother and killed him."[89]

We must beware of anger; it can destroy a lot of things. Whenever we feel the urge to dispel the anger hormones,

---

89 Genesis 4:6-8 AMP

we must never give in to it. At the same time, we must carefully access the situation. When we take action in anger, it can lead to an unpleasant consequence that could harm us or anyone around us. "Stop being angry! Turn from your rage! Do not lose your temper— it only leads to harm."[90]

Jealousy: Jealousy is simply the display of low self-esteem, arrogance, pride, and insecurity; a feeling that makes one conclude the other person is better off, or their actions are better off. This is a very dangerous lane to tread; it can lead man into doing despicable and unacceptable things. Rather than succumb to such feelings, why not self-evaluate what to do better to be in that position, or just ask the other person for what they did that can serve as a guide. Most times, when we find other persons where we had anticipated ourselves to be and we are not there yet, the sense of jealousy kicks in. As humans, it is normal to react that way, but it is dangerous to operate in that mindset beyond the moment it was perceived. It could engineer the development of negative energy that could form our decision or behavior.

Cain's display of jealousy towards his brother, Abel, led to killing his brother making him the first murderer in history (of the Bible) which brought upon him shame and reproach.

"And now you are cursed from the ground, which has

---

90 Psalms 37:8

34

opened its mouth to receive your brother's [shed] blood from your hand. When you cultivate the ground, it shall no longer yield its strength [it will resist producing good crops] for you; you shall be a fugitive and a vagabond [roaming aimlessly] on the earth [in perpetual exile without a home, a degraded outcast]."[91]

Being jealous of others is not a good attribute, it leads to envy and such behavior could lead to execution of bad things, and bad things only get people into trouble. "Surely resentment destroys the…, and jealousy kills the simple."[92]

BENEFITS AND DISBENEFITS OF CAIN'S ATTRIBUTES

God First: When you put God first before other things, God honors you in return by giving you the first place in His life. "…for those who honor me I will honor."[93] "And you will love the Lord your God with all your heart…"[94]

"Seek first God's kingdom…"[95] When we do this, God adds to us whatever we need even without asking Him sometimes. Putting God first connotes making everything that matters to us secondary, while we make those things that matter to Him the priority. Doing this puts us on the frontline with

91 Genesis 4:11-12 AMP
92 Job 5:2
93 1 Samuel 2:30 AMP
94 Deuteronomy 6:5 AMP
95 Matthew 6:33 WEB

God for honor, favor, blessings, and preservation.

"Truly I tell you," Jesus replied, "no one who has left home or brothers or sisters or mother or father or children or fields for me and the gospel will fail to receive a hundred times as much in this present age: homes, brothers, sisters, mothers, children and fields—along with persecutions— and in the age to come eternal life."[96] All through the scriptures, everyone who made God a priority enjoyed the honor of God.

Giving: Giving to others around you makes the world a better place. The hand of the giver is always on top, and a giver never lacks because God will always supply their needs through others. "Give, and it will be given to you. "A good measure, pressed down, shaken together, and running over, will be poured into your lap..."[97]

When we make giving a lifestyle, extending our hands to others, we secure a place in the heart of God with a reward. "Whoever is kind to the poor lends to the LORD, and he will reward them for what they have done."[98] Among many other benefits, it secures our connection to the giver of all things, God.

The act of giving is not a one-time thing and is not limited

---

96 Mark 10:29-30
97 Luke 6:38
98 Proverbs 19:17

to cash gifts or other things like time, presence, prayer, love, encouragement, empathy, and support are what many people need. All these acts of giving make a beautiful environment.

Anger: Anger is not a good thing; it presents men with the opportunity to make bad decisions even when they are good people because their judgment at that moment of anger is clouded. People's decision-making skills in the moment of anger is impeded, and any action taken at that moment could lead to grave consequence. "For anger slays the foolish man, and jealousy kills the simple (naïve)."[99]

We must exercise patience whenever we find ourselves exhibiting anger, no matter how hurt we may be. Once a wrong decision or action is taken, it may not be reversible; and it could cause some damages we may eventually regret. Even when anger is channeled positively, it is still important to always review things before any decision is made.

Jealousy: Every bad behavior always has bad consequences. Being Jealous of others is not a good attribute, if a man is not careful, it will position him for failure, embarrassment, or disgrace. It has the capacity to make man form resentment or hatred toward other people, which could potentially lead to the conception of wrong ideas that may lead to harming others, or things, and eventually harming ourselves either

---

99 Job 5:2 AMP

physically or emotionally. Note, bad energy will always attract the same. If jealousy is not controlled, it may lead to attracting like minds that could eventually lead us astray[100]

"For wherever there is jealousy and selfish ambition, there will be disorder and every kind of evil."[101]

Never be jealous of others, it leads to wrong decision-making that may eventually have regrettable consequences.

Prayer: Lord, grant me the grace and power to give to others who may be in need around me. Also, I pray for grace and wisdom to control my anger, and not to be jealous of others.

---

100 Proverbs 13:20
101 James 3:16 TLB

Chapter 4

DANIEL

---◆◇◇◉◇◇◆---

Daniel was a native of Judea, a righteous man full of integrity and honesty. Daniel had 3 friends, named Hananiah, Mishael, and Azariah. Daniel and his 3 friends were taken away by a king called Nebuchadnezzar to Babylon. On their arrival at Babylon, Daniel's name was changed to "Belteshazzar," while his other 3 friends went by the name "Shadrach," "Meshach," and "Abednego." The purpose of the name change was to create an identity crisis for these 4 Hebrews boys. However, this attempt by the king never materialized because these boys knew who they were from within. Our real identity is on our inside, and nobody can take it away except we choose to give it up.

Daniel was a very intelligent young man who loved God. He loved to read books and prayed always. "…I Daniel understood by books..."[102] "Daniel was a very smart and intelligent boy. He was found to be better than all his peers."[103]

No matter where we find ourselves in life, we must never compromise our real identity to conform to the world around us. Our conformity should be centered on and around God. Daniel and his 3 friends became celebrities for this reason[104]

ATTRIBUTES OF DANIEL AND LESSONS

Studious: Daniel was a man of knowledge. He loved to read books which was why he was loved and preferred above others because of his vast knowledge in many areas of life. Daniel's studious life made him relevant in six different governments. They could not do without him. You also can be like Daniel, or a better version of Daniel if you decide to study and build yourself up. "Study to shew thyself approved..."[105]

Integrity: Daniel was a man of integrity. He always stood by the truth, and refused to compromise his integrity for gifts. He always stood on the right side, and never played games or gimmicks. God expects us to the truthful,

---

102   Daniel 9:2 KJV
103   Daniel 1:4, 20
104   Daniel 3:16-30; 6:4-28
105   2 Timothy 2:15 KJV

trustworthy, display integrity and most importantly, our lives should reflect our spoken words. "Daniel chose not to sell his integrity for riches, and God helped him because of that singular action."[106] "People with integrity walk safely, but those who follow crooked paths will be exposed."[107]

Love of God: Daniel was a man who loved God. He always identified with the things of God even at the expense of his life. He was always ready to put God first at the expense of his own life. He was never afraid to excuse himself from the things that do not glorify God. "Daniel decided and asked those in place of authority not to defile himself because God frowns at such behavior."[108] When we love God, He loves us in return by showing us secrets that will make us stand out amid the multitude. "The things that nobody has ever thought of, imagined or seen before are the things God secretly tells those who genuinely love Him."[109]

"Then was the secret revealed unto Daniel in a night vision. Then Daniel blessed the God of heaven."[110]

Prayer: Daniel was a man of prayer. He identified and lived a life characterized by prayer, even at the expense of his life. He knew the importance and the benefits of prayer. God expects us to always pray to Him because it is one

---

106   Daniel 1:8-9 Paraphrased
107   Proverbs 10:9
108   Daniel 1:5-8 Paraphrased
109   2 Corinthians 2:9-10 Paraphrased
110   Daniel 2:19 BRG

of the channels by which we can communicate with Him, convey our concerns, secure His guidance in instruction, and importantly, live an empowered life. "Now when Daniel learned that the decree had been published, he went home to his upstairs room where the windows opened toward Jerusalem. Three times a day he got down on his knees and prayed, giving thanks to his God, just as he had done before."[111]

"Present your case," says the LORD. *"Set forth your arguments," says Jacob's King."*[112]

BENEFITS OF DANIEL'S ATTRIBUTE

Studious: Daniel was committed to reading books because it has a lot of rewards. When we set apart time to read, we are consciously developing our minds and brains. When we develop our minds with books, we are building capacity that will set us apart from others who decided to spend all their time playing. Continuous learning makes you relevant in the present and the future like Daniel who was relevant in different governments. When we subscribe to learning, capacity is developed and knowledge increases. Reading is like giving a plant the necessary nutrients it needs to keep growing and remain fresh. Reading makes you

---

111   Daniel 6:10
112   Isaiah 41:21

knowledgeable, and it brings honor. King David attested to the fact that his studious life made him better than his teachers[113]

Integrity: Like Daniel, God expects us to live a life of integrity. A life worthy of emulation by those around us. A life that paints the picture of who God is to those who may not know Him. We enjoy a life of peace when we walk in integrity. "Better *is* the poor who walks in his integrity Than one perverse *in his* ways, though he *be* rich."[114] "The wicked flee though no one pursues, but the righteous are as bold as a lion."[115] Integrity promotes and exalts people.

"The integrity of the upright guides them, but the unfaithful are destroyed by their duplicity."[116]

Love of God: Daniel as a young boy loved God and His ways. He was always ready to put God before himself and above all other things he was engaged in. He was not afraid of demonstrating his love for God in the public. "A decree was issued that everyone should only ask the king for what they want and not pray to God, but Daniel who will never compromise his place with God chose to stand for God by praying to Him instead of the small gods of the land."[117] When you stand for God in love, you enjoy

---

113   Psalms 119:99
114   Proverbs 28:6 NKJV
115   Proverbs 28:1
116   Proverbs 11:3
117   Daniel 6:6-10 Paraphrased

protection, honor, and promotion and earn His love in return. "Daniel was punished for praying to God, but God defended Daniel, gave him honor, promotion and favor with the king."[118] That is what loving God can do for us.

Prayer: God expects us to always pray because it is one of the secure communication lines to Him. When we pray to God concerning the issues of our lives, He responds by giving us instructions, guidance, and revelation to solve that situation. When the king could not understand his dream, Daniel went back to God, and God explained the dream to Daniel. "…Then was the secret revealed unto Daniel in a night vision. Then Daniel blessed the God of heaven."[119] "Call to me and I will answer you and tell you great and unsearchable things you do not know."[120] Praying prevents us from getting stranded, it boosts our confidence in God and empowers us to live above all situations. "As he was praying, the appearance of his face changed, and his clothes became as bright as a flash of lightning."[121]

Prayer: Lord, help me to love You with all my heart; live a life of integrity; live a life characterized by prayer, and importantly live a studious life that will distinguish me.

---

118   Daniel 6:8-25 Paraphrased
119   Daniel 2:19 KJV
120   Jeremiah 33:3
121   Luke 9:29

44

Chapter 5

ELIJAH

Elijah was a Tishbite, he hailed from Gilead. He was a prophet of God with authority and power. Elijah was an obedient man, he loved to pray because he understood the essence of prayers as a channel to be in dominion and command authority[122] Elijah, as a conveyor of God's word, trusted and believed every spoken word of God. No wonder he delivered every of God's messages to the recipients without any doubt. "For this is what the LORD, the God of Israel, says: 'The jar of flour will not be used up and the jug of oil will not run dry until the day the LORD sends rain on the land.'"[123] Elijah's trust in God made him like a mountain that could not be removed because God was with him. "Those who trust in the LORD are like Mount

---

122   James 5:17-18
123   1 Kings 17:14

Zion, which cannot be shaken but endures forever. As the mountains surround Jerusalem, so the LORD surrounds his people both now and forevermore."[124] Elijah was used by God to deliver messages to His people either as an instruction or warning because he made himself available for God[125] When we make ourselves available for God, He will make a sign and wonder out of us.

ATTRIBUTES OF ELIJAH

Availability: Elijah was a man who made himself available to be used by God. God is always looking for a man to undertake or carry out His agenda. "I looked for someone among them who would build up the wall and stand before me in the gap on behalf of the land so I would not have to destroy it, but I found no one."[126] Our availability for the things of God creates a platform where we can be used by God to do amazing things, and as a result; God makes a wonder out of us.

"What are we going to do with these men?" they asked. "Everyone living in Jerusalem knows they have performed a notable sign, and we cannot deny it."[127] "I know you need all these things everyone is running after. However, I can give you all those things, just make yourself available for

---

124 Psalms 125:1-2
125 Ezekiel 22:30
126 Ezekiel 22:30
127 Acts 4:16

the things of the kingdom first and I will add those desires of yours to you cheaply."[128] In our contemporary days, one of those individuals who made themselves available to be used by God is Bishop David Oyedepo. In his words, "I found the jackpot of life in Matthew 6:33" When you are sold out to God, He makes you stand out among men. "Come, follow me," Jesus said, "and I will send you out to fish for people." At once they left their nets and followed him."[129] And immediately they left their nets and followed him. Making every other thing secondary to the pursuit of God is what guarantees the fulfillment of destiny. "A man named Levi, who was a tax collector, left everything and followed Jesus, and he was privileged to host Jesus in his home. When we make ourselves available, divine visitation is guaranteed."[130]

Prayer: Elijah was a man of prayer. He prayed with authority and confidence in God. It is important to know that our confidence in prayer unto God is what guarantees the returns on our investment on the prayer altar. "Therefore I tell you, whatever you ask for in prayer, believe that you have received it, and it will be yours."[131]

Elijah exercised his confidence in prayer, and his confidence yielded tremendous results that made men marvel. "[36] At

---

128 Matthew 6:32-33 Paraphrased
129 Mark 1:17-18
130 Luke 5:27-28 Paraphrased
131 Mark 11:24

the time of sacrifice, the prophet Elijah stepped forward and prayed: "LORD, the God of Abraham, Isaac and Israel, let it be known today that you are God in Israel and that I am your servant and have done all these things at your command. [37] Answer me, LORD, answer me, so these people will know that you, LORD, are God, and that you are turning their hearts back again." [38] Then the fire of the LORD fell and burned up the sacrifice, the wood, the stones and the soil, and also licked up the water in the trench.[39] When all the people saw this, they fell prostrate and cried, "The LORD— he is God! The LORD—he is God!"[132]

It is important that we approach God with confidence on our prayer altar because it guarantees a response from God. "Let us then approach God's throne of grace with confidence, so that we may receive mercy and find grace to help us in our time of need."[133]

Obedience: Elijah was a man of obedience. He followed every single instruction God gave him. His trust and commitment to God secured His divine presence always. "Then the word of the Lord came to him:"[134]

Elijah never hesitated at the instance of instructions, he

---

132   1 Kings 18:36-39
133   Hebrews 4:16
134   1 Kings 17:8

obeyed every detail of the instruction, and it resulted in provisions. "Our total obedience to God's instruction guarantees unending supernatural supplies, and honor. But when we choose not to be obedient, we suffer the consequence. God is not interested in partial obedience, but total and absolute obedience."[135] Jonah chose to engage in partial obedience, but he suffered the consequence.[136]

Confidence: Elijah was a man who lived a life of confidence in God. He believed every word of God that was delivered to Him. Every time a word came from God, he acted because he knew that God will never lie. God told Elijah to go into hiding for three years because there was going to be a drought as a result of King Ahab's disobedience to God's law. Without hesitation, Elijah departed, and God provided for him during those three years of drought.[137] Our confidence in obedience guarantees sufficiency during dry seasons. We must not leave any room for doubt when we deal with God because it will hinder our access to the flow of grace that will sustain our confidence in Him. "But blessed is the one who trusts in the LORD, whose confidence is in him."[138]

---

135 Deuteronomy 28:1-13 Paraphrased
136 Jonah 1:1-17
137 1 Kings 17:33-34; 18:1-6
138 Jeremiah 17:7

BENEFITS OF ELIJAH'S ATTRIBUTES

Availability: Elijah and many other prophets of God chose to make themselves available when God called them. It was a personal choice they made, and they never regretted it. Psalm 65:4 "Blessed are those you choose and bring near to live in your courts! We are filled with the good things of your house, of your holy temple."[139] Even though God called us, He will never make it obligatory to make ourselves available. God called out for people to do His bidding, unfortunately at that moment, God did not find anyone. We must understand that it is a privilege to be called or chosen by God to do His bidding. God has the capacity to replace anyone who feels he or she is too big to do His will. "I tell you, "He replied, "if they keep quiet, the stones will cry out."[140] We must humble ourselves because God delights and uses the humble to achieve great feats. Our availability guarantees supernatural supply and brings honor[141] Nehemiah made himself available; he was instrumental in the rebuilding of the walls of Jerusalem and God honored and favored him in return. Our availability initiates our access to a realm of favor.

---

139   Psalms 65:4
140   Luke 10:40
141   1 kings 18:1-13, Luke 22:35

"Thou shalt arise and have mercy upon Zion: for the time to favor her, yea, the set time, is come. For thy servants take pleasure in her stones and favor the dust thereof."[142]

Prayer: Prayer is an integral part of our Christian life. The essence of prayer cannot be over-emphasized. "One day Jesus was praying in a certain place. When he finished, one of his disciples said to him, "Lord, teach us to pray, just as John taught his disciples."[143] Prayer makes things happen for our benefit when done in accordance with God's Word. Prayer puts you in a place of authority over any unpleasant situation. Elijah was a man of prayer, he exercised his authority over the weather "Elijah was a human being, even as we are. He prayed earnestly that it would not rain, and it did not rain on the land for three and a half years. Again, he prayed, and the heavens gave rain, and the earth produced its crops."[144] Prayer helps you enjoy seamless victory over any unwanted situation. Jabez prayed in order to exercise his authority over the situation because he was tired of it. "Jabez cried out to the God of Israel, "Oh, that you would bless me and enlarge my territory! Let your hand be with me and keep me from harm so that I will be free from pain. And God granted his request."[145] Also, prayer helps us keep the communication line between us and God because He

142   Psalms 102:13-14
143   Luke 11:1
144   James 5:17-18
145   1 Chronicles 4:10

always speaks to us. "Call to me and I will answer you…"[146] Therefore, we must never be weary on the prayer altar.

Obedience: Elijah was the epitome of obedience in his walk with God. Every time God spoke to Elijah, he moved regardless of what the message could have been. Obedience retains the presence of God around us because disobedience is a branch of sin and God will not hang around those who do things that do not please him. ""Why do you call me, 'Lord, Lord,' and do not do what I say?"[147] Obedience makes rich, guarantees a continuous flow of heavenly presence, divine protection, promotion, favor, honor, exemption, and guidance. When we obey God's word/instructions delightsomely, it automatically activates and duplicates in our life the goodness of heaven here on earth because we are His ambassadors, representing heaven here on earth. If we continue to do and represent the interest of heaven as commanded, we have nothing to worry about.

Confidence: Elijah was a man of confidence, even amid opposition. He was never afraid but demonstrated his confidence in God. This was why he was not moved when he had a confrontation with the priest of Baal.

Our demonstration of confidence in God guarantees constant victories, the opposition regardless, and it

146   Jeremiah 33:3
147   Luke 6:46

eliminates shame and ushers in honor. In the midst of a dire and uncertain situation, Elijah proved that having confidence in God will always guarantee victory, defeat the enemy, give you victory, and make you a celebrity. "Then the fire of the Lord fell and burned up the sacrifice, the wood, the stones and the soil, and licked up the water in the trench. When all the people saw this, they fell prostrate and cried, "The Lord—he is God! The Lord—he is God!"[148] We must learn and build the capacity to have confidence in God because it is our highway out of unpleasant situations into victory and good report.

Our level of confidence in God determines our level of victory. The three Hebrew boys demonstrated absolute confidence in God even when their lives were at stake, and God showed up for them. "Shadrach, Meshach and Abednego replied to him, "King Nebuchadnezzar, we do not need to defend ourselves before you in this matter. If we are thrown into the blazing furnace, the God we serve is able to deliver us from it, and he will deliver us from Your Majesty's hand. But even if he does not, we want you to know, Your Majesty that we will not serve your gods or worship the image of gold you have set up."[149]

---

148 1 Kings 18:38-39
149 Daniel 3:16-18 NIV

Their confidence in God made them a celebrity in a strange land because God was with them, and as a result, they enjoyed promotions because God was pleased with their confidence in Him. "Then King Nebuchadnezzar leaped to his feet in amazement and asked his advisers, "Weren't there three men that we tied up and threw into the fire?" They replied, "Certainly, your Majesty. He said, "Look! I see four men walking around in the fire, unbound and unharmed, and the fourth looks like a son of the gods." Nebuchadnezzar then approached the opening of the blazing furnace and shouted, "Shadrach, Meshach and Abednego, servants of the Most High God, come out! Come here!" So, Shadrach, Meshach and Abednego came out of the fire, and the satraps, prefects, governors and royal advisers crowded around them. They saw that the fire had not harmed their bodies, nor was a hair of their heads singed; their robes were not scorched, and there was no smell of fire on them. Then Nebuchadnezzar said, "Praise be to the God of Shadrach, Meshach and Abednego, who has sent his angel and rescued his servants! They trusted in him and defied the king's command and were willing to give up their lives rather than serve or worship any god except their own God. Therefore, I decree that the people of any nation or language who say anything against the God of Shadrach, Meshach and Abednego be cut into pieces and their houses be turned into piles of rubble, for no other god can save in this way." Then the king promoted Shadrach,

Meshach and Abednego in the province of Babylon."[150] We must never compromise or yield our confidence in God to fear, doing that leaves us vulnerable to the enemy.

Prayer: Lord, I know I cannot do it by myself, but by your Spirit engrace me to build and demonstrate my confidence in you, be available to you, while I engage my prayer altar to your glory.

---

150 Daniel 3:24-30 NIV

Chapter 6

FESTUS

Festus was a Roman procurator, someone who represents others in a court of law. He was in a place of authority because of the office he occupied, he held the tenets of his office highly by allowing the truth of law to prevail without circumventing the process to favor one above others. He demonstrated responsibility in discharging his duties. Festus took up the case of Paul the Apostle of Jesus when the Jews accused him of blasphemy. However, Festus did not bow to the pressure of the Jews who came to accuse Paul but decided to let the truth of the law prevail. Whenever we are privileged to occupy a position of authority, we must remember to be just and fair to everyone who is under us because our actions determine and shapes every event and outcome of everyone committed to our care.

"Festus said: "King Agrippa, and all who are present with us, you

see this man! The whole Jewish community has petitioned me about him in Jerusalem and here in Caesarea, shouting that he ought not to live any longer. I found he had done nothing deserving of death, but because he made his appeal to the Emperor, I decided to send him to Rome. But I have nothing definite to write to His Majesty about him. Therefore, I have brought him before all of you, and especially before you, King Agrippa, so that as a result of this investigation I may have something to write. For I think it is unreasonable to send a prisoner on to Rome without specifying the charges against him."[151]

ATTRIBUTES OF FESTUS

Authority: Festus demonstrated reverence and authority to his office. He knew that as a public officeholder, his actions, words, and decisions matter a lot. The actions of those who sit in positions of authority have the capacity to determine or shape the outcome of situations or people's lives. He was very careful in discharging his duties without being biased even when the Jews tried to make him do their bidding. The Jews sought a favor from Festus so that they would have the upper hand to destroy Apostle Paul, but Festus, a noble man countered that gesture from the Jews.

All of us have been charged with an office of authority, therefore we must discharge our privileged duties in fairness to others. "God blessed us, and gave us the staff of authority to rule."[152]

---

151 Acts 25:24-27 NIV
152 Genesis 1:28 Paraphrased

Responsibility: Festus was truthful to his office and those he represented. He discharged his duties with high regard even when the Jews tried to influence his decision[153]. We must ensure that we are responsible towards our assignment because we are accountable to God and not man.

"Whatever you do, work at it with all your heart, as working for the Lord, not for human masters,"[154] We must not be afraid to speak or stand by the truth always whether people's lives are dependent on it or not. Our goal should be to please God, and not man.

Truthfulness: Festus demonstrated a level of sincerity and truthfulness when he handled the situation of Apostle Paul. He was a procurator; he understood the law and what his office stood for. He gave Apostle Paul the opportunity to defend himself, even though he could have used his authority to deliver what the Jews wanted.

"*2 where the chief priests and the Jewish leaders appeared before him and presented the charges against Paul. 3 They requested Festus, as a favor to them, to have Paul transferred to Jerusalem, for they were preparing an ambush to kill him along the way. 4 Festus answered, "Paul is being held at Caesarea, and I myself am going there soon. 5 Let some of your leaders come with me, and if the man has done anything wrong, they can press charges against him there."*[155]

---

153 Acts 25:1-9
154 Colossians 3:23 NIV
155 Acts 25:2-5 NIV

As leaders, we must ensure we let everyone have equal access to all available provisions without subjugating anyone. "As a leader, you must be a perfect example after the order of Jesus discharging your duties within its confines, in trustworthiness and in honor authority in fairness and sincerity without being in fear of any mortal man."[156]

BENEFITS OF FESTUS ATTRIBUTES

Authority: Occupying a place of authority is a privilege. Therefore, we must uphold the dictates of the office in truth and dignity as a representative of the people. When our duties are discharged with dignity and honor, and in respect for the people, we enjoy honor, favor, blessings, and promotions. Most importantly, we put smiles and confidence on their face and in their heart.

When the righteous are in authority, the people rejoice; But when a wicked *man* rules, the people groan."[157]

Responsibility: Leadership equals responsibility. As a leader who is responsible for discharging his or her assignments, he is bound to enjoy promotions, honor, relevance, and wealth. "Do you see any truly competent workers? They will serve kings rather than working for ordinary people."[158]

---

156 Titus 1:7-14 Paraphrased
157 Proverbs 29:2 NKJV
158 Proverbs 22:29

" In every matter of wisdom and understanding about which the king questioned them, he found them ten times better than all the magicians and enchanters in his whole kingdom."[159] "Now Daniel so distinguished himself among the administrators and the satraps by the exceptional qualities that the king planned to set him over the whole kingdom."[160] All these benefits come at a cost, we must be willing to pay the price in order to experience and enjoy the blessings.

Trustworthiness: Festus demonstrated trustworthiness in the discharge of his official duties. Even when he was caught between making a political decision that could help his office, he held onto the tenets of the law guiding his office and decision. As a result, he was able to give Apostle Paul a chance to live. As a leader, people must be able to trust us with what has been committed into our hands because we will all give an account of our activities to God. In order to enjoy God's commendation, we must discharge those duties in the fear of God. "The LORD detests dishonest scales, but accurate weights find favor with him."[161]

Like the parable of the gold, different individuals had the opportunity to make a difference, unfortunately, only two out of the three succeeded in discharging their privileged

---

159 Daniel 1:20 NIV
160 Daniel 6:3 NIV
161 Proverbs 11:1

duties well while one failed. Everyone got rewarded according to their service with a commendation from their master.

"...His master replied, 'Well done, good and faithful servant! You have been faithful with a few things; I will put you in charge of many things. Come and share your master's happiness!'"[162]

We all can enjoy God's commendation like Abraham if we stay faithful to our privileged given assignment[163]

Prayer: Lord, as a privileged leader, grant me the grace to be just, truthful, honest, and respectful to others in discharging my duties to the authority and those around me.

---

162   Matthew 25:21 NIV
163   Genesis 18:19

Chapter 7

GEHAZI

Gehazi was a mentee of Prophet Elisha and was privileged to enjoy a position of power, but was ultimately corrupt. However, he lost his credibility due to covetousness and greed when he decided to use his position to extort Naaman, the Syrian general afflicted with leprosy. Gehazi's act of greed brought upon him and his lineage a generational punishment. He was afflicted with the sickness of general Naaman, which was also transferred to his entire family. Lack of contentment will always result in bad behaviors that could eventually bring about shame.

Gehazi was privileged to experience God's power at work in the life of Elisha, that is, he where resided God's power and glory domiciled, yet his heart was somewhere else. Unfortunately, his acts of foolishness caused him the honor and power of God he could have manifested like his mentor, Elisha. Gehazi was unable to perform the miracles his masters did because his heart was never connected to that of Elisha, all his thoughts were centered on what he could get for himself from his master's visitors.

"Gehazi, the servant of Elisha the man of God, said to himself, 'My master was too easy on Naaman, this Aramean, by not accepting from him what he brought. As surely as the LORD lives, I will run after him and get something from him.'"[164]

"Gehazi went on ahead and laid the staff on the boy's face, but there was no sound or response. So Gehazi went back to meet Elisha and told him, "The boy has not awakened.""[165] The dead boy was brought back to life through Elisha's intervention. Everyone who subscribes to worldly distractions and bad habits like Gehazi will always end up in regret and shame.

ATTRIBUTES OF GEHAZI

Stewardship (Dedication): Gehazi was privileged to serve with a great man of God, Prophet Elisha, who was used by God to do miracles. It was an opportunity for Gehazi to grow and learn the ways of God through his master, but his heart was always in a different place. We all have been called to serve, and we must ensure we stay focused on our assignment(s) because that is the only way

---

164   2 Kings 5:20 NIV
165   2 Kings 4:31 NIV

we can learn, grow, and get rewarded. "…Let my people go, that they may serve Me."[166] Unfortunately, Gehazi lost focus because of his inability to put under subjection the needs of the flesh. No doubt, our body will always crave what it desires, but we must discipline ourselves to bring it under subjection. "But I discipline my body and bring it into subjection, lest, when I have preached to others, I myself should become disqualified."[167] Our focus should be on how to effectively discharge our duties in order to touch lives and be rewarded.

"If therefore thine eye be single, thy whole body shall be full of light."[168]

Everyone who desires to be a leader will have to subscribe to the demands of attaining a place of leadership. One of those ways is servanthood. Being a servant gives the platform to learn, acquire and develop leadership skills. This could be formal or informal. In Gehazi's situation, he had the opportunity to become like his master through the informal way of learning but his priority was misplaced.

"…Whoever wants to be a leader among you must be your servant."[169]

Covetousness: Gehazi as a steward cultivated and nurtured a bad habit. He was covetous. No matter the level of good you may have done, if you give room to a bad habit, it

---

166 Exodus 8:1 NKJV
167 1 Corinthians 9:27 NKJV
168 Matthew 6:22 KJV
169 Matthew 20:26

will gradually grow and destroy the good in you. And when that good is no more, shame is inevitable. Gehazi could not curb his habit of covetousness so he ended up in shame and destruction. "Let your conversation be without covetousness; and be content with such things as ye have…"[170] Covetousness is taking an unnecessary interest in other people's belongings or the urge to be their person for a wrong purpose.

Greed: Gehazi fell a victim to greed because he could not keep his eyes off other people's things. He coveted the gifts his master rejected from his visitors "But Gehazi, the servant of Elisha the man of God, said, Behold, my master hath spared Naaman this Syrian, in not receiving at his hands that which he brought: but, as the LORD lives, I will run after him, and take somewhat of him."[171] Greed is dangerous. It will lead to lying, stealing, and taking what does not belong to you. This could ultimately lead to disrepute and shame. "Then he said to them, "Watch out! Be on your guard against all kinds of greed; life does not consist in an abundance of possessions."[172] We must learn to be content and grateful for what we have, and the level we are per time. A life of integrity will always bestow upon people honor, favor, blessings, and promotions.

Lying: "So Gehazi followed after Naaman. And when

---

170 Hebrews 13:5 KJV
171 2 Kings 5:20 KJV
172 Luke 12:15 NIV

Naaman saw him running after him, he lighted down from the chariot to meet him, and said, is all well? And he said, all is well. My master hath sent me, saying, Behold, even now there be come to me from mount Ephraim two young men of the sons of the prophets: give them, I pray thee, a talent of silver, and two changes of garments. And Naaman said, be content, take two talents. And he urged him, and bound two talents of silver in two bags, with two changes of garments, and laid them upon two of his servants; and they bare them before him. And when he came to the tower, he took them from their hand, and bestowed them in the house: and he let the men go, and they departed. But he went in and stood before his master. And Elisha said unto him, where comest thou, Gehazi? And he said, thy servant went no whither."[173]

Gehazi became a liar because he needed to hide his bad habit from his master; he thought nobody noticed his action. He was wrong. God sees everything even when we think we are alone. His eyes run to and fro the earth."[174] God revealed Gehazi's action to Prophet Elisha "... but he revealeth his secret unto his servants the prophets."[175]

We must learn to be contented with what we have and not covet other people's properties. Doing this will keep us from unnecessary lies.

---

173   2 Kings 5:21-25 KJV
174   2 Chronicles 16:9
175   Amos 3:7 KJV

BENEFITS AND DISBENEFITS OF GEHAZI'S ATTRIBUTES

Stewardship: Like Gehazi, we have been called to a life of stewardship by God. "And the LORD spoke to Moses, "Go to Pharaoh and say to him, 'thus says the LORD: "Let My people go, that they may serve Me.""[176] Service to God, our environment, and humanity is an opportunity for development and growth. Everyone genuinely in service must undergo a set of training in order to master what is required of him or her. As stewards in training, we have the privilege to access the trainer's capacity, and subsequently build on the knowledge transferred by the trainer, while we can also operate in the grace at work in the trainer if we truly commit to it. In the case of Gehazi, he was in training with Prophet Elisha, and he had the opportunity to operate in the same capacity as his master. "Elisha said to Gehazi, "Tuck your cloak into your belt, take my staff in your hand and run…"[177] He was privileged to do the same thing his master would do.

Service brings honor, promotion, blessings, favor, fruitfulness, preservation, longevity, and fulfillment when it is done with a genuine heart[178]. In our various communities today, there are individuals who have rendered their service

---

176   Exodus 8:1 NKJV
177   2 Kings 4:29 NIV
178   Exodus 23:25-31

genuinely to God and humanity. As a result, they have been honored. Everyone has the same opportunity to serve God and make a difference.

Covetousness: Covetousness is a bad habit. God does not want that for His children because it is not His nature. "But among you there must not be even a hint of sexual immorality, or of any kind of impurity, or of greed, because these are improper for God's holy people."[179] A life of holiness and purity is the hallmark of every child of God. We must never allow ourselves to covet the riches of others. "Fret not thyself because of evildoers, neither be thou envious against the workers of iniquity. For they shall soon be cut down like the grass, and wither as the green herb. Instead, let your focus be on God."[180] Covetousness destroys, humiliates, and brings dishonor. "Achan went against God's instruction, took an accursed item. His act of covetousness brought punishment upon Joshua and the people of Israel. However, when the truth was uncovered, Achan was punished, and he brought disgrace and dishonor to his family. Eventually, his bad behavior cost him his life."[181]

---

179 Ephesians 5:3 NIV
180 Psalm 37:1-2 KJV
181 Joshua 7:1-26 paraphrased

The truth will always be unveiled. It is better not to engage in the act of unrighteousness because the consequences are grave.

Greed: Gehazi was greedy, and as a result, he brought upon himself sickness, shame, and disgrace. Our actions have the capacity to bring upon us generational punishment. Most times, people who knew nothing about the action will also suffer the consequences. That is why it is important to think twice before making a wrong decision or taking a step that could potentially hurt our loved ones. "The leprosy therefore of Naaman shall cleave unto thee, and unto thy seed forever. And he went out from his presence a leper as white as snow."[182] Today, everyone born into this world indirectly suffers the consequences of the decision the first man and woman made in the Garden of Eden "God punished everyone that was involved in the act of disobedience, and the punishment was not limited to them alone, but generations unborn."[183] So, we must be wise and put on the thinking cap before any decisions that will influence our actions are made.

Lying: Lying became the nature of Gehazi because he needed to cover up his bad actions "But he went in and stood before his master. And Elisha said unto him,

---

182   2 Kings 5: 27 KJV
183   Genesis 3:14-19 paraphrased

whence comest thou, Gehazi? And he said, thy servant went nowhere. He lied to protect his image despite his actions, unfortunately for him, his master knew all that had transpired. And he said unto him, went not mine heart with thee, when the man turned again from his chariot to meet thee? Is it a time to receive money, and to receive garments, and olive yards, and vineyards, and sheep, and oxen, and menservants, and maidservants?"[184] Such actions may be a secret for a moment; the truth will be revealed at some point. "For nothing is hidden that will not be made manifest, nor is anything secret that will not be known and come to light."[185]

God does not like liars and will not listen to them. "The Lord detests lying lips, but he delights in people who are trustworthy."[186] Remember, you cannot serve two masters, you either love one or hate the other[187]

Satan is the father of lies[188] , while God is righteous[189]. Never be afraid to tell the truth even when you are caught doing something bad, or you discovered what you did is wrong. Being honest could save you from any intended

---

184   2 Kings 5:25-26 KJV
185   Luke 8:17 ESV
186   Proverbs 12:22 NIV
187   Matthew 6:24
188   John 8:44
189   Psalm 145:17 and Psalm 119:137

punishment. "People who conceal their sins will not prosper, but if they confess and turn from them, they will receive mercy."[190] "Truthful lips endure forever, but a lying tongue is but for a moment."[191]

Prayer: Lord, give me the grace to be committed to a life of stewardship, and to be contented with what I have, refraining from bad companies and a lying lip. Amen.

---

190   Proverbs 28:13
191   Proverbs 12:19 NIV

Chapter 8

HANNAH

Hannah was the wife of Elkanah, an Ephraimite but did not have children. She was a woman of prayer. She made a yearly visit with her husband to Shiloh to pray, worship, and make sacrifices to God. This was her yearly routine because she believed an encounter with God will terminate her childlessness. During her difficult times, she was unhappy, which is normal for people when they are faced with an unwanted situation. Of course, she was also mocked for being childless[192].

However, she remained steadfast in prayer despite all the mockeries and the plan of the enemy to rob her of her desired encounter with God. Like Hannah, God expects us to trust Him in all situations and for all things without

---

192 1 Samuel 6 & 7

giving up in our pursuit of answers. "…You who call on the Lord, give yourselves no rest and give him no rest till he establishes Jerusalem and makes her the praise of the earth. She was committed to God as her only source of hope and help throughout her ordeal. Only those who endure to the end receives the crown of glory."[193] "For surely there is an end; and thine expectation shall not be cut off."[194]

ATTRIBUTES OF HANNAH

Prayer: Hannah was a woman who believed so much in prayer. She went to Shiloh with her family to pray to God yearly. It was like a tradition for her family and also an opportunity to fellowship with God because they believed Shiloh ground to be a place of encounter where all impossibilities become possible with God. "This man went up from the city yearly to worship and sacrifice to the Lord of hosts in Shiloh…"[195]

"The Lord continued to appear at Shiloh, and there he revealed himself to Samuel through his word."[196] An encounter with the Word is what changes abnormalities around our lives to the supernatural that is characterized by testimonies.

When we commit to trusting God with all our problems,

---

193   Isaiah 62:6-7 NIV
194   Proverbs 23:18 KJV
195   1 Samuel 1:3 NKJV
196   1 Samuel 3:21 NIV

He is able to turn them around. One of those ways is to reach out in prayer. God expects us to stand in the place of prayer, reminding Him of those prophecies that have been spoken concerning us[197] While we pray for things to change for us, we must also remember that praying for others and the interest of God's kingdom also guarantees answers to our personal desires also. "And I sought for a man among them that should make up the hedge and stand in the gap before me for the land, that I should not destroy it: but I found none."[198]

We must ensure we make ourselves available on the altar of prayer, because it does not only change things, but it changes people, ushers in blessings, and builds a defense mechanism around us. "Keep on asking, and you will receive what you ask for. Keep on seeking, and you will find. Keep on knocking, and the door will be opened to you"[199] Hannah's persistence on the altar of prayer secured her much desired testimony[200]

Trust: Our consistent visit to the same place for a particular service is a justification that we have some level of connection or satisfaction with the place, and we trust them enough to offer what we desire. That was Hannah's approach throughout her waiting time. She continually

197 Isaiah 43:26
198 Ezekiel 22:30 KJV
199 Matthew 7:7
200 Luke 18:2-8

went back to God because she judged God faithful, that He is the only one who could proffer a solution to her problem. The same is expected of us by God, our absolute trust must be in Him. "Those who know your name trust in you, for you, O Lord, do not abandon those who search for you."[201]

Job demonstrated his trust in God throughout his predicament. He chose to trust God because he knew only God could deliver him. He waited continually on God in prayer and trust, and his change came. "If a man die, shall he live again? All the days of my appointed time will I wait, Till my change come"[202]

"After Job had prayed for his friends, the Lord restored his fortunes and gave him twice as much as he had before."[203]

We must never allow our focus to shift from God; any attempt to do that can put us in a difficult position where God may not respond to us. "Anyone who doubts is unstable, and such will not get anything from God."[204] And remember, no man can receive anything except what God gives him[205]. So, it is wise to keep trusting in God like Hannah because He has never changed, and He is not limited in capacity like a man.

---

201   Psalm 9:10
202   Job 14:14 KJV
203   Job 42:10 NIV
204   James 1:6-8 paraphrased
205   John 3:27

Unhappiness: Hannah, due to her situation, wore about the garment of unhappiness and was of a sorrowful spirit. She allowed her being childless to overwhelm and empty her tank of joy. "Hannah was bittered in her soul, and she prayed to God."[206] Even though she did a good thing by praying, she did it the wrong way. Her being unhappy stood as a barrier. The Bible says we should enter His gate with thanksgiving, and His court with praise[207] It may seem difficult but God expects us to be joyful always. It takes joyfulness to experience the fullness of God.

"Though the fig tree does not bud and there are no grapes on the vines, though the olive crop fails and the fields produce no food, though there are no sheep in the pen and no cattle in the stalls, yet I will rejoice in the Lord, I will be joyful in God my Savior. The Sovereign Lord is my strength; he makes my feet like the feet of a deer; he enables me to tread on the heights."[208]

Access to God is limited when we are surrounded by the cloud of unhappiness because God only inhabits a joyful environment. We should make it a lifestyle to live a joyful life, the negative situation regardless. It may be painful, but our state of joyfulness connects us to the voice of God that will lead us out of our unwanted situation. "Ye shall have a song, as in the night when a holy solemnity is kept;

---

206   1 Samuel 1:10
207   Psalm100:1-4
208   Habakkuk 3:17-19

and gladness of heart, as when one goes with a pipe to come into the mountain of the LORD, to the mighty One of Israel. And the LORD shall cause his glorious voice to be heard…"[209]

We must beware of joy stealers or else they will make us lose sight of God's plan for us. Hannah was a victim of joy stealers but the moment she realized the danger of being unjoyful, her breakthrough came. "And Hannah's adversary provoked her sore, and make her afraid … So, she provoked her, and she cried and did not eat."[210] Hannah switched from being an unhappy prayer person to a happy prayer person, and immediately her story changed. We must remember that our right attitude or disposition in what we do with God is key to experiencing His hand, not the exercise itself.

"And he did that which was right in the sight of the LORD, but not with a perfect heart."[211]

Integrity: Hannah was integrity personified in her walk with God. She committed herself to every of her spoken word and covenants she made with God. She did not renege on her words to God.

---

209 Isaiah 30: 29-30
210 1 Samuel 1: 6-7
211 2 Chronicles 25:2

"She vowed to God, and she fulfilled her vow."[212] We are expected to maintain a life of integrity because God loves those who are committed to their words "Lying lips are an abomination to the Lord, but those who act faithfully are his delight."[213]

"All you need to say is simply 'Yes' or 'No'; anything beyond this comes from the evil one."[214] A life of integrity brings us honor before God and man. "She returned to fulfil what she said to God."[215] It is unacceptable and a display of lack of integrity to make a commitment and go back on it without considering the other party involved. It is not who we are as children of God, it is better not to commit yourself in words than to commit and fail.

"It is better to say nothing than to make a promise and not keep it."[216]

People take us at our word that is why we must be truthful always. "Show yourself in all respects to be a model of good works, and in your teaching show integrity, dignity."[217] We must strive to be like Hannah who returned. Today, many of us are guilty of not returning after getting blessed by God.

---

212 1 Samuel 1: 11
213 Proverbs 12:22
214 Matthew 5:37
215 1 Samuel 1:24-28 paraphrased
216 Ecclesiastes 5:15
217 Titus 2:7

BENEFITS AND DISBENEFITS OF HANNAH'S ATTRIBUTES

Prayer: Hannah had a lifestyle of prayer and was very fervent because she believed in the potency of prayer, and its capacity to change situations. Hannah made us understand that the altar of prayer is a place where we can relate with God for a desired change of story.

"Then you will call on me and come and pray to me, and I will listen to you."[218]

God is ever ready to listen all we need to do is play our part by engaging the prayer altar which will supernaturally turn our captivity around. "Until now you have asked for nothing in My name; ask and you will receive, so that your joy may be made full."[219]

When we pray, we experience transformation just as Jesus was transformed when he prayed[220]. Praying to God with all our heart in faith consistently guarantees testimonies, turnarounds, and victories that become the norm in our lives. "If my people, who are called by my name, will humble themselves and pray and seek my face and turn from their wicked ways, then I will hear from heaven, and I will forgive their sin and will heal their land."[221] Prayer is

---

218 Jeremiah 29:12
219 John 16:24
220 Matthew 17:2
221 2 Chronicles 7: 14

not an option but a requirement to have access to God and take command of every situation. We are admonished by the Word of God to pray always, everywhere, and without ceasing because it is one of the heavenly key mysteries God gave to us[222]

Trust: Hannah's trust in God was evident in her action. She channeled all her energy towards God in prayer, and not man, not even her spouse because she understood that only God could give children and not man; not even her husband. If man was able to give children, she could have conceived from the day she met with her husband.

"Every good and perfect gift is from above, coming down from the Father of the heavenly lights, who does not change like shifting shadows."[223] Children are good gifts, and they are from the Lord. "Behold, children are a gift of the LORD, the fruit of the womb is a reward."[224] Hannah channeled her efforts into prayer because she trusted God to reward her for her labor on the prayer altar. "The laborer is worthy of his reward"[225] When we trust God with all our hearts without shifting focus or putting our trust in man, we get rewarded with testimonies, victories, breakthroughs, blessings, and many more.

---

222   Luke 18:1, 1 Thessalonians 5:16-18, 1 Timothy 2:8
223   James 1: 17
224   Psalm 127:3
225   1 Timothy 5:18

"But blessed is the one who trusts in the Lord, whose confidence is in him. They will be like a tree planted by the water that sends out its roots by the stream. It does not fear when heat comes; its leaves are always green. It has no worries in a year of drought and never fails to bear fruit."[226] Unending and all-around freshness with fruitfulness becomes a norm when you trust in God.

Unhappiness: We are called to a life of happiness, and not unhappiness. Many times, we allow circumstances and situations to deprive us of our real identity. We were made in God's image, and because we carry His DNA, we are expected to demonstrate and pattern our lives after Him. God is a happy God, even when men had evil intentions; He couldn't help but laugh. "The kings of the earth prepare for battle; the rulers plot together against the LORD and against his anointed one... But the one who rules in heaven laughs, the Lord scoffs at them."[227] When we allow unhappiness to cloud our real identity, we may lose out of the real plan of God per time. For several years, Hannah prayed to God, which is good but in an unacceptable way. She prayed in sorrow, and unhappiness. You can do the right thing but in the wrong way. This method can place a limit on our results or the expected outcome. But when Hannah changed her approach on the prayer altar, her story

---

226 Jeremiah 17:7-8
227 Psalm 2:2, 4

changed. "… And her countenance was no longer sad, and they rose to worship God… and the Lord visited her."[228]

God cannot hang around murmurers, complainers, or in an environment where the atmosphere is sad. We are expected to guard our joy with all our being because it is what guarantees the presence of God, and when we have God's presence; we have everything. Jesus reminded us about the importance of keeping our joy amid unwanted and negative situations because it is the key to enjoying and entering into that victory that has been obtained for us.

"These things I have spoken unto you, that in me ye might have peace. In the world ye shall have tribulation: but be of good cheer; I have overcome the world."[229]

When we are in a state of joyfulness, we are able to experience and retain God's presence, hear His voice, and ultimately secure revelation that will engender ceaseless triumph

Integrity: God is a just God; He abides by His Word to perform; will never go back on them because His integrity is at stake. "Then he said: "Praise be to the LORD, the God of Israel, who with his own hand has fulfilled what he

228   1 Samuel 1:18-19
229   John 16:23

promised with his own mouth to my father David."[230] God expects us to operate in the same fashion, to be trustworthy with our spoken words and actions. Hannah demonstrated a lifestyle of integrity.

Hannah vowed to God and she returned to fulfill her vows. God always expects this from us, whether when we are dealing with Him or our families, friends, colleagues, or even strangers. He is pleased with those who practice integrity. "To the faithful you show yourself faithful; to those with integrity you show integrity."[231]

When we live a life of integrity, we secure God's backing, and He vouches proudly and testifies of our integrity like He did for Job[232] A life of integrity secures for us posterity, protection, blessings, honor, and favor with God and man "The righteous who walks in his integrity, blessed are his children after him!"[233] However, if our activities are without integrity, we set ourselves up for shame, disgrace, poverty, and failure.

However, if we follow the path of integrity, we are able to lift our heads in pride, with our chests out, and ultimately

---

230   1 Kings 8:15
231   2 Samuel 22:26 NLT
232   Job 1:8; 2:3
233   . Proverbs 20:7

say with boldness before God and man "Vindicate me, O LORD, for I have walked in my integrity, and I have trusted in the LORD without wavering."[234]

Prayer: Lord, give me the strength to commit to a life of prayer, while I live in integrity and do away with all forms of unhappiness.

---

234   Psalm 26:1

Chapter 9

ISAAC

Isaac was the miracle son and only child Sarah had for Abraham after a long wait together as a couple. Isaac's birth was a miracle because his parents gave birth to him at a very old age of 100 years and 90 years respectively. Medically speaking, they had gone past the age of childbearing. "Abraham and Sarah were both very old by this time, and Sarah was long past the age of having children."[235]

It is a miracle because God said it, and it happened. Every time God says something to and about us, we must trust Him; because he will do it. "So is my word that goes out from my mouth: It will not return to me empty but will accomplish what I desire and achieve the purpose for which

---

235 Genesis 18:11

I sent it"[236] Isaac was a covenant child; God had planned to fulfil every word He said to Abraham his father[237]

Isaac was forty years old when he got married to his wife, Rebekah. They were blessed with twins, Esau and Jacob. Isaac was an obedient man. He followed every instruction God gave to him just like his father, and because of his act of obedience; he enjoyed God's presence always[238] Anyone who wants to experience God's presence must subscribe to obeying and following His instructions.

Isaac was a very hardworking man, in the midst of an economic downturn, he continued to do his job without giving excuses, and because of this, he was blessed exceedingly in the midst of scarcity[239] Hard work does not kill, it dignifies and brings plenty of returns in blessings. Hard work will always result in success and blessings if we don't give up. However, if we choose otherwise, poverty is inevitable. "…Hard work brings profit, but mere talk leads only to poverty."[240]

He was passionate about his work even in the midst of envy and strife from the enemy, he continued to work, and he refused to get distracted. Hard work and success will draw criticism and anger from lazy and visionless individuals, but

---

236 Isaiah 55:11
237 Genesis 17:19
238 Genesis 26: 2-6
239 Genesis 26:12-14
240 Proverbs 14:23

never pay attention to them; they are a source of distraction; their only goal is to find someone who will end like them before they move to the next person. Our focus should be on the goal and pursuit of the assignment before us.

ATTRIBUTES OF ISAAC

Covenant child: Isaac was a covenant child, and God's plan was to make a great person out of him. Like Isaac, we are also children of promise, but we must align with the demands of God to experience the promises of God in our lives.

"And we, [believing] brothers and sisters, like Isaac, are children [not merely of physical descent, like Ishmael, but are children born] of promise [born miraculously]."[241]

Everything God Said about him came to pass because God's Word will never fall to the ground, He will never lie or deny Himself. God's plan is to make greatness out of all of us in life. "Before I formed you in the womb I knew you, before you were born, I set you apart; I appointed you as a prophet to the nations."[242]

We must have it at the back of our minds, and constantly remind ourselves that we are children of the covenant created by God to fulfill a great purpose before the enemy

---

241 Galatians 4:28 AMP
242 Jeremiah 1:5

will deceive us and displace us. "For I know the plans I have for you," declares the LORD, "plans to prosper you and not to harm you, plans to give you hope and a future."[243]

Obedience: Isaac was a man of obedience; he obeyed every of God's instructions. His obedience kept him in favor with God and he was exceedingly blessed and protected from all assaults of the enemy. When you follow God's instructions, you secure His presence which guarantees all your needs. Obedience guarantees the fulfillment of God's plan for our lives. There are times those instructions may not look logical to us, but if it is God who gave the instruction, it is imperative we follow because God does not operate like a man. He knows the outcome of every situation from the beginning.

"And if they obey, they will be successful and happy from then on"[244]

Hard work: Isaac was a very hardworking man; he never had any reason not to do that which God committed to his hand as an assignment. He was always excited about his job even when the enemies came to harass him over his properties. Isaac continued to do his job despite the disturbance from the lazy people around him, he refused to allow their actions to deter him, he remained focused and he became very rich. Distractions will always come at some point in our life, but we should never allow that to

---

243   Jeremiah 29:11
244   Job 36:11 CEV

deter or shift our focus. The focus should be on the finish line ahead "Brothers and sisters, I do not consider myself yet to have taken hold of it. But one thing I do: Forgetting what is behind and straining toward what is ahead"[245] A wise man once said, it's better to subscribe to the pain of hard work than the pain of regret. "Hard work will give you power; being lazy will make you a slave"[246]

BENEFITS OF ISAACS ATTRIBUTES

Covenant Child: As covenant children, we have been destined by God to be great. However, subscribing to the things and ways of God is what guarantees fulfillment. Negative forces will contest the fulfillment of God's plan for our lives but having God on our side will secure the much-needed victory. The only way we can have God on our side is to pitch our tent with Him, and it is only possible by doing His will.

"If it is unacceptable in your sight to serve the LORD, choose for yourselves this day whom you will serve whether the gods which your fathers served that were on the other side of the river, or the gods of the Amorites in whose land you live; but as for me and my house, we will serve the LORD."[247]

---

245   Philippians 3:13
246   Proverbs 12:24
247   Joshua 24:15

Our beloved Jesus' destiny was contested, but God came through for Him. The place of understanding the covenant is what brings us into the reality of the greatness, blessings, glory, honor, and authority that God has packaged for all His children before birth. All of God's God creations are destined to fulfil destiny in a grand style, except those who choose otherwise because we are of creation of choice. God will never impose His will on any of His creation.

"I call heaven and earth to witness against you today, that I have set before you life and death, blessing and curse. Therefore, choose life, that you and your offspring may live"[248]

Operating with this mindset empowers God's children to fulfill their destiny no matter the obstacles.

"Have this attitude in yourselves which was also in Christ Jesus."[249] Have the right and positive mentality.

Obedience: Obedience triggers and moves God into action to pour out limitless blessings that can never be imagined. Abraham was a recipient of this order of blessings because of obedience. Everyone has a right to enjoy the same, but it is anchored on obedience. God is no respecter of any man, neither is he a partial God, whatsoever he did to one would

---

248 Deuteronomy 30:19
249 Philippians 2:5

be done for the other as long as what is required is done[250] If we do the same thing Abraham did, we are certain to experience the same.

"...and said, "By Myself (based on Who I Am) I have sworn [an oath], declares the LORD, that since you have done this thing and have not withheld [from Me] your son, your only son [of promise],"[251]

A key component of our walk with God is obedience, it initiates access into the realm of divine guidance every time the face of God is sought after in your journey of life. And when we obey God, we show the sincerity and the genuineness of our love for him. In so doing, we pivot ourselves to keep enjoying the unchanging love of God.

"Whoever has my commands and keeps them is the one who loves me. The one who loves me will be loved by my Father, and I too will love them and show myself to them."[252]

Though life is characterized by a series of battles, being on God's side in obedience guarantees victory.

Hard work: The place of work in our journey in life cannot be overemphasized. Having something to do as work, in summation, is a sign of responsibility, engaging our creative mind, and enjoying successes at different stages of our life.

---

250 Acts 10:34
251 Genesis 22:16 AMP
252 John 14: 21

God, the Creator of all things was a worker. We saw Him in action during the creation of heaven and earth. "For in six days the LORD made the heavens and the earth, the sea, and all that is in them, but he rested on the seventh day."[253] Jesus is a testament that God was a worker, and He also worked. "But Jesus answered them, "My Father has been working until now [He has never ceased working], and I too am working."[254]

When God made the first man, Adam, He also gave him work to do, "The LORD God took the man and put him in the Garden of Eden to work it and take care of it."[255] Work does not kill, but it brings the creativity of God out of everyone who cares to engage.

Having something to do helps you plan for now and the future. It is an avenue to secure the blessings of God and help others who are in need.

"The LORD will open the heavens, the storehouse of his bounty, to send rain on your land in season and to bless all the work of your hands. You will lend to many nations but will borrow from none."[256]

It doesn't matter how small or low paying the work may be, get something to do, and being faithful to it will always open the door for bigger ones. "Whatever your hand finds

---

253 Exodus 20:11
254 John 5:17
255 Genesis 2:15
256 Deuteronomy 28:12

to do, do it with all your might."[257] God only blesses the works of our hand and not what people hand to us as gifts to get by our daily needs. "Give generously to them and do so without a grudging heart; then because of this the LORD your God will bless you in all your work and in everything you put your hand to."[258]

Prayer: Lord, grant me the grace to walk in the understanding of Your covenant for my life, and help me to live a life of obedience and hard work. Amen.

---

257 Ecclesiastes 9:10
258 Deuteronomy 15:10

Chapter 10

JOSEPH

J oseph, the dreamer, as many called him was the eleventh of twelve sons from his father, Jacob, and the first of his mother, Rachel. He lived with his family in Canaan before being sold as a slave to Egypt after a failed attempt to take his life by his brothers. He had a younger brother called Benjamin; they were the only two children their mother Rachael bore for their father. Joseph had other half-brothers and sisters namely Reuben, Simeon, Levi, Judah, Dan, Naphtali, Gad, Asher, Issachar, Zebulun, and Dinah. As his father's favorite, he made him a beautiful coat of many colors, and Joseph loved to care for the sheep of his father. Joseph was a man full of love, he loved his entire family regardless of their bad attitude toward him. God expects us to love everyone around us as He loves us because love is the only thing that can diffuse bad or tense situations, deflate negative energy, and make the world a happy and loving place.

"A new command I give you: Love one another. As I have loved you, so you must love one another."[259]

We are commanded by God to love all men, and only those who obey God's commandment are loved by Him. It is okay not to be friends with everyone because friendship is by choice; and we have the right to choose friends that will impact our lives positively and cut away those friends that will lead us into a path of destruction. Love is of the heart, so we can love people from distance.

Joseph lived a happy and forgiving life even when his brother sold him to a merchant as a slave in Egypt because they did not like the dream Joseph had about all of them bowing down to him. Joseph was full of God's wisdom, feared God, and he obeyed God's instruction. "Love bears all things, believes all things, hopes all things, endures all things"[260]

ATTRIBUTES OF JOSEPH

Happiness: Joseph was a happy person; he never gave room for unhappiness even when things will not go the

---

259   John13:34
260   1 Corinthians 13:7

way he wanted or planned. His happy attitude made many become fond of him and love him. Even while he was in prison, many sought his help every time they had concerns. Only happy people can notice the sad countenance of others to the point of checking on them, that was Joseph's way of life. "Joseph saw some prisoners unhappy, and he helped them." A wise man said, "What you don't have, you can't give."[261]

Joseph enjoyed the presence of God to the point that his master, Potiphar, testified that the Lord was with Joseph, and everything he did prospered. A wise man said, "When you are joyful, you become full of God, and when you are full of God, His presence makes the difference in your life." "The Lord was with Joseph so that he prospered, and he lived in the house of his Egyptian master… But while Joseph was there in the prison, the Lord was with him; he showed him kindness and granted him favor in the eyes of the prison warden."[262]

He found favor in Potiphar's sight because of his demeanor[263] Our way of life, character, and demeanor can have a positive or negative impact on others, so it is important to live our lives to please God, and to help others.

---

261 Genesis 40:5-7 paraphrased
262 Genesis 39:2, 21
263 Genesis 39:4-5

Wisdom: Joseph was a man who operated in the wisdom of God, this rare gift and ability of his brought him favor with God and man[264] God's presence was always with Joseph, and that presence made him enjoy favor to the point of becoming a notable person in a strange land[265] Anyone who subscribes to the dictates of God in love can also enjoy the same privileges as Joseph, only if a way into the heart of God is found. One of the ways we can find our way to the heart of God is to be a people lover regardless of their background, language, creed, or beliefs.

Joseph, through his wisdom, saved the entire nation of Egypt from famine. Pharaoh testified of Joseph's wisdom. The wisdom of God is propelled to fruition through revelation, and it takes only the lovers of God to access those revelations that will drive the application of the wisdom. "Then Pharaoh said to Joseph, "Since God has revealed the meaning of the dreams to you, clearly no one else is as intelligent or wise as you are."[266] "The LORD confides in those who fear (Love) him; he makes his covenant known to them."[267] God's wisdom is available to anyone who loves Him, and it can be accessed by asking.

---

264 Genesis 39:2-3
265 Genesis 39:3-6 & 21-23
266 Genesis 41:39
267 Psalm 25: 14

"If any of you lacks wisdom [to guide him through a decision or circumstance], he is to ask of [our benevolent] God, who gives to everyone generously and without rebuke or blame, and it will be given to him."[268]

Fear of God: Joseph was a man who practicalized and exemplified the fear of God. The fear of God is said to be the beginning of wisdom[269] When one walks in the fear of the Lord, His presence is retained because God is pleased with anyone who lives a righteous life, and as a result, peace is established. "When a man's ways please the Lord, he makes even his enemies to be at peace with him."[270]

Being in fear of the Lord does not mean to be afraid, but to respect and honor whatsoever He has commanded. God's presence guarantees and secures favor, blessings, honor, promotion and victories just like Joseph experienced and enjoyed. Joseph demonstrated his fear (love) for God by turning down those things that looked compelling and appealing to the flesh by putting his body under subjection to honor God. "...How then could I do such a wicked thing and sin against God?"[271] He forsook all for God, and God decorated Joseph. Potiphar's wife told lies against him, but God came through and fought for Joseph because he honored Him. No matter what the situation may look

---

268 James 1:5 AMP
269 **Proverbs 9:10**
270 **Proverbs 16:7**
271 **Genesis 38:9b**

like, it is imperative we remain on the side of God in truth and in honor of Him with our words and actions. Man is limited in capacity and ability when trouble arises, but God will never forsake any of His children as long as they are on His side. Even in prison, God was with Joseph until he was set free.

"Joseph's master took him and put him in prison, the place where the king's prisoners were confined. But while Joseph was in the prison, the Lord was with him; he showed him kindness and granted him favor in the eyes of the prison wardens."[272] God will never leave or forsake you[273]

Gift: All of God's creations were created to fulfill a purpose, none of them were created to fill or occupy a vacuum. Everyone has been wired at creation with the necessary components that will enable them to achieve and fulfill purpose. Like Joseph, he was gifted with the interpretation of dreams. His first encounter with his gift was when he dreamt about his family, but they never liked the outcome of Joseph's dream[274] Not everyone will like or be fascinated by our unique gift(s), we must never allow anyone's negative opinions about God's plan and vision for our life deter or discourage us. Everyone is entitled to his or her opinion about others, the only opinion that matters is that of God. We must align and hold onto whatever God

---

272 Genesis 39: 20-21
273 Hebrews 13:5, Deuteronomy 31:6, and Joshua 1:5
274 Genesis 37:5

has designed us for and neglect the naysayers. Dislikes and negative opinions are part of the spices of life, they are there to spice up our journey. We should not allow any of those things to dampen our spirit or discourage us, rather use them as rungs of a ladder to keep climbing. "How horrible it will be for you when everyone says nice things about you."[275] Avoiding distraction is key to growth, we must remain undistracted in order to reach the summit as designed by God for our lives.

Joseph never got discouraged even when his brothers sold him into slavery because of his gift, rather he was focused, and he kept engaging his gift until he was announced and honored in a strange land. "… After they had been in custody for some time, each of the two men—the cupbearer and the baker of the king of Egypt, who were being held in prison—had a dream the same night, and each dream had a meaning of its own, …"We both had dreams," they answered, "but there is no one to interpret them."[276] All dreams came to pass just as Joseph had said to them in his interpretation. King Pharaoh also had a dream that Joseph interpreted and as a result was given the highest honor in the Land[277] That is what gifts can do if focus is maintained, avoiding mere talks and gossip by men.

---

275 Luke 6:26
276 Genesis 40: 4- 20
277 Genesis 41:1-57

"Do you see someone skilled in their work? They will serve before kings; they will not serve before officials of low rank."[278]

BENEFITS OF JOSEPH'S ATTRIBUTES

Happiness: Cultivating and living a genuinely happy life contributes to the outcome of situations around our lives. Achieving this requires the help and empowerment of God because life will throw our way sometimes things that may look big for us to handle.

"Though the fig tree does not bud and there are no grapes on the vines, though the olive crop fails, and the fields produce no food, though there are no sheep in the pen and no cattle in the stalls, but I will rejoice in the Lord, I will be joyful in God my Savior. The Sovereign Lord is my strength; he makes my feet like the feet of a deer; he enables me to tread on the heights."[279]

Unhappiness blocks our access to the presence of God, and the ability to access the secrets of God that can propel us into a world of unlimited breakthroughs.

Joseph was a happy man even in prison; he demonstrated and exemplified a life of happiness. His happy attitude made him realize some prisoners around the prison were unhappy "When Joseph saw them the next morning, he noticed that they both looked upset. "Why do you look

---

278 **Proverbs 22:29**
279 Habakkuk 3:17-19

so worried today?" he asked them"[280] His happy life kept his mind clear of depression even in prison, as a result, he was able to put his gift to work. It is dangerous to lose our joy, we must not allow any unwanted circumstances dampen our spirits; it has the capacity to rob us of our peace. Hannah is a perfect example of an individual who lost her joy because of her barren situation. Hannah had been praying to God for a testimony, though she did the right thing by praying, but she did it yearly in bitterness. However, the moment she switched from been unhappy in prayer, she got her testimony. "…and her countenance was no longer sad. And they rose up in the morning early and worshipped before the LORD… and came to their house to Ramah, Elkanah knew Hannah his wife; and the LORD remembered her."[281]

Joyfulness of heart gives access to God, and when that access is secured, great things happen. "Serve the Lord with gladness! Come into his presence with singing! Know that the Lord, he is God! It is he who made us, and we are his; we are his people, and the sheep of his pasture." [282] And as a sheep of his pasture, he makes the grass green for us always[283]

---

280 Genesis 40: 6-7
281 1 Samuel 1:18-19
282 Psalm 100: 2-3
283 Psalms 23:2

As long as we don't allow the situation to rob us of our happiness, the presence of God that puts us above all things is guaranteed. Joseph traded this secret, and he enjoyed the favor of God.

WISDOM

The journey of life requires wisdom in order to navigate successfully through the unpredictable uncertainties of life. When we operate in God's wisdom, we are able to overcome those things that affect the world. Operating in divine wisdom creates a platform that will enable men to seek out our knowledge and ideas. Divine wisdom is available to every of God's children, those who are ready to reverence and honor God in their hearts[284]

It is one thing to have wisdom, and another to use it right. The right application of wisdom with results is what distinguishes us from others. Joseph reverenced God in his heart, he forsook everything that will bring dishonor to the name of God; this made him the carrier of God's wisdom. This wisdom of his brought him honor, promotions, and blessings.

---

284 Proverbs 4:7; 8:1-35

King Solomon also enjoyed and operated in God's wisdom during his time on earth, as a result, he commanded honor and riches. From different countries, people came to listen to Solomon's wisdom[285] God's wisdom makes a showpiece out of a man and brings honor.

FEAR OF THE LORD (LOVE)

The fear of the Lord (Love) gives us access to the person of God. Our genuine love of God is what guarantees access to the secrets of God that enables us to stand out among men. Joseph's love for God kept him from doing things that God detested "And how should I do this great wickedness, and sin against God?"[286]

When we genuinely love God, we are empowered to please him. Pleasing God equals doing and obeying his commandments, and it gives us access to the knowledge of God that will make us do exploits. "However, as it is written: "What no eye has seen, what no ear has heard, and what no human mind has conceived the things God has prepared for those who love him."[287] The love of God sets apart for exploits, it brings honor, promotions, and blessings.

---

285   1 Kings 4: 34
286   Genesis 39:9
287   2 Corinthians 2:9

107

The three Hebrew boys refused to bow to another small god because of their love for God, and God beautified their lives in a strange land. "…But even if he does not, we want you to know, Your Majesty, that we will not serve your gods or worship the image of gold you have set up."[288] A genuine demonstration of our love for God makes us indestructible and guarantees the continuous presence of God. "When you pass through the waters, I will be with you; and when you pass through the rivers, they will not sweep over you. When you walk through the fire, you will not be burned; the flames will not set you ablaze."[289]

We must guard our love of God jealously without allowing anything to stand in the way (Romans 8:35-39).

Gift: The parable of the talent told by Jesus in Matthew 25:14-30 talked about certain individuals who were equipped by their master to carry out a particular assignment with tools (gifts) given to them. Unfortunately, some engaged with all their hearts and got rewarded, some engaged with little commitment, and got a little reward, while some never engaged, but lost their reward. God has equipped everyone, including you and me with a gift or talent. Those gifts or talents are meant to be engaged to the glory of God, and for our own profiting as rewards and blessings. When gifts

---

288 Daniel 3:18
289 Isaiah 43:2

are channeled toward the right course, God is delighted, and it brings an abundance of blessings and rewards. "A man's gift opens doors for him and brings him before great men."[290] Anyone who engages his or her God-given gift (Talent) like Joseph will experience and enjoy open doors of honor, blessings, favor, and without doubt, puts such an individual before kings, presidents, and men of influence. Joseph engaged his God-given gift of dream interpretation and this brought him before the number one person in the whole of Egypt at that time, and he was blessed and well-decorated[291] Peradventure those gifts or talents are yet to be discovered, go to God in prayer the giver of those gifts, and He will reveal it through the help of the Holy Spirit "But God has revealed it to us by the Spirit. The Spirit searches all things, even the deep things of God."[292]

All God's-given gifts are gateways to a world of exploits and blessings through different times and seasons as long as we are connected to Him in truth and spirit. Daniel's gift made him relevant in different governments, and he got rewarded for it (Daniel 1-6). Gift(s) must never be left dormant; it should be engaged continually until the set season of honor appears "…Invest this for me while I am gone."[293]

---

290 Proverbs 18:16
291 Genesis 41:1-44
292 1 Corinthians 2:10
293 Luke 19:13 NLT

Prayer: Lord, help me to keep my joy alive in the midst of difficult circumstances, engaging the gift You have given to me to Your glory; loving and operating in Your wisdom continually. Amen.

Chapter 11

KNOWLEDGE

Knowledge is said to be powerful, and a tool for liberation from any form of unwanted situation or ignorance. The right application of acquired and relevant knowledge will always alter any form of status quo in a man's life as long as a desire for change is imminent.

"My people are destroyed for lack of knowledge, because you have rejected knowledge..."[294]

Acquisition of knowledge must be continuous in order to stay relevant and current. Many claim they know enough to remain in charge, but in most cases they don't, while some

---

294 Hosea 4:6

don't even know, and are not willing to commit themselves to learning. "Those who think they know something do not yet know as they ought to know."[295]

Regardless of where we find ourselves in these categories of people, the common denominator is that acquisition of knowledge is important, and no one can know it all because learning is continuous and progressive. Acquiring knowledge could be formal or informal, it is imperative to commit to learning because it gives an advantage and stands you out among others[296] Daniel understood by books, and he was relevant in many governments. Those who commit to mental development will always discover hidden things that will distinguish them.

It is said that "When you stop learning, you start stinking." That is, people can smell ignorance, and it is rare to see anyone who wants to associate with an ignorant person. The apostles were perceived to be ignorant, but on their return, the crowd took note that something was different about them[297] They had gone to develop themselves at the feet of Jesus. Transformation will always put the spotlight on you!

It is important we develop ourselves and build capacity because that is the only way we can be in command of life

---

295   1 Corinthians 8:2
296   Daniel 6:3; 9:2
297   Act 4:13

situations, live a good life free of subjection, create wealth, liberate others of captivity, and most importantly discern between what God is saying and what the devil (The enemy) is saying to avoid confusion.

Knowledge creates a path to understanding and empowers with the skills required to navigate the paths of life regardless of what the known or the unknown may bring. They could be tough and difficult moments, hindrances, rejections, and setbacks, among many other issues of life. When we subscribe to learning, there is an assurance that at some point, the circle of mediocrity or any unpleasant situation will be broken.

"In the first year of his reign I Daniel understood by books the number of the years..."[298]

The absence of knowledge or limited knowledge puts us at risk of oppression, suppression, failure, limitation, and poverty. Our minds must be developed to the maximum capacity progressively in order to fashion a way out of any situation we don't like.

It is important to note that not just any quest for knowledge is relevant, but the one that will transform our mind, and make us a voice in our world. There is so much junk knowledge (information) out there, rather than build us,

---

298   Daniel 9:2

they put us further into captivity, limitation, poverty, or even destroy us. It is wisdom to know what to take in and what to trash.

"Give me wisdom and knowledge, that I may lead this people, for who is able to govern this great people of yours?"[299]

Solomon knew knowledge plays a key role in succeeding in whatever field or calling we find ourselves in, so he asked God for a deposit of knowledge. We must search for relevant knowledge that will make us a success. Jesus, as an example, showed us that seeking knowledge is key to a world of exploits, honor, and relevance. "And He was handed the book of the prophet Isaiah. And when He had opened the book, He found the place where it was written of him…"[300]

"Let the elders that rule well be counted worthy of double honor, especially they who labor in the word and doctrine."[301]

Being knowledgeable is not a function of age, but a function of responsibility on the part of everyone who desires to build capacity. Remember, knowledge is power, and readers are said to be leaders.

---

299 2 Chronicles 1:10
300 Luke 4:17
301 1 Timothy 5:17

ATTRIBUTES OF KNOWLEDGE

Authority: One of many attributes of man at creation by God is to be in place of authority. Authority was conferred on man by God, but most people are not aware of their position of authority, which is why they are living or existing as subjects in their domain.

"And God said, let us make man in our image, after our likeness: and let them have **Dominion** over the fish of the sea, and over the fowl of the air, and over the cattle, and over all the earth, and over every creeping thing that creeps upon the earth."[302] It will only take a man or woman who has built capacity in his or her area of interest to dominate and be in command.

The place of knowledge is very important, and it cannot be overemphasized, because the absence of relevant knowledge puts man in a tight, obscure, and condescending situation.

"They know not, neither will they understand; they walk on in darkness: all the foundations of the earth are out of course. I have said, ye are gods; and all of you are children of God. But ye shall die like men and fall like one of the princes."[303]

---

302 Genesis 1:26-28 (Emphasis added)
303 Psalms 82:5-7

We are a product of divine authority positioned to oversee the affairs of life. But when we don't know really know who we are, we are subjected to the dictates of life. Apostle Paul emphasized the importance of knowledge in order to assume our place or authority.

"But I say that so long as the heir is a child, he differeth nothing from a bondservant though he is lord of all; but is under guardians and stewards until the day appointed of the father. So, we also when we were children, were held in bondage under the rudiments of the world."[304]

It is important to note that being mature to be in authority is not a function of age but relevant knowledge and corresponding capacity. In most cases, anyone who subscribes to relevant mental development will always be considered ahead of others to be in charge of things. We have situations where individuals oversee and coordinate those far older than them.

"Joash was seven years old when he became king, and he reigned in Jerusalem forty years."[305]

Knowledge is said to be light, and many are in the darkness looking for someone to lead them out of every dark situation they are subjected to. Our place of authority is

---

304 Galatians 4:1-3
305 2 Chronicles 24:1

waiting for us, all we need to do is identify the relevant knowledge that will get us there. Jesus said, "I have seen where it is written of me..."[306]

Through learning and study, we can discover our identity, then embark on the journey to fulfillment with the help of God. People assume authority over different things, some have authority over organizations, institutions, families, religious gatherings, and many more. The most important authority to have is the authority over our lives with the ability to dictate and take charge. Having authority over our lives will help us manage our lives accordingly. If we can successfully be in control of our lives, then we have positioned ourselves to take on other levels of authority.

"No, I strike a blow to my body and make it my slave so that after I have preached to others, I myself will not be disqualified for the prize."[307]

Honor: It sets apart for preferential treatment. When we are valuable to those around us, making impacts, touching lives, and changing the status quo, men will naturally bestow honor on us. Honor is an offshoot of knowledge. When we are knowledgeable (skilled) to the point where we become a solution, honor is accorded to us because of our impact.

---

306 Hebrews 10:7 paraphrased
307 1 Corinthians 9:7

"Let the elders that rule well be counted worthy of double honor, especially they who labor in the word and doctrine."[308]

Permit me to say honor is honorable. If we desire to live a life of honor, we must make our lives count by building capacity that will affect the lives of others and our environment.

Joseph enjoyed honor in a strange land (Egypt) because he was able to proffer a way out of a problem; his life impacted many and he, as a result, was loved and sought after. Joseph was able to gather intel through the help of God on the dream of Pharaoh, and the intel ended up in favor of the Egyptians. As a result, Joseph was honored.

"And the thing was good in the eyes of Pharaoh, and in the eyes of all his servants. And Pharaoh said unto his servants, can we find such a one as this is, a man in whom the Spirit of God is? And Pharaoh said unto Joseph, Forasmuch as God hath shewed thee all this, there is none as discreet and wise as thou art: Thou shalt be over my house, and according unto thy word shall all my people be ruled: only in the throne will I be greater than thou. And Pharaoh said unto Joseph, See, I have set thee over all the land of Egypt. And Pharaoh took off his ring from his hand, and put it upon Joseph's hand, and arrayed him in vestures of fine linen, and put a gold chain about his neck; And he made him to ride in the second chariot which he had; and they

---

308   1 Timothy 5:17

cried before him, Bow the knee: and he made him ruler over all the land of Egypt. And Pharaoh said unto Joseph, I am Pharaoh, and without thee shall no man lift up his hand or foot in all the land of Egypt."[309]

All through the scriptures, we saw men subscribing to relevant knowledge in order to make an impact in their environment. Daniel[310], Apostle Paul[311], Jesus[312], and Peter and John[313] are a few of the many who enjoyed honor as a result of their impact on the world around them.

"Wherefore God also hath highly exalted him and given him a name which is above every name. That at the name of Jesus every knee should bow, of things in heaven, and things in earth, and things under the earth."[314]

Wealth: It is God's will for us to prosper and live a life of beauty. However, the good things in life don't come cheap. We must engage the law of labor which is acceptable in the spirit realm and the physical realm in order to position ourselves for wealth. A man who is not ready to engage in the law of labor will remain poor or die poor. Wealth is not just having plenty of money in your bank account but having all that makes life worthwhile. When we go for

---

309   Genesis 41:37-44 KJV
310   (Daniel 9:2, Daniel 2:46-49)
311   (2 Timothy 4:13)
312   (Luke 4:16-20)
313   (Acts 4:13-20)
314   Philippians 2:9-10 KJV

relevant knowledge in any area of our calling or career, we set ourselves up for success. However, it is important to also seek out relevant knowledge in other areas of our lives where we desire beauty and greatness. It could be living a healthy life, marriage, parenting, or spirituality.

"...So exercise yourself spiritually, and practice being a better Christian because that will help you not only now in this life, but in the next life too[315]. The Bible is the source of all God has for our lives. When we search it and read other relevant books that address our peculiar situations; our lives will be the epitome of success that others want to learn from. Note, challenges will come in our quest to establish wealth for ourselves, but it will take knowledge to overcome those challenges.

Jesus was faced with a life situation from the Devil but because of His knowledge of what was written; he was able to defeat the devil.

"He humbled you, causing you to hunger and then feeding you with manna, which neither you nor your ancestors had known, to teach you that man does not live on bread alone but on every word that comes from the mouth of the LORD."[316]

---

315   1 Timothy 4:8 LB
316   Deuteronomy 8: 3

"...But He answered and said, "It is written man shall not live by bread alone... and the devil left Him for a while."[317]

Our tool to disengage the devil from manipulating or disturbing our lives is to build capacity that will enable us to take charge of situations.

Relevance: Change is said to be constant, and at some point, it will always happen. No one can prevent change from happening, it may be restricted but will eventually happen. The Pharisees, Sadducees, and their cohorts fought against the fulfillment of prophecy, and the acceptance of Jesus and His gospel due to hypocrisy and inadequate knowledge. Against all odds, the change still took place.

"Which none of the princes of this world knew: for had they known it, they would not have crucified the Lord of glory."[318]

In essence, when we have adequate and relevant knowledge, we will not resist change; rather we will embrace it because it will always bring beauty. Daniel subscribed to reading and this made him relevant in different governments. Governments were changed, but Daniel's relevance was prevalent all through.

"There is a man in your kingdom who has the spirit of the holy gods in him. In the time of your father, he was found to have insight

---

317 Matthew 4:4-11
318 1 Corinthians 2:8

and intelligence and wisdom like that of the gods. Your father, King Nebuchadnezzar, appointed him chief of the magicians, enchanters, astrologers and diviners. He did this because Daniel, whom the king called Belteshazzar, was found to have a keen mind and knowledge and understanding, and the ability to interpret dreams, explain riddles and solve difficult problems. Call for Daniel, and he will tell you what the writing means."[319]

Our knowledge and skills make us relevant. However, we must strive to keep developing ourselves in order not to become obsolete. The more current we are, the more relevant we become. Apostle Paul subscribed to constant personal development, and as a result; he became the greatest of the apostles of Jesus.

"For I am the least of the apostles and do not even deserve to be called an apostle, because I persecuted the church of God. But by the grace of God, I am what I am, and his grace to me was not without effect. No, I worked harder than all of them—yet not I, but the grace of God that was with me."[320]

Freedom: Mental freedom is the bedrock of our physical freedom. Men may create a physical barrier that limits or hinders us, but if our mind is liberated, other forms of freedom will follow. In order to experience the reality of any freedom we desire; we must first liberate our minds. Our minds can be liberated by acquiring relevant and

---

319 Daniel 5: 11-12
320 1 Corinthians 15:9-10

purposeful knowledge that will establish total freedom. When we fail to know what we ought to know, we create room for limitation, barriers, or mediocrity.

"Therefore my people are gone into captivity, because they have no knowledge: and their honorable men are famished, and their multitude dried up with thirst."[321]

The Eunuch just couldn't comprehend what was wrong with him until his mind was liberated.

"And Philip ran thither to him, and heard him read the prophet Esaias, and said, understand thou what thou read? And he said, how can I, except some man should guide me? And he desired Philip that he would come up and sit with him..."[322]

And when his mind was liberated, his freedom was established. The Bible recorded that he went his way rejoicing. This is what we enjoy when we develop our mental capacity; freedom is established, peace is established, and most importantly, joy is established.

"...And the Eunuch went on his way rejoicing."[323]

---

321 Isaiah 5:13
322 Acts 8:27-39
323 Acts 8:39

Authority: When we are full of knowledge, we are positioned for greater things because of our capacity, and ability. "The hand of the diligent bears rule..."[324]

Naturally, the world will always look for a man or woman who is able to lead them to their desired destination. It will only take someone who has built themselves or someone willing to be built up to fit into the categories of those that are been sought after for solutions. Nobody assumes a place of authority by chance, an effort must be made to assume it. Some do it cunningly, while some do it in a dignified manner. Remember, everything obtained by pretense will always collapse in the long run. So, we must strive to be honest in the quest for knowledge and attainment of authority.

How we coordinate ourselves in a place of authority will determine whether our names will be written on the hearts of men even when we are gone. Most importantly, we are privileged to become a book that people can learn from and pattern their lives after.

Honor: "Then King Nebuchadnezzar prostrated before Daniel and paid him honor and ordered that an offering and incense be presented to him. The king said to Daniel, "Surely your God is the God of gods and the Lord of kings

---

324 Proverbs 12:24

and a revealer of mysteries, for you were able to reveal this mystery." Then the king placed Daniel in a high position and lavished many gifts on him. He made him ruler over the entire province of Babylon and placed him in charge of all its wise men."[325]

When we are able to provide solutions to people's problems, we get honored in return because we have been able to do for them what they could not do by or for themselves. It will take a man and woman of knowledge to proffer solutions that will bring an end to the problems of others. Joseph was able to achieve the same and honor was bestowed upon him. Honor brings acceptance, beauty, elevation, breaks protocols, and releases blessings.

Relevance: The world is constantly in need of solutions to problems. If we position ourselves to provide those sought-after solutions, men will always look for us. Recommendations will be made by others because of our proven track record and ability to deliver. Daniel was recommended to different governments in Babylon because of his knowledge and ability. Nobody remains relevant by chance, a price of diligence and self-development must be paid in order to assume the seat of relevance.

"There is a man in thy kingdom, in whom is the spirit of the holy gods; and in the days of thy father light and understanding and wisdom, like the wisdom of the gods,

---

325 Daniel 2:46-48

was found in him; whom the king Nebuchadnezzar thy father, the king, I say, thy father, made master of the magicians, astrologers, Chaldeans, and soothsayers."[326]

Daniel attained this seat of relevance because he took responsibility for self-development. He made us understand that he constantly subjected himself to self-development. Relevance will always stand us out from the crowd, bestow honor, promotion, and bring us riches.

Wealth: Genuine wealth comes by self-development by the enabling of God, through acquisition and application of right and relevant knowledge. Everyone has a gift in them, but those gifts must be honed in order to trade them for profit. Peter, despite being a great fisherman, needed to be schooled by Jesus on how to be a good fisher of men.

Genuinely gotten wealth creates stability, rest, progress, and sustenance. Every creation of God wants the benefits of wealth, however; they don't drop on people's laps. People engage their God-given ability in a right and honest way to become wealthy.

"Wealth gained by dishonesty will be diminished, but he who gathers by labor will increase."[327]

326 Daniel 5:11
327 Proverbs 13:11

Everyone who cheated their way to success will always suffer the consequences. So, if we desire to be wealthy all-round, we must subscribe to acquiring relevant knowledge that will help us attain it. It could be the prosperity of our health, life, career, marriage, finance, academics, or any other desire we may have. There is a price to pay, and everyone who is committed to genuinely paying the price will always come out victorious.

"And I am certain that God, who began the good work within you, will continue his work until it is finally finished on the day when Christ Jesus returns."[328]

God will always play His part, all we need is to do our own part in order to experience the blessings that will desire.

Freedom: "So if the Son sets you free, you will be free indeed."[329]

Our quest for a beautiful and glorious life is partly anchored on freedom. Man can be physically free, while his mind is still in captivity. No matter the level of physical freedom we have, if our mind is not liberated, we are as good as being in captivity. Why? Our mind is what sets the pace for our physical manifestation.

---

328 Philippians 1:6
329 John 8:36

"Be careful how you think; your life is shaped by your thoughts."[330]

We set our minds free by what we feed them, and that is why we must seek relevant knowledge that will liberate our minds and propel us to our destination. No matter the level of physical limitation, if the mind is liberated; the physical manifestation will follow suit.

Freedom is a platform for advancement, creativity, ingenuity, and a ticket to a world of exploits filled with beautiful things.

The Bible reflected on the power of freedom that was exhibited by men. Their mind was liberated, and they were able to think and bring their thought to pass. A wise man once said, "If you can think it, you can become it as long as you are taking corresponding action."

"But the LORD came down to look at the city and the tower the people were building. "Look!" he said. "The people are united, and they all speak the same language. After this, nothing they set out to do will be impossible for them! Come, let's go down and confuse the people with different languages. Then they won't be able to understand each other."[331]

---

330   Proverbs 4:3 GNT
331   Genesis 6:5-11

Their thoughts became restricted, and the power of their mind was also held in captivity. Our mind is a goldmine and the biggest asset. We must protect its freedom.

Prayer: Oh Lord, I ask for the grace to take responsibility in studying Your Word and other relevant materials that will enhance my understanding and build the capacity that will enable a purposeful life.

Chapter 12

LUKE

Luke was an Evangelist, the author of the Gospel of Luke and the Book of Acts. He was a trained physician[332] who dedicated his life to the spread of the gospel of Jesus even though he was not a direct witness to the ministry of Jesus. He availed himself of books that opened him up to the ministry of Jesus[333]. He was Apostle Paul's traveling companion and became a disciple of Apostle Paul.

ATTRIBUTES OF LUKE

Companionship: Luke understood the importance of good association and teachers. He positioned himself under the ministry of Apostle Paul to carry out kingdom

---

332 Colossians 4:14
333 Colossians 4:14

assignments. Paul refers to Luke as his fellow worker in God[334], and testified that Luke was with him in ministry work. "Only Luke is with me. Get Mark and bring him with you, because he is helpful to me in my ministry."[335] Our life is a representation of the association we move with. "As iron sharpens iron, so one person sharpens another."[336] The Bible admonished that we walk with the wise in order to become wise[337]. The character and actions of those within our circle will always rob off on us no matter the level of our spirituality. Luke was a wise man; he knew hanging around Apostle Paul would be beneficial to his life. The outcome of our lives is largely dependent on the choices we make, and friendship is one of those choices. A wise man once said, "Friendship is not by force, but by choice." Friends can make or destroy. There is an account in the Bible about an account of certain individuals who were friends. Ammon had a friend named Jonadab who taught David's son, Amnon, how to materialize the evil intention in his mind. Unfortunately, Amnon paid the price with his life[338]. We have a glorious destiny, and we cannot afford to be careless with it. Choose wisely. Even Jesus carefully selected his twelve disciples. In the days of the disciples, when the work of God became enlarged, they carefully selected individuals who possessed the same trait that will

---

334 Philemon 1:24
335 2 Timothy 4:11
336 Proverbs 27:17
337 Proverbs 13:20
338 1 Samuel 13: 1-32

help them further the cause of the assignment. "Brothers and sisters, choose seven men from among you who are known to be full of the Spirit and wisdom. We will turn this responsibility over to them."[339]

Therefore, it is wise to choose those we associate with and disassociate from those who may slow down our journey to greatness.

The Evangelist: Luke was an Evangelist. He wrote one of the four gospels. It was regarded as one of the four gospels because their writings proclaimed the "good news" (or gospel) of Jesus Christ. Luke was devoted to proclaiming and writing about the ministry of Jesus to teach others His ways even though he was a physician by profession. "Many have undertaken to draw up an account of the things that have been fulfilled among us, just as they were handed down to us by those who from the first were eyewitnesses and servants of the word. With this in mind, since I myself have carefully investigated everything from the beginning, I too decided to write an orderly account for you, most excellent Theophilus, so that you may know the certainty of the things you have been taught."[340]

Regardless of our chosen field or career path, we all have been called to be evangelists in the ministry of Jesus. "Ye have not chosen me, but I have chosen you, and ordained

---

339 Acts 6:3
340 Luke 1:1-4

you, that ye should go and bring forth fruit, and that your fruit should remain..."[341]   We have a duty to reconcile every soul who is yet to hear about Jesus back to Him, either by evangelizing, preaching the gospel, sharing gospel materials, and all other avenues that will draw the attention of many to Jesus. "And all things are of God, who hath reconciled us to himself by Jesus Christ, and hath given to us the ministry of reconciliation."[342]

Our job, family, career, or other personal engagement should not hinder our spiritual calling and assignment. We are ambassadors for Christ, and we must carry out our duty. "We are therefore Christ's ambassadors, as though God were making his appeal through us. We implore you on Christ's behalf: Be reconciled to God."[343] Our goal is to seek first His kingdom (Matthew 6: 32-33), and other things we are looking for will be added to us as a reward. Jesus affirmed that everyone who put Him first by forsaking every other thing will be rewarded. Mark 10:29a

Studious: Luke demonstrated the importance of being studious. Reading and learning reveals to us history and past events, enhances our thoughts, and builds our mind. Reading creates a platform for empowerment, avails the opportunity to build capacity, and also teach or help others understand. "Many people have set out to write accounts

341   John 15:16
342   2 Corinthians 5:18 KJV
343   2 Corinthians 5:20 KJV

about the events that have been fulfilled among us. They used the eyewitness reports circulating among us from the early disciples. Having carefully investigated everything from the beginning, I also have decided to write an accurate account for you, most honorable Theophilus, so you can be certain of the truth of everything you were taught."[344]

Luke took his time to read the accounts of those that were before him and, as a result, his confidence and understanding opened and he was able to impart others with his acquired knowledge. He positioned himself with Apostle Paul who was also a reader and a student of the Bible, and it paid off. "Suddenly, Festus shouted, "Paul, you are insane. Too much study has made you crazy!"[345] "When you come, bring the cloak that I left with Carpus at Troas, and my scrolls, especially the parchments."[346] Readers are writers, they are always inspired. As readers, we position ourselves for influence and authority. It is often said that knowledge is light, and when we have light; we take dominion over all forms of dark situations. Throughout the Bible, men of influence were students and reader of books. Daniel understood by books (Daniel 9:2) Jesus, our perfect example, was also a reader "And there was delivered unto him the book of the prophet Esaias. And when he had opened the book, he found the place where it was written about him and his purpose." Luke 4:17-18

344 Luke 1: 1-3
345 Acts 26:24
346 2 Timothy 4:13

BENEFITS OF LUKE'S ATTRIBUTES

Companionship: Relationship is significant in our quest to fulfill purpose in life. The kind of relationship we are involved in is a function of our choice. Luke was a man of wisdom, he decided to pitch his tent with one of the greatest Apostles, Paul. They were both companions and study mates, which impacted their ministry greatly. "Only Luke is with me. Bring Mark with you when you come, for he will be helpful to me in my ministry."[347] They only surrounded themselves with men of like minds because they had a mission to fulfill and were not willing to mess it up. Same for us, the outcome and the current state of our lives are dependent on those we have associated with in the past, or presently. It is never too late to shake off friends whose vision do not align with ours.

"Therefore, since we are surrounded by such a great cloud of witnesses, let us throw off everything that hinders and the sin that so easily entangles. And let us run with perseverance the race marked out for us."[348]

When we choose friends wisely, we can remain focused in pursuit of our goals like Luke and Paul. Right friends help us arrive at our destination quickly, they impart our lives positively, and they challenge us and bring out the best in us. The right company brings us into a place of honor,

347 2 Timothy 4: 11
348 Hebrews 12:1

influence, and impact. Daniel and the three Hebrew boys were a perfect example of good companions; they were able to influence themselves not to buy into those things that do not glorify God, and in the end, they were honored and celebrated.

"Shadrach, Meshach, and Abednego, answered and said to the king, O Nebuchadnezzar, we are not careful to answer thee in this matter... Then the king promoted Shadrach, Meshach, and Abednego, in the province of Babylon."[349]

Evangelist: We have been called to a life of service by God. It is a call to duty, and we must undertake the task if we want to experience the blessings, honor, and beauty that come with it. Our service to God in whatever area He called us is rewarding[350] "Then Jesus asked them, "When I sent you without purse, bag or sandals, did you lack anything?" "Nothing," they answered."

There are many avenues we can serve God, yielding our lives to His service, seeking first His kingdom by promoting what it stands for and preaching the gospel through evangelism. Undertaking this assignment positions us for supernatural blessings. "Ye have not chosen me, but I have chosen you, and ordained you, that ye should go and bring forth fruit, and that your fruit should remain that whatsoever ye shall

---

349 Daniel 3:16, 30
350 Luke 22:35

ask of the Father in my name, he may give it you."[351] If we genuinely play our part, our rewards of honor, and supernatural supplies, are guaranteed. "But first and most importantly seek (aim at, strive after) His kingdom and His righteousness [His way of doing and being right—the attitude and character of God], and all these things will be given to you also."[352] It is important we identify with our God-given assignment, and as we do so He honors us in return.

Studious: To an extent, our lives reflect what we have fed our minds or feasted on as information. Information is power; it enlightens, keeps us informed, and gives us a voice and a place amid the multitude. Luke made a choice to live a studious life. He said everything he shared as knowledge with others was a result of him taking responsibility to read the things that were documented before his time. Reading gave him a place, and others learned from him. No wonder he was a study mate of Apostle Paul who was regarded as a crazy person because of too much reading[353]. Therefore, we must potion ourselves and avail ourselves of the necessary materials (books) that will transform our minds and position us for exploits.

Living a studious life makes us relevant, current, a knowledge bank people can draw from, and most importantly, gives us

---

351 John 15:16
352 Matthew 6:33 AMP
353 Acts 26:24

a voice and makes us a wonder among many with rewards to show for it. "Let the elders that rule well be counted worthy of double honor, especially they who labor in the word."[354] Our dominance in life is anchored on God's approval due to the capacity we have built over time, while our acceptance and celebration by man in life is a function of our built capacity that affects them positively. Building capacity takes away shame, ushers us into honor, affluence, respect, and success. "Show me someone who does a good job, and I will show you someone who is better than most and worthy of the company of kings."[355]

"Study to shew thyself approved unto God; a workman that needs not to be ashamed..."[356]

"Study this Book of Instruction continually. Meditate on it day and night so you will be sure to obey everything written in it. Only then will you prosper and succeed in all you do."[357] Therefore, in life, to experience growth either spiritually or in our fields of endeavor; we must subscribe to continuous learning.

Prayer: Lord, I desire to live a studious life, give me the inner strength to commit myself to building capacity.

---

354 1 Timothy 5:17
355 Proverbs 22:29
356 2 Timothy 2:15 KJV
357 Joshua 1:8

Chapter 13

MARY & MARTHA

Martha and Mary Magdalene were sisters who had a brother named Lazarus; they lived in Bethany, close to Jerusalem, and were friends of Jesus. Martha and Mary taught us lessons about hospitality and priority. When Jesus came to their home, Mary sat at the feet of Jesus to learn from Him, while Martha was busy putting meals together. No doubt, there was nothing wrong with the action of Martha, she was simply trying to ensure their guests were well taken care of. However, we must learn to prioritize our time from the things that are of utmost importance to the least important. To Mary, sitting at the feet of Jesus was the most important then, because such opportunities don't come always.

Jesus was quick to mention the need to prioritize as Martha told Jesus to scold Mary to help her instead of just sitting down at His feet.

"But Martha was cumbered about much serving, and came to him, and said, Lord, dost thou not care that my sister hath left me to serve alone? bid her therefore that she help me. And Jesus answered and said unto her, Martha, Martha, thou art careful and troubled about many things: But one thing is needful: and Mary hath chosen that good part, which shall not be taken away from her."[358]

We have to identify the things that are of uttermost importance and attend to them because those things are what determine the outcome of our life. And when we miss it, it may be hard to recover or catch up with it.

Mary loved Jesus so much that she dedicated her life to His service as a priority. Even in death, and the resurrection of Jesus, she never gave up on seeking God "… The one you seek is no longer here."[359] This is what God expects of us, to seek His kingdom first[360]

There are many avenues we can seek God, making Him the priority. This includes His Word, prayer, fellowship, and in service to others by reaching out to any unsaved soul in the harvest field; telling them about God.

---

358 Luke 10:40-42
359 Mark 16 1-6 paraphrased
360 Matthew 6:33

Mary Magdalene's love for Jesus was so great that she was still dedicated even in His death. "And they say unto her, Woman, why weepest thou? She saith unto them, because they have taken away my Lord, and I know not where they have laid him. And when she had thus said, she turned herself back and saw Jesus standing, and knew not that it was Jesus. Jesus saith unto her, Woman, why weepest thou? whom seekest thou? She, supposing him to be the gardener, saith unto him, Sir, if thou have borne him, hence, tell me where thou hast laid him, and I will take him away. Jesus saith unto her, Mary. She turned herself, and saith unto him, Rabboni; which is to say, Master. Jesus saith unto her, touch me not; for I am not yet ascended to my Father: but go to my brethren, and say unto them, I ascend unto my Father, and your Father; and to my God, and your God. Mary Magdalene came and told the disciples that she had seen the Lord, and that he had spoken these things unto her."[361]

We can prioritize our lives like Mary so that God will be delighted to testify of our love for Him. Her dedication earned her the privilege to be the first to see Jesus after He was resurrected. That is the highest honor she would have ever asked for. When we live a zealous life for Jesus,

---

361 John 20:11-13

He honors us in return "…Those who honor me I will honor." Mary honored Jesus with her presence, and she was honored in return."[362]

These sisters also taught us that we must keep trusting God, no matter the negative situation because consistency in trusting God is key to unleashing the supreme power and authority of God.

When their brother, Lazarus, was sick and died; they sent for Jesus. "Then Martha, as soon as she heard that Jesus was coming, went and met him: but Mary sat still in the house. Then said Martha unto Jesus, Lord, if you have been here, my brother wouldn't have died. But I know that even now, whatsoever thou wilt ask of God, God will give it thee."[363] The fire of our trust in God must keep burning at its peak, and never go down, neither should we waver in our trust because God will never fail.

ATTRIBUTES OF MARY MAGDALENE AND MARTHA

Hospitality: One of the lessons Jesus taught us was to be hospitable. When we have genuine love in our hearts, we will easily love others and look out for their wellbeing. "Thou shalt love thy neighbor as thyself."[364] "For I was

---

362   1 Samuel 2:30
363   John 11: 3, 20-22 KJV
364   Matthew 22:39

hungry, and you gave me something to eat, I was thirsty and you gave me something to drink, I was a stranger and you invited me in, I needed clothes and you clothed me, I was sick and you looked after me, I was in prison and you came to visit me.' "Then the righteous will answer him, 'Lord, when did we see you and did all these? The King will reply, 'Truly I tell you, whatever you did for one of the least of these brothers and sisters of mine, you did for me.'"[365] We must look out for others in love, care for them and use our resources to serve God with those around us. Martha dedicated her resources to serving Jesus, and the same is expected of us.

"Six days before the Passover, Jesus came to Bethany, where Lazarus lived, whom Jesus had raised from the dead. Here a dinner was given in Jesus' honor. Martha served, while Lazarus was among those reclining at the table with him. Then Mary took about a pint of pure nard, an expensive perfume; she poured it on Jesus' feet and wiped his feet with her hair."[366] The resources and other things God gave us are not only meant for our benefit and family, but other people around us that may need help. "Is it not to share your food with the hungry and to provide the poor wanderer with shelter— when you see the naked, to clothe them, and not to turn away from your own flesh and blood?"[367]

---

365 Matthew 25:35-40
366 John 12:1-3
367 Isaiah 58:7

We need to always do good to one another[368]. Being hospitable is a choice, and we are a reflection of the choices we make. Remember, we reap what we sow[369]

Zealous: Our passion must be first and foremost channeled toward the things of God. God is the source of all things; when we commit ourselves to Him, He takes care of every other thing. "So don't worry about these things, saying, 'What will we eat? What will we drink? What will we wear?' These things dominate the thoughts of unbelievers, but your heavenly Father already knows all your needs. Seek the Kingdom of God above all else, and live righteously, and he will give you everything you need."[370]

Mary was so dedicated and committed to one of the most important things about God, His Word. No wonder they were able to trust God to bring their brother Lazarus back from the dead. "Then said Martha unto Jesus, Lord, if thou have been here, my brother would not have died. But I know that even now, whatsoever thou wilt ask of God, God will give it thee."[371]

God's Word has the capacity to make all things happen for us the way we want them. However, we must dedicate out life to Him in order to experience His power.

---

368 1 peter 4:8-9
369 Galatians 6:7
370 Matthew 6:31-33
371 John 11:21-22 KJV

"Do not be slothful in zeal, be fervent in spirit, serve the Lord."[372]

Our strength in God and our passion for His things are what guarantee our access to an unlimited world of possibilities. David, Daniel, Apostle Paul, are other examples of men who were zealous for God, and they were rewarded.

"For though I preach the gospel, I have nothing to glory of: for necessity is laid upon me; yea, woe is unto me, if I preach not the gospel! For if I do this thing willingly, I have a reward:"[373]

We must never let it get to a point where anyone would compel us to do the things of God. It must be done willingly, cheerfully and lovingly. Doing this brings us closer to God. "But if I say I'll never mention the LORD or speak in his name, his word burns in my heart like a fire. It's like a fire in my bones! I am worn out trying to hold it in! I can't do it!"[374]

Like Mary and other patriarchs or matriarchs in the Bible, we can also borrow a leaf from them and be fervent in prioritizing and serving God.

---

372   Romans 12:11
373   1 Corinthians 9: 16-17 KJV
374   Jeremiah 20:9

Faith: One of the many ways to connect with God is our faith. Whatever we desire of God is released on the platform of our faith in God. "Then he touched their eyes and said, 'According to your faith let it be done to you'"[375]

"For without faith it is impossible to please God..."[376]

Pleasing God is the gateway to our world of unlimited access to His plan and beauty for our lives.

Mary and Martha demonstrated their unwavering trust in God when their brother died, as a result, they received their dead back to life. Their testimony of faith enlisted them among the faith hall of fame which described how women received their dead back to life.

Our faith which is built and sustained on the Word of God has the capacity to do what men think is not possible. Even in the case of Lazarus, he was already dead for four days, with a decomposed body but Jesus brought him back to life. We must continually grow in faith because challenges of life come in different forms and sizes, so we need our faith to be ready to confront whatever negative things life throws at us. Our faith can be built by learning at His feet (Reading and meditating on His Word, attending a word-based church, and fellowshipping with like-minded

---

375 Matthew 9:29
376 Hebrews 11:6

individuals). "Consequently, faith comes from hearing the message, and the message is heard through the word about Christ."[377]

We must never be complacent in our faith walk with God because any attempt to sleep spiritually could expose us to the enemy who is always looking for ways to defeat us. "Be alert and of sober mind. Your enemy the devil prowls around like a roaring lion looking for someone to devour."[378] We must guard our faith like a precious asset because it is very valuable to our victory in life. "For everyone born of God overcomes the world. This is the victory that has overcome the world, even our faith."[379]

BENEFITS OF MARY MAGDALENE AND MARTHA

Hospitality: When we live a hospitable life, we create an environment of happy people. "Every day they continued to meet in the temple courts. They broke bread in their homes and ate together with glad and sincere hearts, praising God and enjoying the favor of all the people. And the Lord added to their number daily those who were being saved."[380] Mary and Martha's hospitable lifestyle brought

---

377 Romans 10:17
378 1 Peter 5:8
379 1 John 5:4
380 Acts 2: 46-47

them into love and favor with God. "Now Jesus loved Martha, and her sister, and Lazarus."[381]

Our show of love and care for others attracts love in return. When we care for others, God is happy about it. "He who has a [a]generous eye will be blessed, for he gives of his bread to the poor."[382]

Every time we reach out to others around us, we do it unto God, and God blesses us in return "Whoever is kind to the poor lends to the LORD, and he will reward them for what they have done."[383] We must not let our giving or hospitality be only motivated by what we will get in return, but the joy we bring to their faces should be our core motivation.

"Do not neglect to do good and to share what you have, for such sacrifices are pleasing to God."[384]

Ultimately, when God is pleased with us, every other thing follows suit. "When the LORD takes pleasure in anyone's way, he causes their enemies to make peace with them."[385]

Zealous: Being zealous for God means being genuinely committed to His course. Mary was committed to learning the Word of God among other things. She saw it a great

---

381 John 11:5
382 Proverbs 22:9
383 Proverbs 19:17
384 Hebrews 13:16
385 Proverbs 16:7

deal because it has its benefits. "Jesus showed us how Mary made a choice to sit at His feet to learn forsaking all other things that people thought were priorities[386] When we commit ourselves wholly to the things of God, God in turn commits Himself to our own things.

God is aware of all our desires, while others may be struggling to get those things that seemed important than God, and while they may be man's daily needs, we should choose to commit ourselves first to His vision for the world, and those things that seemed like a priority in needs will be added to us[387]. That is, we won't struggle to acquire or get what others who are not committed are struggling to get." Mary chose the Word, and it helped build her faith.

When we serve God, we enjoy His presence, and His presence brings about fulfilment, achievement, honor, and success. "Then the disciples went out and preached everywhere, and the Lord worked with them and confirmed his word by the signs that accompanied it."[388] "The seventy-two returned with joy and said, "Lord, even the demons submit to us in your name."[389] Those are some of the blessings we enjoy among others when we are committed to the service of God. Our service to God guarantees

---

386   Luke 10: 38-42
387   Matthew 6: 31-33
388   Mark 16:20
389   Luke10: 17

longevity, preservation, and supernatural supplies[390] We must therefore use our God-given gift (talent) and strength to promote and propagate the gospel of God's Kingdom. King David said he would rather be a doorkeeper in God's house than associate with idle ones and not do anything for God. Doing something for God sets us apart for honor, secures posterity, and guarantees trans-generational blessings.

Faith: Faith is a force that triggers the supernatural. It is said that until a force is applied to an object, it remains in the state of rest. Faith is a force that when applied to the spoken Word of God, triggers a reaction that propels the power of God to make things happen.

The Scripture referenced the faith of Abraham and how it triggered the release of his desire[391] Faith empowers what man thinks and as a result does the unbelievable, with proofs that cannot be denied. "What are we going to do with these men?" they asked. "Everyone living in Jerusalem knows they have performed a notable sign, and we cannot deny it."[392]

---

390 Exodus 23:25-26
391 Romans 4:16-20
392 Acts 4:16

Our faith makes us notable among men because of the proof it generates, simply because we chose to partner with God of all possibilities.

"Jesus said unto him, if thou canst believe, all things are possible to him that believeth."[393] Every time we engage our faith, God moves on our behalf; and of course, His move will always culminate in what eyes have not seen or ears heard before. Like Mary and Martha expressed their faith in God after the death of their brother, we must also endeavor to put our faith to work, the circumstances regardless because God will never leave or forsake us.

God looks for a son or daughter who can throw caution into the wind when it comes to expressing their faith without displaying fear because He has equipped us with the spirit of boldness. "For God hath not given us the spirit of fear; but of power, and of love, and of a sound mind."[394]

Genuine love eliminates doubt, God wants us to trust Him because it is the gateway to securing and moving His hand into action. Faith must be built to the point where it remains rested in God amid turbulent situations because He has our back. "God has said, "Never will I leave you; never will I forsake you."[395]

---

393   Mark 9:23 KJV
394   2 Timothy 1:7
395   Hebrews 13:5

Our faith will always guarantee access to the power of God, destroy barriers, commit God's integrity, engender exploits, and peace.

Prayer: Lord, help me to love others around me unconditionally, be zealous for your kingdom, and build unwavering faith in You.

Chapter 14

NEHEMIAH

Nehemiah was an official in the Persian court of King Artaxerxes where he served as the king's cupbearer[396] He was upright in character, and by the privilege of his position, he had access to the king. Nehemiah was a compassionate man whose heart panted for the freedom of God's people who were in captivity. "I inquired of the people of God, and I was to about their deplorable state. And it came to pass, when I heard these words, that I sat down and wept, and mourned certain days, and fasted, and prayed before the God of heaven."[397]

Nehemiah's compassionate and loving nature pushed him to request a favor from the king in order to render any help

---

396   Nehemiah 1:11
397   Nehemiah 1: 1-4 paraphrased

within his capacity to the people of God after hearing about their deplorable state in Judah. God saw the genuineness of his heart and He granted him favor with the king.

A wise man once said, "When it is in your heart, God will put it in your hand" No doubt, God saw the genuine burden on Nehemiah's heart, and He made sure avenues to deal with the burden were made available. When we genuinely have God's agenda on our hearts, which includes the welfare of others, He will see to it that we succeed with those good intentions. It wouldn't cost God anything to make it happen, providing every resource that may be needed, including human resources. In Nehemiah's case, God through the king provided all he needed because the hearts of kings are in God's hand, and He will turn them wherever He wills[398]

The king granted him permission and favor because God was involved and at the center of it. "And the king granted me favor, according to the good hand of my God upon me."[399] God expects us to have compassion, while we also show love for others because this is nature, also an avenue to bring hope and restore joy to the brokenhearted.

"Finally, all of you, be like-minded, be sympathetic, love one another, be compassionate and humble."[400]

---

398 Proverbs 21:1-3
399 **Nehemiah 2:8b**
400 **1 Peter 3:8**

"Because of the Lord's great love we are not consumed, for his compassions never fail. They are new every morning; great is your faithfulness."[401]

ATTRIBUTES OF NEHEMIAH

Compassion: The greatest gift God gave us was his Son, Jesus, for our sakes. God had compassion on us even in our failed and sinful state, He wanted a better life for us, so he was moved with compassion and love as He gave the life of His only Son to reconcile us back to God's intended original state as designed by God before the fall of the first man, Adam.

"For God so loved the world that He gave His only begotten Son, that whoever believes in Him should not perish but have everlasting life."[402]

God expects us to demonstrate His kind of nature to others around us. "Be kind and compassionate to one another."[403]

Nehemiah demonstrated the nature of God by showing compassion for his brethren and the things of God.

"And they said unto me: The remnants that are left of the captivity there in the province are in great affliction and reproach: the wall of Jerusalem also is broken down, and the gates thereof are burned with fire. And it came to pass,

---

401   Lamentations 3:22-23
402   John 3:16
403   Ephesians 4: 32

when I heard these words, that I sat down and wept, and mourned certain days, and fasted, and prayed before the God of heaven."[404] Nehemiah's compassionate level was so high that he stood in the place of prayer for the people of God. God is always looking for someone whose heart pants after others in compassion, and when He finds one, He empowers them for the assignment with rewards.

"And it came to pass, when I heard these words, that I sat down and wept, and mourned certain days, and fasted, and prayed before the God of heaven… Let thine ear now be attentive, and thine eyes open, that thou mayest hear the prayer of thy servant, which I pray before thee now, day and night, for the children of Israel thy servants."[405]

"I looked for someone among them who would build up the wall and stand before me in the gap on behalf of the land so I would not have to destroy it, but I found no one."[406]

We must always express compassion to others around us who may be challenged or going through difficult times because we have the nature of God with the capacity to be a blessing to others.

"Therefore, as God's chosen people, holy and dearly loved, clothe yourselves with compassion, kindness, humility, gentleness and patience."[407]

---

404   Nehemiah 1:3-4
405   Nehemiah 1:4, 6
406   Ezekiel 22:30
407   Colossians 3:12

Love: Our totality is embedded in love. Love enables us to fulfill our purpose, care for other people and our environment besides ourselves. No matter what we have, do, or become, without love; it is meaningless. "If I could speak all the languages of earth and of angels, but didn't love others, I would only be a noisy gong or a clanging cymbal. If I had the gift of prophecy, and if I understood all of God's secret plans and possessed all knowledge, and if I had such faith that I could move mountains, but didn't love others, I would be nothing. If I gave everything I have to the poor and even sacrificed my body, I could boast about it; but if I didn't love others, I would have gained nothing."[408]

Our love for others creates a room for others to feel and experience the nature of God. Nehemiah demonstrated his love for others, the reason why he was no longer comfortable living in the palace while the people of God and their possessions things were in ruins.

"And they said unto me, the remnants that are left of the captivity there in the province are in great affliction and reproach: the wall of Jerusalem also is broken down, and the gates thereof are burned with fire. And it came to pass, when I heard these words, that I sat down and wept, and mourned certain days."[409]

"Love is patient and kind. Genuine love seeks to see

---

408   1 Corinthians 13:1-3
409   Nehemiah 1:3-4

others happy, and successful, importantly, it makes the world a better place to live in, foster unity, harmony, and pleasantness."[410] Self-love is important, but we must extend the same love beyond ourselves as God as commanded.

"… Love your neighbor as yourself. There is no commandment greater than this."[411]

Passion: "Wherever your treasure is, there the desires of your heart will also be."[412] Our passion for something is spurred by our love for it. Nehemiah could not but express his love for God and His people through the demonstration of his passion. He was not happy about the state of the well-being of God's people, and how the house was in ruin. "…The king said unto me, why is thy countenance sad, seeing thou art not sick? This is nothing else but sorrow of heart. Then I was very sore afraid, "And said unto the king: why should not my countenance be sad, when the city, the place of my fathers' sepulchers, lies waste, and the gates thereof are consumed with fire?"[413]

When we are genuinely passionate about something, all our focus, energy, and resources will be channeled toward it in order to ensure it is in good condition, and when it is broken, there is pain or displeasure that comes with it.

---

410 1 Corinthians 13:4-7 paraphrased
411 Mark 12:31
412 Matthew 6:21
413 Nehemiah 2:2-3

In other words, we are poised to give all it takes to keep it in good condition or ensure it is fixed when broken. This is what God wants for us; to be passionate about His creations and His kingdom. "For the hurt of the daughter of my people I am hurt. I am mourning."[414] The above scripture demonstrates the passion God has for our all-round wholeness, the same is expected of us just like the king stated and expressed his passion for God saying that he would rather be a doorkeeper in God's house than any other thing[415] Also, he said he will never sleep until he finds a place of worship made available for God[416]. When we are genuinely passionate about something, nothing will be able to stop us until we see the passion materialize. Nehemiah was confronted and mocked for daring to do what was good, he did not allow the negative reaction or comments from men to limit or hinder his desire to attain greatness[417] Men will talk, mock, or plan to stand in our way, but we have a choice; either we succumb to men or pursue passionately with all our trust in God because God will never let us fail. We must not be moved by men but by our love for God which is rewardable. Nehemiah and his team were mocked, but they remain focused on their mission. "But it came to pass, that when Sanballat heard that we builded the wall, he was wroth, and took great indignation, and mocked the Jews... So built us the wall; and all the wall was joined

---

414   Jeremiah 8:21
415   Psalm 84: 10
416   Psalm 132:4-5
417   Nehemiah 2:19-20

together unto the half thereof: for the people had a mind to work. And the conspired to hinder us, but we prayed unto God."[418]

Apostle Paul said, "How terrible for me if I didn't preach the Good News! Apostle Paul was driven by his passion for God throughout his lifetime. To the weak I became weak, that I might win the weak. I have become all things to all people that by all means I might save some."[419]

Like Nehemiah, we must ensure our heart is constantly panting after the good of God's Kingdom. Nehemiah succeeded in rebuilding the walls of Jerusalem[420], and he was honored in return. Our passion will always bring about positive change, accomplishment, blessings, and honor.

Commitment: One of the driving forces to see our passion materialize is our ability to commit and totally immerse ourselves in that passionate vision, distractions, or hindrances regardless. "The light of the body is the eye (Vision): if therefore thine eye be single, (being focused) thy whole body shall be full of light."[421] Nehemiah was so committed to the restoration of God's glory and the beauty of his people. He was willing to lay aside his job to take on the burden of others. As a cupbearer, he was committed to

---

418   Nehemiah 4:1-10 Paraphrased
419   1 Corinthians 9:16, 22
420   Jeremiah 6:15
421   Matthew 6:22 Emphasis Added

the course of others. He prayed, fasted, sought for solutions to the problem God's people were facing.

Nehemiah began to engage corresponding actions in line with his passion and vision[422] We are also expected to make corresponding moves in line with our vision or passion. It is a demonstration of our commitment and responsibility toward the realization of the goal. "And I arose in the night, I and some few men with me; neither told I any man what my God had put in my heart to do at Jerusalem: neither was there any beast with me, save the beast that I rode upon. And I went out by night by the gate of the valley, and we began to put plans in place to build because everyone was happy and strengthened for the assignment."[423] In order to succeed in our vision, mission, and passion, we must make moves for things to fall into place. A wise man once said, "Until a force is applied to an object in a state of rest, no change will occur." The force of commitment is key in our quest to succeed. Abraham had to move from where he was before he experienced a change in his situation. He had to commit himself to move out of his usual and comfort zone "By faith Abraham, when called to go to a place he would later receive as his inheritance, obeyed and went, even though he did not know where he was going."[424]

We must borrow a leaf from Nehemiah who did not just

---

422 Nehemiah 1:5-18
423 Nehemiah 2: 12-18 Paraphrased
424 Hebrews 11:8

develop a passion for a change but committed himself by putting plans in place and executing those plans. "Nehemiah put his job on the line to seek support from the king for all that he would need to achieve his goal."[425] We must not be complacent, rather we should seek support in line with the dictates of God in ensuring that our passion materializes. "Do you not know that in a race all the runners run, but only one gets the prize? Run in such a way as to get the prize."[426]

"Let us not become weary in doing good, for at the proper time we will reap a harvest if we do not give up."[427] We should remain committed like Nehemiah, and the wall we desire to build will surely be completed, if we faint not.

BENEFITS OF NEHEMIAH'S ATTRIBUTE

Compassion: Being compassionate is a demonstration of love at work in us. Every compassionate person will always look out for the good of others, not just themselves only. Nehemiah expressed and demonstrated his compassion through a show of love and concern for the broken wall of Jerusalem that was in ruin, and the people of God that were in captivity. He began to pray and find ways he can possibly help those that were in trouble. He prayed to God for help and he approached the king for everything he

---

425   Nehemiah 2:5-9 Paraphrased
426   1 Corinthians 9:24
427   Galatians 6:9

could possibly need as resources to lift the displaced people of God out of their present situation into a better one. "O Lord, I beseech thee, let now thine ear be attentive to the prayer of thy servant, and to the prayer of thy servants, who desire to fear thy name: and prosper, I pray thee, thy servant this day, and grant him mercy in the sight of this man. For I was the king's cupbearer."[428]

Those who are compassionate are never tired of doing it because they love others like themselves. We must not be tired of doing good because it has lots of benefits for the doer and the recipients. We must remember that it is not the wish of anyone to be in a bad situation, therefore; we must show love and support because our good will always be rewarded while hope and joy are restored to the recipients. "You cannot fool God, so don't make a fool of yourself! You will harvest what you plant."[429] God rewards everyone according to whatever they sow as a character.

"Look, I am coming soon! My reward is with me, and I will give to each person according to what they have done."[430] Like Nehemiah and other patriarchs who have shown compassion on others by lifting them up, we must bring ourselves to do the same because it will make the world a better place to co-habit, be happy, progress, and prosper. "Pray for peace in Jerusalem. May all who love this city prosper."[431]

---

428   Nehemiah 1:11
429   Galatians 6:7
430   Revelation 22:12
431   Psalm 122: 6

The good we desire for others will always come back to us. Job was an example, he prayed for his friends, and he experienced the blessings of God. "And the LORD turned the captivity of Job, when he prayed for his friends: also the LORD gave Job twice as much as he had before."[432]

Love: Love is one of the greatest assets God gave to us. When we genuinely have love in our hearts, we are able to love others around us because we genuinely have the nature of God. Love is powerful, and it helps us overcome every form of negative energy and report around us. Genuine love helps us stand with others in their difficult times. The love Nehemiah had for God and His people was the driving force behind the rebuilding of the wall that was in ruin and the restoration of God's people. "And they said unto me, the remnants that are left of the captivity there in the province are in great affliction and reproach: the wall of Jerusalem also is broken down, and the gates thereof are burned with fire. And it came to pass, when I heard these words, that I sat down and wept, and mourned certain days."[433] True love will always move us to have compassion for others. Loving others helps us defeat any negative vibes the world may throw or present to us. Love helps us conquer hate, pride, self-centeredness, and most importantly, love never fails[434]. If we truly love God, then we must love everyone around us because that is the only confirmation that we

---

432   Job 42:10
433   Nehemiah 1:3-4
434   1 Corinthians 13: 4-8

truly love God just as He loved us[435] "Most important of all, continue to show deep love for each other, for love covers a multitude of sins."[436] We can also demonstrate our love for others to our prayers, material support, showing kindness, and looking out for them.

Passion: Our passion is what drives and propels us toward the realization of our goals and vision. It is what gives us the inner strength to keep pursuing those goals. Without passion, there is a possibility that the steam will fade away, and this could be detrimental to our journey or quest to see our goals attained. When Nehemiah made up his mind to ensure that the people of God are restored to their original state and the broken city is rebuilt; he began to put plans together by praying, reaching out to the kind for favor and resources, and training men that will help in the assignment. Our passion must be incorporated with actions, those actions are what fuel our passion to keep going until we attain the desired result. Nehemiah was driven by love, compassion, and the change he envisaged for others. Apostle Paul, our perfect example, was so passionate that he was willing to give his life for the love of others. "For to me, living means living for Christ, and dying is even better."[437]

"How terrible for me if I didn't preach the Good News!"[438] *Apostle*

---

435 1 John 4:20
436 1 Peter 4:8
437 Philippians 1:21
438 1 Corinthians 9:16, 22

Paul was driven by his passion for God throughout his lifetime. To the weak he became weak, that he might win the weak. He became all things to all people that by all means, he might save some. When we are passionate about something and take corresponding actions, the outcome will be success, honor, blessings, and accomplishments. "See thou a man diligent in his business? He shall stand before kings; he shall not stand before mean men."[439] Our passion is what drives our diligence. Just like Nehemiah, he was diligent; and his diligence fueled his passion until he accomplished his goal. "So we rebuilt the wall till all of it reached half its height, for the people worked with all their heart."[440] "So on October 2 the wall was finished—just fifty-two days after we had begun. Our passion engenders speed in our quest to reach our goal."[441]

Commitment: The commitment shown towards an assignment is what determines the outcome and the quality. Being committed is a sign of responsibility, and it will always result in the materialization of a set goal. Nehemiah was committed to building the wall, and the restoration of God's people. His commitment made him pray to God, took time from his job, and sought for resources that will aid him in accomplishing his goal. "O Lord, I beseech thee, let now thine ear be attentive to the prayer of thy servant, and to the prayer of thy servants, who desire to fear thy name: and prosper, I pray thee, thy servant this day, and grant him mercy in the sight of this man. For I was the

---

439 Proverbs 22:29
440 Nehemiah 4:6
441 Nehemiah 6:15

king's cupbearer."[442] He prayed and approached the king for the necessary support he could get[443]. When we are truly committed to a course, we don't fold our arms, we engage in corresponding actions. Being productively committed will always result in an accomplishment like Nehemiah completed the wall. Paul shared with us the result of his commitment "I have fought the good fight, I have finished the race, I have kept the faith. Now there is in store for me the crown of righteousness, which the Lord, the righteous Judge, will award to me on that day—and not only to me, but also to all who have longed for his appearing."[444]

Our ability to stay committed to that course will always result in accomplishment, success, honor, and reward.

"Therefore, my beloved brethren, be ye steadfast, unmovable, always abounding in the work of the Lord, forasmuch as ye know that your labor is not in vain in the Lord."[445] Our commitment will always bring us into favor with God and man and promotion.

Nehemiah enjoyed the promotion from being a cupbearer in the king's palace to become a governor because of his passion.

---

442 Nehemiah 1:11
443 Nehemiah 2: 4-9
444 2 Timothy 4:7-8
445 1 Corinthians 15:58

"Moreover, from the twentieth year of King Artaxerxes, when I was appointed to be their governor in the land of Judah, until his thirty-second year—twelve years—neither I nor my brothers ate the food allotted to the governor."[446]

Prayer: Lord, empower me to love others unconditionally, and stir up in me the love for Your house

---

446 Nehemiah 5:14

Chapter 15

OBED-EDOM

Obed-Edom hailed from the tribe of Levi. A man who received reverenced, and honored the presence of God in his home. He was willing to care for the Ark of God even though Uzzah was struck dead due to his carelessness around the Ark of God.

"And the anger of the Lord was kindled against Uzzah, and God struck him down there because of his error, and he died there beside the ark of God."[447]

Obed-Edom demonstrated his genuine love and pure heart for God by accepting the Ark in his home. God expects us to love Him with all our hearts in reverence and honor. Like Obed-Edom, situations should not determine how we love

---

447   1 Samuel 6:7

or care for the things of God. Our love for God and His kingdom should be unconditional no matter the situation we find ourselves in. Nothing should be able to separate us from the love of God.

"Who shall separate us from the love of Christ? Shall tribulation, or distress, or persecution, or famine, or nakedness, or peril, or sword? As it is written, for thy sake we are killed all day long; we are accounted as sheep for the slaughter. Nay, in all these things we are more than conquerors through him that loved us. For I am persuaded, that neither death, nor life, nor angels, nor principalities, nor powers, nor things present, nor things to come, nor height, nor depth, nor any other creature, shall be able to separate us from the love of God, which is in Christ Jesus our Lord." [448]

Obed-Edom demonstrated his unwavering love for God in honor and boldness, the reason why what befell Uzzah was not able to stop him from welcoming the Ark of God into his house; even when King David refused to take the Ark. As a result, he became a more than a conqueror in every area of his life. Romans 8: 38 paraphrased "Because of our genuine love for God, we are more than a conqueror." Our genuine love for God changes our unwanted and negative situations. God rewarded Obed-Edom and his household awesomely for harboring the Ark.

"So David was not willing to take the ark of the Lord into the city of David. But David took it aside to the house of Obed-Edom the

---

448   Romans 8:35-39 KJV

Gittite. And the ark of the Lord remained in the house of Obed-Edom the Gittite three months, and the Lord blessed Obed-Edom and all his household."[449]

Our commitment and genuine love for the things of God is what sets us apart for beauty and the glory of God. "Because he loves Me, I will deliver him; because he knows My name, I will protect him."[450]

ATTRIBUTES OF OBED-EDOM

Reverence for God: Obed-Edom was a man of Integrity; he did not renege when it came to the things of God. He was willing to put everything on the line to ensure the things of God retain their dignity and honor. "So David was not willing to take the ark of the Lord into the city of David. But David took it aside to the house of Obed-Edom the Gittite. And the ark of the Lord remained in the house of Obed-Edom the Gittite three months, and the Lord blessed Obed-Edom and all his household."[451] Our glory is embedded in our reverence and love for the things of God. "The Lord favors those who fear (love and reverence) Him..."[452]

---

449 2 Samuel 6:10-11
450 Psalm 91:14
451 2 Samuel 6:10-11
452 Psalm 147: 11

173

"Therefore, since we receive a kingdom which cannot be shaken, let us show gratitude, by which we may offer to God an acceptable service with reverence and awe."[453]

When we reverence God in our all ways, observing and abiding by His word, He honors us in return. "So the church throughout all Judea and Galilee and Samaria enjoyed peace, being built up; and going on in the fear of the Lord and in the comfort of the Holy Spirit, it continued to increase."[454]

As a people, we must ensure we live in fear (reverence) of the Lord because it holds the key to a world of supernatural blessings. Joseph in Genesis lived in the Fear of the Lord, and God blessed him in a foreign Land. "How can I do this wickedness, and sin against my God... The Lord was with him; he showed him kindness and granted him favor..."[455] He honored God by not engaging in what could possibly bring mockery to his God, and God rewarded him for that. When we demonstrate our love and honor for God, no matter the pressure we are faced with, God honors us in return.

"Those who honor me I will honor, but those who despise me will be disdained. Obed-Edom was honored by God, and his entire household was blessed."[456]

---

453   Hebrews 12:28
454   Acts 9:31
455   Genesis 39:9, 21
456   1 Samuel 2:30

Boldness: The boldness of Obed-Edom was a demonstration of his love for God. God emboldens His lovers. "God didn't give us a cowardly spirit but a spirit of power, love, and good judgment."[457] He was a God-fearing man, and he showed proper reverence for the Ark, unlike Uzzah who got punished due to his carelessness because of familiarity; he got so used to the Ark because the Ark was in his father's house for a period of 20 years[458] Despite knowing about the fate of Uzzah, Obed-Edom welcomed and accommodated the Ark. As children of God, we are expected to always show courage regardless of the prevailing circumstances. Obed-Edom had nothing to fear, he was as bold as a lion. "...The righteous is as bold as a lion."[459] Our boldness in God may put us in difficult positions with fellow humans but it is rewarding. When we choose to stand for God, we stand out among men. The three Hebrew boys demonstrated their love, reverence and boldness for God. "Shadrach, Meshach, and Abednego, answered and said to the king, O Nebuchadnezzar, we are not careful to answer thee in this matter. If it be so, our God whom we serve is able to deliver us from the burning fiery furnace, and he will deliver us out of thine hand, O king. But if not, be it known unto thee, O king that we will not serve thy gods, nor worship the golden image which thou hast set up."[460] As a reward for their boldness and love

---

457 2 Timothy 1: 7
458 1 Samuel 7:1-2
459 Proverbs 28:1
460 Daniel 3:16-18

for God, they were honored by God, and the King. God showed up, and the King had no choice but to honor them.

"God showed up amid tough situation for the three boys, they were rescued; and the king made a decree throughout the territory of Babylon that every living thing must honor and worship the God of the three Hebrew boys."[461] This is what our boldness can do when we stand for, and with God. Obed-Edom accepted the Ark with boldness even when King David rejected it[462] and God honored and embarrassed the house of Obed-Edom with blessings that the entire city of Jerusalem under the kingship of David heard about it[463]

Honor/ Service: One of the numerous ways we can enjoy and experience the goodness of the Lord is the mystery of Kingdom service. Obed-Edom was committed to kingdom service, he harbored the Ark of the Lord at the time when everyone refused it and he was rewarded[464] Kingdom service grants us access to the treasure room of God without stress.

---

461 Daniel 3: 25-30 Paraphrased
462 1 Chronicles 13:13-14
463 2 Samuel 6:12
464 1 Samuel 6:10-11

176

"But first and most importantly seek (aim at, strive after) His kingdom and His righteousness [His way of doing and being right— the attitude and character of God], and all these things will be given to you also"[465]

Genuinely putting the things of God first in service opens over our lives the windows of heaven with transgenerational blessings "If they listen and serve Him, they will end their days in prosperity, and their years in happiness."[466] "Blessed are those who fear the Lord, who find great delight in his commands. Their children will be mighty in the land; the generation of the upright will be blessed. Wealth and riches are in their houses, and their righteousness endures forever."[467] "Our genuine service to God secures supernatural provisions, preservation, longevity and fruitfulness."[468]

Obed-Edom was committed to the service of the Ark of God for three months, and God blessed him. Part of Obed-Edom's blessings were the gifts of children. Our service secures posterity for our generations yet unborn. Our service must be willing, not with compulsion or murmuring before it can be rewarded. Obed-Edom accepted the responsibility

---

465 Matthew 6:33 AMP
466 Job 36:11
467 Psalm 112:1-3
468 Exodus 23:23-25

willingly with whatever inconvenience that came with it because he must have viewed having the Ark in his home as a high honor and privilege, and God rewarded his attitude. Willingness and joyful attitude towards kingdom service are always beneficial[469] His unwavering commitment for three months was rewarded.

"Therefore, my dear brothers and sisters, stand firm. Let nothing move you. Always give yourselves fully to the work of the Lord, because you know that your labor in the Lord is not in vain."[470]

BENEFITS OF OBED-EDOM'S ATTRIBUTES

Reverence: Reverence is the display of honor, respect, or profound adoring. Obed-Edom exemplified how to reverence God even when the circumstances surrounding the Ark of God was not welcoming. Everyone including King David were not ready to take in the Ark of God, but Obed-Edom out of honor and respect for God; he took into his home the Ark.

Obed-Edom's reverence for God brought him into favor with God, and God blessed him and his entire household. Every time we honor God, we find favor with Him. One person's singular action brought about a change of story for an entire family. God is always looking for that one man to bless as a result of his commitment to Him. "I looked

---

469   Psalm 100:2, 1 Chronicles 26:9
470   1 Corinthians 15:8

for someone among them who would build up the wall and stand before me in the gap on behalf of the land so I would not have to destroy it, but I found no one."[471]

If we can make ourselves available like Obed-Edom, God will be delighted because of our interest in and love for Him. We can reverence God by being obedient to His instructions from the pages of the Bible, and when we do; we enjoy preservation, overflowing blessings, divine guidance, divine presence, and most importantly, honor. Joseph was a recipient of all these blessings in a strange land because he chose to reverence God in his heart and before men by not sinning against God.

"No one is greater in this house than I am. My master has withheld nothing from me except you, because you are his wife. How then could I do such a wicked thing and sin against God? But while Joseph was there in the prison, the Lord was with him; he showed him kindness and granted him favor in the eyes of the prison warden. So, the warden put Joseph in charge of all those held in the prison, and he was made responsible for all that was done there. The warden paid no attention to anything under Joseph's care, because the Lord was with Joseph and gave him success in whatever he did." [472]

We must never compromise our integrity or allow our location, circumstance, or people to determine our stand for God. Obed-Edom, just like Joseph, stood for God in

---

471 Ezekiel 22: 30
472 Genesis 39:9, 21-23

reverence by putting God first and he was decorated. Our lives can also reflect the glory and beauty of God if we can stand for Him when others are willing to compromise their stand. "Those who honor me I will honor."[473] There is no other greater honor than the one God confers on us. Therefore, we must ensure our lives brings reverence to the name of God.

Boldness: Fear is one of the wiles the enemy uses to take advantage of the situation and also to disarm us. As a creation of God, we have His nature of boldness in our DNA. "I said, 'you are "gods"; you are all sons of the Most High."[474]

This is who we are, bold children of God. Obed-Edom was bold enough to take into his home the Ark of God despite what happened to Uzzah. We must never allow fear to dominate our minds because we risk losing our stand, respect, dignity, and blessings. Obed-Edom's boldness brought about supernatural blessings into his home; the blessing was so much that he became the talk of the town. Boldness in God guarantees victory, the release of blessing, proffers honor, celebration and promotion. David, just like Obed-Edom, demonstrated his boldness in God when he came face to face with Goliath who was defiling the army of God. The expression of David's boldness gave the

---

473   2 Samuel 2: 30
474   Psalm 82:6

Israelites victory over Goliath and the philistines. "I have killed a bear and lion with my bare hands, so defeating you Goliath will be cheap for me. You have come to fight me with a sword, but I come to you in the name of God who gave the wisdom to create that weapon. So, David prevailed over the Philistine with a sling and with a stone, and smote the Philistine, and slew him; but there was no sword in the hand of David."[475]

His confidence gave him victory. The enemy will try to intimidate us with what may seem impossible, but we must remember that we have a God of all possibilities. David's victory brought about celebration the same way the city of David heard about the testimonies of God's blessings in the house of Obed-Edom. "Now King David was told, "The LORD has blessed the household of Obed-Edom and everything he has, because of the ark of God." So, David went to bring up the ark of God from the house of Obed-Edom to the City of David with rejoicing."[476]

Our boldness gives us a voice, attracts people to us, builds our confidence, and gives us a place amid the multitude.

Honor/Service: One of the fastest ways to become a leader is service; it is also an avenue to be blessed by God and man. When we make ourselves useful to others, we

---

475   1 Samuel 17:20-55
476   2 Samuel 6:12

get rewarded in return either materially or with a change of level. In service, we learn and grow. Obed-Edom was in service for God for three months, and his fame went abroad with lots of blessings.

"The Ark of the LORD remained there in Obed-Edom's house for three months, and the LORD blessed Obed-Edom and his entire household."[477] *He was not weary, he kept on with servicing God's agenda. Our continuous and unbroken commitment to God's Agenda secures favor for us. "Thou shalt arise and have mercy upon Zion: for the time to favor her, yea, the set time, is come. For thy servants take pleasure in her stones and favor the dust thereof."*[478]

Obed-Edom was favored of the Lord, and his fame went abroad. King David heard and he wanted the Ark back. Obed-Edom became an important person, setting the pace for kingdom service among his tribe. A genuine and honorable service secures longevity, all round fruitfulness, sound health, career breakthroughs, pleasure, prosperity and blessing[479]. We should have at the back of our minds that every service rendered in truth and love is bound to be rewarded. We must remain steadfast like Obed-Edom in order to receive our reward of service. "Therefore, my dear brothers and sisters, stand firm. Let nothing move you. Always give yourselves fully to the work of the Lord, because you know that your labor in the Lord is not in

---

477   2 Samuel 6:11
478   Psalm 102:13-14 KJV
479   Exodus 23: 25-26, Job 36:11

vain."[480] "And, behold, I come quickly; and my reward is with me, to give every man according as his work shall be."[481]

Prayer: Lord, give unto me the wisdom to reverence You in all my endeavors, while I also serve You in truth without fear.

---

480   I Corinthians 15:18
481   Revelation 22:12

Chapter 16

PAUL

Paul the Apostle was one of the disciples of Jesus who did not meet Jesus face to face; I mean physically, he wasn't part of the disciples of Jesus during his ministry days. However, he was completely committed to the teachings and the spread of the gospel more than the other apostles before him who were privileged to walk with Jesus side by side. Paul became committed after the encounter with Jesus on his way to Damacus[482]

Paul was formerly known as Saul of Tarsus, and was a lawyer by profession. He persecuted Christians because he acted in ignorance but after his encounter with Jesus, he was convinced, converted, and became an addict for the gospel of Christ.

---

482 Acts 9:1-30

"Meanwhile, Saul was uttering threats with every breath and was eager to kill the Lord's followers. So, he went to the high priest. He requested letters addressed to the synagogues in Damascus, asking for their cooperation in the arrest of any followers of the Way he found there. He wanted to bring them—both men and women—back to Jerusalem in chains. As he was approaching Damascus on this mission, a light from heaven suddenly shone down around him. He fell to the ground and heard a voice saying to him, "Saul! Saul! Why are you persecuting me? Who are you, lord?" Saul asked. And the voice replied, "I am Jesus, the one you are persecuting! Now get up and go into the city, and you will be told what you must do."[483]

Sometimes, our actions are a result of ignorance. That is why knowledge is very important, it brings light and the light removes the dark cloud of ignorance. Paul acted in ignorance during those years before he encountered the light of God. Like Paul, everyone has the same opportunity; at no point should we condemn ourselves, rather we should ask God for help. God is interested in using everyone as a steward to propagate the gospel of Jesus. Paul and other disciples began to preach the gospel and peace reigned in the cities. He did not allow his past to define his present situation, neither his future. "This one thing I do, forgetting

---

483 Acts 9:1-6

those things which are behind, and reaching forth unto those things which are before, I press toward the mark for the prize."[484]

We must not allow our past to dictate what happens in our present or the future. It is detrimental and bad for our progress because our path has been designed to keep advancing and not retrogress or remain at the same point. Apostle Paul was a visionary, a studious individual, who craved for knowledge, and was passionate and dedicated to the advancement of the gospel.

"I am a Jew, born in Tarsus of Cilicia, but brought up in this city, educated at the feet of Gamaliel according to the strictness of the law of our fathers, being ardent and passionate for God just as all of you are today."[485]

Our genuine encounter with Jesus, with the quest for knowledge, has the capacity to change our lives either spiritually, career wise, and every other aspect of our lives.

ATTRIBUTES OF PAUL

Knowledge: "An intelligent heart acquires knowledge, and the ear of the wise seeks knowledge."[486] Knowledge is the springboard that propels us toward our desired goal. As the above verse of the Bible states, it is wisdom to acquire

---

484 Philippians 3:13
485 Acts 22: 3
486 Proverbs 18:15

knowledge because it will help us have control of situations. Apostle Paul was a man of knowledge, he craved for knowledge to the point where men began to testify about his wealth of knowledge. "At this point Festus interrupted Paul's defense. "You are out of your mind, Paul!" he shouted. "Your great learning is driving you insane."[487]

"Bear in mind that our Lord's patience means salvation, just as our dear brother Paul also wrote you with the wisdom that God gave him. He writes the same way in all his letters, speaking in them of these matters. His letters contain some things that are hard to understand..."[488]

When we acquire relevant knowledge, men take note of us and bless us. In Acts of the Apostles, the people testified of what the acquisition of relevant knowledge did to the apostles. "Now when they saw the boldness of Peter and John, and perceived that they were unlearned and ignorant men, they marveled; and they took knowledge of them, that they had been with Jesus."[489]

The apostles chose to acquire knowledge at the feet of Jesus, as a result; people had no choice but to acknowledge the once perceived ignorant men had experienced a makeover by being with the master. Knowledge is light, and the level of light we have is what determines the level of darkness

---

487   Acts 24:26
488   2 Peter 3:15-16
489   Acts 14:13

we can dispel. Therefore, it will take relevant acquired knowledge to dispel anything that represents darkness around our life. According to Jesus, learning brings rest, and rest is what everyone desires[490] That is why learning cannot be over-emphasized. Knowledge transforms, illuminates, and brings us into favor with God and man.

"Let the elders that rule well be counted worthy of double honor, especially they who labor in the word and doctrine."[491]

Take note of the statement "labor in the word" from the above verse, it connotes the acquisition of knowledge. Fervency and right labor in the acquisition of knowledge confer on us honor. Apostle Paul demonstrated this virtue throughout his lifetime. No wonder he was greater than the apostles that were before him.

"The cloak that I left at Troas with Carpus, when thou comest, bring with thee, and the books, but especially the parchments."[492]

Apostle Peter testified of the knowledge of Paul how it was difficult to comprehend his words[493] Jesus, our perfect example, was keen on knowledge acquisition because it helps with self-discovery and liberates.

---

490 Matthew 11:29
491 1 Timothy 5:17
492 2 Timothy 4:13
493 2 Peter 3: 16

"And there was delivered unto him the book of the prophet Esaias. And when he had opened the book, he found the place where it was written of him..."[494]

We must commit ourselves to learning because it brings understanding, and the understanding of something is what puts us in command.

Daniel, a high ranking official of a State still made out time to read. We must not allow anything limit or stop our learning. "In the first year of his reign I, Daniel, understood by the books..."[495]

A wise man once said, "When you stop learning, you start dying." Not necessarily physical death but death of being relevant. Unfortunately, lack of relevance in society or to people means we have become valueless and dispensable. "A wise man is full of strength, and a man of knowledge enhances his might."[496]

Kingdom Driven: Apostle Paul was a man dedicated to service; he was committed to service on both sides of the world. That is, he was passionate about persecuting Christians, and after he had encountered Jesus, he engaged the passion positively. We have been called to a life of service; service to God, humanity, and society. "Let My

---

494   Luke 4:17-21
495   Daniel 9: 2
496   Proverbs 24:5

people go, that they may serve Me…"[497] Every genuine service carries reward, and it creates channels for us to experience the blessings associated with it.

"You shall serve the LORD your God, and He shall bless your bread and water. I will also remove sickness from among you. No one shall suffer miscarriage or be barren in your land; I will fulfill the number of your days. Every service we render either to God or to humanity comes with a reward."[498]

"Whoever is kind to the poor lends to the LORD, and he will reward them for what they have done."[499]

"Pray for the peace of Jerusalem: they shall prosper that love thee."[500]

It is important to understand that our service is important to the outcome of things around us. It could be propagating the gospel, helping and supporting mankind, or the environment. Apostle Paul was committed to the gospel of Jesus with every fiber in him. He made sure he reached out to as many as he could in order to help them understand the beauty God had for them[501] "Paul stated that not being in service of the God given assignment to him is like

497 Exodus 7:16
498 Exodus 23:25-26
499 Proverbs 19:17
500 Psalm 122: 6 KJV
501 Colossians 1:24-29

being without life or fulfilment."[502] Service brings us into fulfilment when we see others benefiting from our service. He was able to say boldly how he had fulfilled purpose because he was dedicated to a life of service.

"I have fought a good fight, I have finished my course, and I have kept the faith."[503]

Like Paul, we can also live a life of fulfillment if we are committed to the service of God and others; not just ourselves alone "Not looking to your own interests but each of you to the interests of the others."[504] We must identify our point of service and engage.

Job was a man of service, he was committed to serving humanity, and he felt fulfilled doing it. As a reward, he earned honor and respect from his people.

"Whoever heard me spoke well of me, and those who saw me commended me, because I rescued the poor who cried for help, and the fatherless who had none to assist them. The one who was dying blessed me; I made the widow's heart sing. I put on righteousness as my clothing; justice was my robe and my turban. I was eyes to the blind and feet to the lame. I was a father to the needy; I took up the case of the stranger. I broke the fangs of the wicked and snatched the victims from their teeth."[505]

---

502   I Corinthians 9:16 paraphrased
503   2 Timothy 4:7
504   Philippians 2:4
505   Job 29: 11-17

That is the kind of life we have been called to by God; to be a blessing to others regardless of their background and beliefs. "So then, as we have opportunity, let us do good to everyone."[506] Jesus, during His ministry, also demonstrated and made us understand that His purpose was to serve and to be served. "For even the Son of Man did not come to be served, but to serve, and to give his life as a ransom for many."[507]

It is okay to be served, but it is much better and more honorable to serve because it comes with fulfilment. "In everything I did, I showed you that by this kind of hard work we must help the weak, remembering the words the Lord Jesus himself said: 'It is more blessed to give than to receive.'"[508]

Visionary: A life of vision is a life of purpose, progress, victory, peace, riches, and blessings. "Where there is no vision, the people perish."[509] Vision is what keeps you and I on the path of progress and advancement. The absence of vision limits our growth or change in any area we desire. Vision is the engine that propels us toward the plan and purpose of God for our lives. God has a plan and purpose for our lives, but until we catch the vision, we risk losing out of the blessings. "For I know the plans I have for

---

506   Galatians 6:10
507   Mark 10:45
508   Acts 10:35
509   Proverbs 29:18

you," declares the LORD, "plans to prosper you and not to harm you, plans to give you hope and a future."[510] God has envisioned a life of beauty for us but we must catch the vision, then run with it in order to succeed. "Then the LORD answered me and said, "Write the vision and engrave it plainly on tablets So that the one who reads it will run."[511] Our lives are meant to experience progressive and positive change from time to time but lack of vision can jeopardize the plan of God for us. Vision is the leeway for unstoppable advancement.

"The path of the just has been ordained to keen shining brighter and brighter..."[512]

Paul was a man of vision, he understood that the assignment before him required him to be a visionary, so he laid aside everything that could limit his vision because he knew that without vision he will be limited. "Brothers and sisters, I do not consider myself yet to have taken hold of it. But one thing I do: Forgetting what is behind and straining toward what is ahead."[513] His eyes where focused on the goal ahead of him. Many times, we get distracted in our quest to attain vision, but it is risky. Men and women of vision must never be distracted regardless of what may seem like

---

510   Jeremiah 29:11
511   Habakkuk 2:2
512   Proverbs 4:18
513   Philippians 3:13

distraction around them. Paul understood this, that's why he admonished us to lay aside anything that may limit or end our vision prematurely.

"Therefore, since we are surrounded by such a huge crowd of witnesses to the life of faith, let us strip off every weight that slows us down, especially the sin that so easily trips us up. And let us run with endurance the race God has set before us."[514]

There is a race ahead of us, and it takes focus and concentration to get to the finish line of a given or discovered vision. A wise man once said, "Nobody runs a 100 meters dash race and look backward in the process, doing that could lead to loss of race, reward or the honor that comes with completion, and maybe injury to self or others." So, we must be disciplined in pursuing our vision in order to attain and live a life of fulfilment. God, in His creativity, positioned the eyes strategically in front of the head because the eyes help see ahead, guides our legs which are one of the mechanisms that helps us advance, and plan for whatever may be ahead of us. Paul was so passionate about his vision to see all men saved regardless of color, speech and residence. He was willing to give his life to see vision fulfilled. Men and women of vision die many times before they reach their destination, not necessarily physical death, but barriers, setbacks or limitations. There are times

---

514 Hebrews 12: 1

those things will stand in our way of achieving those goals; they could kill us emotionally, mentally, physically and resources wise. However, men and women who are vision-driven are fired up to continue their journey of vision regardless of those barriers.

"As it is written: "For your sake we face death all day long; we are considered as sheep to be slaughtered." No, in all these things we are more than conquerors through him who loved us. For I am convinced that neither death nor life, neither angels nor demons, neither the present nor the future, nor any powers, neither height nor depth, nor anything else in all creation, will be able to separate us from the love of God that is in Christ Jesus our Lord."[515]

Visionaries are unstoppable, they never throw in the towel; rather they devise other ways to move on in their quest to see their vision fulfilled. Several attempts were made on the life of Paul, but he never gave up.

"I am more. I have worked much harder, been in prison more frequently, been flogged more severely, and been exposed to death again and again. Five times I received from the Jews the forty lashes minus one. Three times I was beaten with rods, once I was pelted with stones, three times I was shipwrecked, I spent a night and a day in the open sea, I have been constantly on the move. I have been in danger from rivers, in danger from bandits, in danger from my fellow Jews, in danger from Gentiles; in danger in the city, in danger in the country, in danger at sea; and in danger from false believers. I have labored and

---

515   Romans 8:36-39

toiled and have often gone without sleep; I have known hunger and thirst and have often gone without food; I have been cold and naked. Besides everything else, I face daily the pressure of my concern for all the churches."[516]

Consistency is the key to vision attainment, so we must remain creatively committed in wisdom if we desire to cross that tape of victory in celebration. "Though the race was not easy or rosy, but I remained committed, so I can conveniently say I have fought the good fight, I have finished the race successfully."[517]

Mentor: Apostle Paul lived a life configured around learning. He was committed to the acquisition of knowledge not just for himself but to inform others by imparting them with the knowledge that will bring a change to their lives.

"I am verily a man which am a Jew, born in Tarsus, a city in Cilicia, yet brought up in this city at the feet of Gamaliel, and taught according to the perfect manner of the law of the fathers, and was zealous toward God, as ye all are this day."[518]

God expects us to keep learning for us to assume the place of authority over all things and situations in order not to be a victim of the enemy. "My people are destroyed for lack of knowledge, because you have rejected knowledge...

---

516 2 Corinthians 11: 23-28
517 2 Timothy 4:7 paraphrased
518 Acts 22:3

"[519] Learning is in stages or phases, for us to learn and understand God has prepared for us a mentor, the Holy Spirit. Jesus told us how the Spirit of God will mentor us in all things till we get to our God-ordained destination.

"But when he, the Spirit of truth, comes, he will guide you into all the truth. He will not speak on his own; he will speak only what he hears, and he will tell you what is yet to come."[520] Therefore, the place of mentorship cannot be overemphasized. Being mentored is not limited to one-on-one with other people. just like the Holy Spirit whom we cannot see but mentors us, we can also mentor ourselves through books written by men of God, sermons, videos, and any other resource materials than can build our capacity.

Apostle Paul gave himself to the mentorship of the Holy Spirit, teachers and books. Jesus, Daniel, and other apostles also gave themselves to mentorship. Mentorship creates the opportunity to learn from those who have passed through our intended route in order not to make similar mistakes made by them and build on what they have learned. Learning from others or being mentored is not a function of age, but a function humility, submitting oneself to the tutelage of individuals who have built capacity over a period with the ability to impart others with such knowledge.

"Thus says the LORD, "Stand by the roads and look; ask for the

---

519   Hosea 4:6
520   John 16:13

ancient paths, Where the good way is; then walk in it, and you will find rest for your souls. But they said, 'We will not walk in it!'[521]

Mentorship is a test of humility, the ability to bring oneself under the guidance of others regardless of our status. "… We know that "We all possess knowledge." But knowledge puffs up while love builds up. Those who think they know something do not yet know as they ought to know."[522]

Apostle Paul made himself available to be mentored by the teachings of others as inspired by the Holy Spirit; he took notes and read books. This attitude made him greater than all other apostles, including the ones that met Jesus face-to-face. His growth in knowledge and capacity empowered him to also mentor others through direct teachings, letters, counseling, and admonitions. Our greatness in life begins with the acquisition of the right and relevant knowledge through direct and indirect mentorship[523]

"For though ye have ten thousand instructors in Christ yet have ye not many fathers: for in Christ Jesus, I have begotten you through the gospel. Wherefore I beseech you, be ye followers of me. For this cause have I sent unto you Timotheus, who is my beloved son, and faithful in the Lord, who shall bring you into remembrance of my ways which

---

521 Jeremiah 6:16
522 1 Corinthians 8: 1-2
523 1 Corinthians 1:1-31

be in Christ, as I teach everywhere in every church."[524] As a people, we must never be too proud to submit ourselves to learning or the mentorship of proven mentors. It is the way out of ignorance and limitations into a life of purpose and fulfillment.

"...when thou comest, bring with thee, and the books, but especially the parchments."[525] Our lives as a mentee began when we were born; we were mentored by parents, families and older siblings. As we grew older, we also became privileged to mentor some younger ones. Therefore, we must never give up our place as a mentee or mentor because those two positions are significant to the outcome of our lives and others.

BENEFITS OF PAUL'S ATTRIBUTES

Knowledge: Paul craved for knowledge because he understood its power. His thirst for knowledge made him stand out to the point that men began to testify to his prowess. "At this point Festus interrupted Paul's defense. "You are out of your mind, Paul!" he shouted. "Your great learning is driving you insane."[526]

Kings and nobles will come to our attention because of our mental capacity and skills that is able to proffer solutions

---

524 1 Corinthians 4:15-17
525 2 Timothy 4:13
526 Acts 26:24

to their concerns or troubles. Relevant Knowledge makes us relevant, indispensable and sought after. When we equip ourselves, we don't struggle to be known, people naturally look for us. Solomon was equipped with the wisdom of God, and multitude looked for him[527] Capacity building brings us peace, rest, promotions, increase, favor, and honor. "Study this Book of Instruction continually. Meditate on it day and night so you will be sure to obey everything written in it. Only then will you prosper and succeed in all you do."[528] The more we acquire relevant knowledge, the more we grow. Growth is essential to our living, but until the principle of growth is engaged, relevance and success will only be a mirage.

Growth is a natural phenomenon; every living thing grows except it experiences some medical impediments. The only growth that happens naturally is our biological growth, every other growth is made to happen. So, anyone who desires growth subscribes to acquiring relevant knowledge in a desired area to initiate the reality of what they desire, and also experience mental freedom. "A wise man is strong; yea, a man of knowledge increases strength."[529] When we stop learning, we stop growing; this could be detrimental to our existence because we can no longer add value to our immediate environment or a larger environment. The Bible described us as the light of the world and the salt

---

527 1 Kings 4:34
528 Joshua 1:8
529 Proverbs 24:5

of the earth. That is, we are agents of change, innovation, new developments, and discoveries. However, those things wouldn't just happen, there is a price to pay and it is the price of mental development.

"Ye are the salt of the earth: but if the salt have lost his savor, wherewith shall it be salted? It is thenceforth good for nothing, but to be cast out, and to be trodden under foot of men."[530]

We can only manifest these attributes when we commit to mental development like Apostle Paul did. Decades after his death, we still reference him and his work. That is what becomes of us even when we are no more, we remain relevant and our work continues to impart and change lives.

Kingdom Service: We have been called into a life of service. Service to God, ourselves, family, friends, neighbors, and society. It is God's desire that all His creation fulfill the purpose they were created for. God's wish is that we have a beautiful future, be in health and wealth for the purpose of His kingdom and humanity[531] God enlists and engages our service to carry out His agenda. He doesn't force anyone but engages those who are ready and willing.

---

530   Matthew 5:13 KJV
531   3 john 2, Jeremiah 29:11

"Then the LORD said to Moses, "Go to Pharaoh and say to him, 'This is what the LORD says: Let my people go, so that they may worship me.'"[532]

Apostle Paul committed himself to the service of God and humanity. His passion was to see that everyone knew about the gospel of Jesus because of the goodness embedded in it. No wonder God granted him the grace required to succeed in the service.

"I succeeded in service because I was available, God gave the grace, and I took advantage of the grace."[533]

Decades after Paul's death, he is still relevant because of his service to God and humanity. Service will bring us relevance, honor, and greatness putting our names in the sand of time. Until Jesus comes, Paul will continue to be a reference point. The same honor is available for anyone who desires to genuinely subscribe to service to God and humanity. For every service rendered, there is a form of appreciation or reward.

"And ye shall serve the LORD your God, and he shall bless thy bread, and thy water; and I will take sickness away from

---

532 Exodus 8:1
533 1 Corinthians 5:10 Paraphrased

the midst of thee. There shall nothing cast their young, nor be barren, in thy land: the number of thy days I will fulfil."[534]

Career and marital breakthroughs, academic success, good health, long life and preservation are part of what we enjoy in service.

Jesus, our perfect example, reminded us that He was here on earth not to be served, but to serve others.

"For even the Son of Man did not come expecting to be served by everyone, but to serve everyone, and to give his life as the ransom price in exchange for the salvation of many."[535]

His genuine service to God and humanity secured Him honor, favor, reverence, authority and power. "Wherefore God also hath highly exalted him and given him a name which is above every name: That at the name of Jesus every knee should bow, of things in heaven, and things in earth, and things under the earth; And that every tongue should confess that Jesus Christ is Lord, to the glory of God the Father."[536]

Those who devout themselves with understanding to the service of God and others never lack.

---

534 Exodus 23:25-26
535 Mark 10:45
536 Philippians 2:9-11 KJV

"But first and most importantly seek (aim at, strive after) His kingdom and His righteousness [His way of doing and being right— the attitude and character of God], and all these things will be given to you also."[537]

God knows our needs, the easiest way to trigger the release of those needs is to be genuine in service to God and those around us.

"God is not unjust; he will not forget your work and the love you have shown him as you have helped his people and continue to help them. We want each of you to show this same diligence to the very end, so that what you hope for may be fully realized. We do not want you to become lazy, but to imitate those who through faith and patience inherit what has been promised."[538]

God spoke about the certainty of our reward of service,

"Behold, I (Jesus) am coming quickly, and My reward is with Me, to give to each one according to the merit of his deeds (earthly works, faithfulness)."[539]

We should be anxious for nothing, but intentionally, and genuinely observe and follow the same pattern as Paul the apostle and other disciples in order to ascend the throne of honor, glory, beauty, power and authority.

---

537 Matthew 6:33
538 Hebrews 6:10-12
539 Revelation 22:12

Apostle Paul saw service as a privilege, and he enjoyed it without any struggle. "So what is my reward? It is to spread the Good News free of charge…"[540]

If we can exhibit this level of joy in service, we secure our place in posterity.

Visionary: Vision is a function of foresight, seeing beyond now, the situation notwithstanding. Apostle Paul was a man of vision shortly after he was called into ministry by Jesus after the encounter on his way to Damascus[541] The desire of Paul was to see many come to the knowledge of Christ the same way he persecuted Christians. He envisioned ways that would help him win souls over to the kingdom of God.

"For though I am free from all men, I have made myself a slave to everyone, so that I may win more [for Christ]. To the Jews I became as a Jew, so that I might win Jews [for Christ]; to men under the Law, [I became] as one under the Law, though not being under the Law myself, so that I might win those who are under the Law. To those who are without (outside) the Law, [I became] as one without the Law, though [I am] not without the law of God, but under the law of Christ, so that I might win those who are without law. To the weak I became [as the] weak, to win the weak. I have become all things to all men, so that I may by all means [in any and every way] save some [by

---

540   1 Corinthians 9:18
541   Act chapter 9

leading them to faith in Jesus Christ]. And I do all this for the sake of the gospel, so that I may share in its blessings along with you."[542]

Permit me to describe Paul as a chameleon; his desire was to succeed in his new assignment. He laid aside his status in order to conform or adjust to people and his surrounding to win for Christ. Men of vision are always focused; on their mind is their goal and not their status. As a man or woman driven by a genuine vision, ideas are birthed which become the fuel for driving the vision. Once the vision gains momentum, goals are achieved that will result in the attraction of favor, progress, breakthroughs, and blessings. As a people, the future of a vision we don't envision cannot become a reality. Those who are genuinely visionary defy the odds, change the status quo, and bring hope to those around them that a change is possible.

Paul defied all odds that were against him, he did not allow his past to hold him down, and he remained focused. Nothing limits true and genuine visionary, the visual of the destination they desire is what drives them.

"No, dear brothers and sisters, I have not achieved it, but I focus on this one thing: Forgetting the past and looking forward to what lies ahead. I press toward the mark for the prize of the high calling of God in Christ Jesus."[543]

---

542 1 Corinthians 9:19-23
543 Philippians 3:13-14

As a man or woman of vision, we become pressers, and goal-getters because we are striving to make a difference. This makes us torch bearers, pacesetters, change makers, and trailblazers, and our name becomes a household name because of the effect of our vision.

We are a creation of purpose, but it will take vision to attain and achieve the purpose. If we can envision, God will bring it to practical fulfillment.

"Before I formed you in the womb, I knew you [and approved of you as My chosen instrument], And before you were born I consecrated you [to Myself as My own]; I have appointed you as a prophet to the nations. The word of the LORD came to me, saying, "Jeremiah, what do you see?" And I said, "I see the branch of an almond tree." Then the LORD said to me, "You have seen well, for I am [actively] watching over My word to fulfill it."[544]

We are not here to fill the vacuum or occupy space but to make things happen.

Mentor: Mentors are guides, teachers, and advisers. A mentor is privileged to help others arrive at a desired destination same as their own or otherwise. As a people of God, we enjoy the mentorship and the ministry of the Holy Spirit. He was given to us after the departure of Jesus for him to help us fulfill our purpose.

---

544 Jeremiah 1:5, 11-12

"But I tell you the truth, it is to your advantage that I go away; for if I do not go away, the Helper (Comforter, Advocate, Intercessor— Counselor, Strengthener, Standby) will not come to you; but if I go, I will send Him (the Holy Spirit) to you [to be in close fellowship with you]."[545]

"Howbeit when he, the Spirit of truth, is come, he will guide you into all truth: for he shall not speak of himself; but whatsoever he shall hear, that shall he speak and he will shew you things to come."[546]

Just as Jesus sent us the third person of the trinity as our mentor, there are earthly mentors God has prepared to help us reach our desired destinations. As Jesus said, it is to our advantage. Having a mentor plays to our advantage, they help us avoid physical pitfalls through guidance, and they help us discover our hidden abilities through the help of the Holy Ghost. When we align ourselves with a mentor, we rarely struggle, fall victim of the unknown because we have them placed in our lives just as we have the Holy Spirit. Having a mentor does not mean we may not have hiccups along the way but having them helps us overcome those hiccups quickly. Jesus mentored the twelve disciples, and men could not but marvel at the outcome of the mentorship program.

---

545 John 16:17
546 John 16:13

"When they saw the courage of Peter and John and realized that they were unschooled, ordinary men, they were astonished, and they took note that these men had been with Jesus."[547] *"Saying, what shall we do to these men? for that indeed a notable miracle hath been done by them is manifest to all them that dwell in Jerusalem; and we cannot deny it."*[548]

Mentees will always have better results to show because they have gone the extra mile to learn from a superior mind. They are billed to be marveled at because of their odd-defying results. As a mentor, we help people succeed, build confidence, attain goals, and progress. In return as a mentor, we get honored, rewarded and celebrated.

Apostle Paul positioned himself as a mentor to many in the Bible time, and he was celebrated and honored. Paul mentored Timothy by equipping him for ministry assignments, empowering him for success, and effectiveness at the church in Ephesus "Unto Timothy, my own son in the faith..."[549]

"For this reason, I have sent to you Timothy, my son whom I love, who is faithful in the Lord. He will remind you of my way of life in Christ Jesus, which agrees with what I teach everywhere in every church."[550]

---

547   Acts 14:13
548   Acts 4:16
549   1 Timothy 1:2
550   1 Corinthians 14:7

As a mentor, people celebrated Paul and blessed him even when he never demanded for it[551] Whichever category we find ourselves, we must be committed to it because it will always impart and change people's lives.

Prayer: Lord, help me to take responsibility in fulfilling purpose. I ask for wisdom and grace to serve You and humanity with all I possess, as I render a helping hand to those around me.

---

551 Philippians 4:16

Chapter 17

QUEEN ESTHER

Q ueen Esther was a Hebrew orphan who had been under the care of her uncle Mordecai ever since the demise of her parents at a very young age. Esther, her uncle Mordecai and other Jews lived in the land of Persia as captives. Esther was a noblewoman, courageous, and well committed to the safety of others, her high social status regardless. As a favored person, Esther became a queen in a strange land, and she used her position to stand against injustice against innocent people.

Esther became the face of the Jewish clan before her husband the king when their lives were threatened. Sometimes, we are placed in a position by God for a reason, we must not allow our temporary status to cloud our thoughts, actions, or judgment "You were placed in this place of honor for a purpose, don't get carried away by all the good things you now enjoy."[552] Rather, we must be observant and know that life is in seasons, and we must act when we have the opportunity before it is late.

Courageous: Esther by divine arrangement became the queen, and wife to the king of Persia; Ahasuerus. According to the law of the land, it is treasonous to appear before the king without being summoned. However, Esther chose to defy that order at the risk of her own life. She placed the need of other Jews before herself. "… I will go unto the king, which is not according to the law, if I perish, I perish."[553] Like Esther, we must understand that God has given us the spirt of boldness to stand against anything that may want to destroy us or limit our access to God's glorious plan. "For God hath not given us the spirit of fear; but of power, and of love, and of a sound mind."[554]

Being bold does not mean arrogance but the ability to maintain one's place in authority over what threatens one's existence. God admonished Joshua four times to remain courageous in order to maintain his ability to defeat the enemy[555]. Fear will only keep us in subjection; hence we must not give in to fear because it is not real. A wise man described fear as False Evidence Appearing Real. Those things we see as giants before us were made by God but

---

552   Esther 4:14 paraphrased
553   Esther 4:15
554   2 Timothy 1:7
555   Joshua 1:1-18

controlled by the enemy to scare us. The good news is that God gave us the sole authority over all those things, therefore; we must assume our place of authority and not fall to fear.

"Behold, I have given you authority to tread on serpents and scorpions, and over all the power of the enemy, and nothing shall hurt you."[556]

In the case of Esther, her giant was the law of the land that forbade her from appearing before the king. However, she chose to conquer the fear. God gave all men wisdom to devise, design and build, but He also reserves the wisdom that can pull down those things that pose threats to us. David said to Goliath, "You come to me with weapons, but I David come against you in the name of God who created and gave wisdom to the creator of your weapon."[557] This should be our mentality; that nothing can destroy us before our time. Esther demonstrated her strength in courage, and it gave her a much needed victory the Jews yearned for. The destiny of many is entwined with ours, so we must not allow fear to rob us of what God has planned for us. "Be strong and courageous. Do not be afraid or terrified because of them, for the Lord your God goes with you; he will never leave you nor forsake you."[558]

"David also said to Solomon his son, "Be strong and courageous, and

---

556 Luke 10:19
557 1 Samuel 17:45 Paraphrased
558 Deuteronomy 31:16

do the work. Do not be afraid or discouraged, for the Lord God, my God, is with you. He will not fail you or forsake you until all the work for the service of the temple of the Lord is finished."[559]

Our victory lies in our courage.

Favor: Queen Esther was a favored child, despite the loss of her parents at a very young age; she had an uncle named Mordecai. He oversaw her upkeep even as captives in Persia. She enjoyed the mentorship and guidance of her uncle to the point where he guided her into queenship. "Esther had not revealed her nationality and family background, because Mordecai had forbidden her to do so."[560]

Esther enjoyed favor in the sight of the king's housekeeper above all other maidens that were chosen. "So it came to pass, when the king's commandment and his decree was heard, and when many maidens were gathered unto Shushan the palace, to the custody of Hegai, that Esther was brought also unto the king's house, to the custody of Hegai, keeper of the women. And the maiden pleased him, and she obtained kindness of him; and he speedily gave her things for purification, with such things as belonged to her, and seven maidens, which were meet to be given her, out of the king's house: and he preferred her and her maids unto the best place of the house of the women."[561] Favor sets

---

559   1 Chronicles 28:20
560   **Esther 2:10**
561   Esther 2:8-9

us apart, it makes people show us a different kind of care, love, and kindness that others may not enjoy. Like Esther, we are created to enjoy favor because it is one of those things that negate the law of labor; when you don't have to labor or struggle for it. God positions people in our way to favor us. The Bible talked about how Jesus enjoyed favor with God, then men[562]. Note that once we are favored of God, men will also favor us. Favor brought Esther to the palace and made her a queen.

"Now when the turn of Esther… And Esther obtained favor in the sight of all of them that looked upon her. And the king loved Esther above all the women, and she obtained grace and favor in his sight more than all the virgins; so that he set the royal crown upon her head and made her queen."[563] Favor brings us into unmerited blessing; Esther appeared to have been the least qualified because of her background. When God is with us, He breaks protocols for our sake. If we can walk in obedience and love with God, He will set His affection over us, and when we are favored of God, men are compelled to favor us.

"For the Lord God is a sun and shield; the Lord bestows favor and honor. No good thing does he withhold from those who walk uprightly."[564]

---

562 Luke 2:52
563 Esther 2:15, 17
564 Psalm 84:11

"And when God is for us, no one can be against us"[565]

Queen: Esther was crowned a queen in a land where she was taken captive[566]. Our location is not the issue or the reason why we are experiencing delay or limitation. It is our lack of connectivity with God. A wise man once said, "There is an allocation for every location, and when we are in our God-ordained location; our allocation will never elude us." Esther was a slave in a foreign land but she still enjoyed her allocation.

Favor will always make room for us where others are being rejected, or experiencing any form of struggle, hindrance, or delay. Favor is like a perfumed ointment that draws people to us regardless of our background because we have one thing working for us, God.

As a queen she assumed a place of authority that comes with honor, beauty, blessings, gifts, help, support, and dominion. Like Esther, we were created by God as kings and queens, therefore; it is important we walk in the understanding of our real and royal status in order to enjoy all the benefits that accompany royalty. "But ye are a chosen generation, a royal priesthood..."[567] We belong to a royal family, the lineage

---

565 Romans 8:31
566 (Esther 2:5-7)
567 1 Peter 2:9 KJV

of God. That's why we must carry ourselves as one, if not we may not experience the reality and the manifestation of our royalty.

"And hath made us kings and priests unto God and his Father; to him be glory and dominion for ever and ever. Amen."[568]

We may not seat on a physical throne as a king, but our lineage is royalty, so we must live it, do it, and express it. If we understand our real and true status as royalty, then we will also enjoy what Esther enjoyed, even much more.

Selfless: Esther was a selfless young lady. A time came when she made a choice to put her own needs behind, while the needs of others became precedent.

"Then Esther bade them return Mordecai this answer, Go, gather together all the Jews that are present in Shushan, and fast ye for me, and neither eat nor drink three days, night or day: I also and my maidens will fast likewise; and so will I go in unto the king, which is not according to the law: and if I perish, I perish."[569] The lives of the Jews who were in captivity in Persia were threatened, but after counsel from her uncle Mordecai; she chose to put her life on the line by going to the king. Such action is against the law of the

---

568   Revelation 1:6
569   Esther 4:15-16

land, no one appears before the king except when they are summoned by the king. When we genuinely care about others, we will always care for them and their needs. "Do not merely look out for your own personal interests, but also for the interests of others."[570] Our demonstration of love and care for the needs of others besides our own is proof of our nature in God.

"Greater love has no one than this: to lay down one's life for one's friends."[571]

Esther's act of selflessness secured the lives of all the Jews and gave them a place and hope in a strange land. "Write ye also for the Jews, as it liketh you, in the king's name, and seal it with the king's ring: for the writing, which is written in the king's name, and sealed with the king's ring, may no man reverse."[572]

We must try everything within our God-given capacity to care for and love others the way we love ourselves.

BENEFITS OF QUEEN ESTHER'S ATTRIBUTES

Courage: Queen Esther was a woman of courage. The story of Esther is part of history today because of her courageous actions in saving the Jews that were in captivity

---

570   Philippians 2:4
571   John 15:13
572   Esther 8:8

in the Land of Persia and were on the verge of destruction at the hands of Haman. Courage puts us on a pedestal of honor, victory, and sometimes martyrdom.

"Yet having learned who Mordecai's people were, he scorned the idea of killing only Mordecai. Instead, Haman looked for a way to destroy all Mordecai's people, the Jews, throughout the whole kingdom of Xerxes."[573]

However, Esther placed all she had on the line, including her life to see others rescued.

"...and so will I go in unto the king, which is not according to the law: and if I perish, I perish."[574]

Being courageous is not a sign of arrogance but the confidence to do what is right to the benefit of others including ourselves. Acts of courage liberate from mediocrity, captivity, fear, and procrastination. Many of us are in some form of bondage, limitation, and breakdown not because God wants that for us, but because we are afraid to make moves. God's plan is to see us fulfill destiny in a grand style. Nothing will drop freely on our laps. If there is any area of our lives where we desire a change or we want to put an end to oppression, we must make a move in boldness to see those desires come to practical reality.

573 Esther 3:6
574 Esther 4:16

"So, Joshua said to the Israelites: "How long will you wait before you begin to take possession of the land that the LORD, the God of your ancestors, has given you?"[575]

Slackness is either a function of an inadequate understanding of what it takes to take the delivery of what belongs to us, or we lack the courage to make a move. Courageous people are never limited no matter the obstacle before them. Like Queen Esther, we must be bold and courageous in order to break through barriers. Courage brings us into the class of those who assume the place of authority, success, power, influence, honor, achievements, and most importantly, riches. We belong to the family of Jesus, therefore; we must represent our status[576]

Jesus was respected because He demonstrated authority without fear, and He has promised that greater things than what He did will we do also[577]

"...but the godly are as bold as lions."[578] *As a child of God, we are only given the spirit of boldness, love, and a sound mind.*

Favor: Favor is a representation of breakthroughs, kindness, a show of affection, or unusual likeness we enjoy, but largely not merited. When one is favored, things just happen for them without struggle or stress because there

---

575   Joshua 18: 3
576   Romans 8:17, Galatians 3:29
577   Mark 1:22, John 14:12
578   Proverbs 28:1

is something about them that people want to identify with. When we are favored by God, men naturally favor us. A wise man once said, "If you pay for everything you own or have, you lack favor." That is, there should be times when people just go out of their way to bless you. When God favored Jesus, men had no choice but to favor Him as well because a smell of favor was placed on him by God.

The smell of favor was upon Queen Esther. When she was brought into the king's palace, she found favor in the eyes of the keeper throughout her stay until she was installed as a queen.

"When the king's order and edict had been proclaimed, many young women were brought to the citadel of Susa and put under the care of Hegai. Esther also was taken to the king's palace and entrusted to Hegai, who had charge of the harem. She pleased him and won his favor. Immediately he provided her with her beauty treatments and special food. He assigned to her seven female attendants selected from the king's palace and moved her and her attendants into the best place in the harem."[579]

Note, many young women were brought but something about her made her the preferred. When God is with you, men naturally favor you. "For you bless the righteous, O Lord; you cover him with favor as with a shield."[580]

---

579   Esther 2:8-9
580   Psalm 5:12

Favor makes us the preferred, takes away the struggle, gets things done cheaply, and delivers to us most times things we don't even qualify for. So, favor is not a function of our qualifications, societal status, or our background. Favor is God-bestowed. When we are favored, it is like the smell of cologne that draws attention every time it's worn. Everything about us becomes likable. Songs of "Pleasing is the fragrance of your perfumes; your name is like perfume poured out. No wonder the young women love you!"[581]

"And I will make the Egyptians favorably disposed toward this people, so that when you leave you will not go empty-handed. Favor breaks protocols and sustains continuous flow of resources."[582]

Queen: As royalty, Queen Esther enjoyed privileges, honor, riches, and she had it the way she wanted it, not at the detriment of others but to help those who were being oppressed[583].

We belong to a royal family of God, so we must exhibit our nature as royalty. We are a royal priesthood[584] and Christ has made us kings and priests unto God[585]. Our position as a king or queen puts us in a place of authority

---

581   Solomon 1:3
582   Exodus 3:21
583   Esther chapters 5&6
584   1 Peter 2:9
585   Revelation 1:6

and power where we enjoy privileges, affluence, honor, and lots of blessings. However, being royalty does not make other people less of a people than us, rather; we are also privileged to be in that position. Therefore, we must do everything within our capacity to promote love, equality, protection, and provision for those who are subject to us rather than oppress or intimidate them.

Selfless: A genuine act of selflessness helps us to consider the needs of other people besides our own. Looking out for their wellbeing, caring for them within our God-given capacity. "Do not merely look out for your own personal interests, but also for the interests of others."[586] Queen Esther was selfless about others who needed help, and she committed herself to it until her goal was attained.

"Then Esther bade them return Mordecai this answer, Go, gather together all the Jews that are present in Shushan, and fast ye for me, and neither eat nor drink three days, night or day: I also and my maidens will fast likewise; and so will I go in unto the king, which is not according to the law: and if I perish, I perish."[587]

Our act of selflessness to others brings hope, peace, and progress to them. Doing this also brings us joy in return when we see the joy on their faces. They reciprocate in love,

---

586 Philippians 2:4
587 Esther 4:15-16

support, and honor. Doing good to others is like doing it to ourselves and God because we belong to the same father - God "'Love your neighbor as yourself.' There is no commandment greater than these."[588]

"...Lord, when did we see you hungry and feed you, or thirsty and give you something to drink? When did we see you a stranger and invite you in, or needing clothes and clothe you? When did we see you sick or in prison and go to visit you?' The King will reply, 'Truly I tell you, whatever you did for one of the least of these brothers and sisters of mine, you did for me.'"[589]

Genuinely helping others gives a feeling of goodness, creates a sense of belonging, and sense of purpose that leads to fulfillment. Our act of kindness will inspire others to do the same which could have a ripple effect that can make the world a better place.

"If you pour yourself out for the hungry and satisfy the desire of the afflicted, then shall your light rise in the darkness and your gloom be as the noonday."[590]

Prayer: Lord, grant me the grace to be selfless towards others, and act in courage, while You surround me with favor.

---

588   Mark 12:31
589   Matthew 25:37-40
590   Isaiah 58:10

Chapter 18

RUTH

R uth was a Moabite who got married to one of the two sons of Elimelech and Naomi who sojourned into the Land of Moab after the king of Judah declared famine in the Land. Shortly after about ten years, Ruth lost her husband, Mahlon. Everyone prays and hopes they live a long life, even with their spouse. Unfortunately, that wasn't the case for Ruth. The loss of her husband would have been devastating and painful to bear.

"They married Moabite women, one named Orpah and the other Ruth. After they had lived there about ten years, both Mahlon and Chilion also died, and Naomi was left without her two sons and her husband."[591]

---

591   Ruth 1:4-5

Despite losing her husband, with no children for him, she decided to commit herself to her mother-in-law who was sorrowful after her loss as a show of her love for her family. Naomi her mother-in-law advised her to go, but she decided to dedicate herself to supporting Naomi during this difficult time.

"And Ruth said, Intreat me not to leave thee, or to return from following after thee: for whither thou goes, I will go; and where thou lodges, I will lodge: thy people shall be my people, and thy God my God: Where thou dies, will I die, and there will I be buried: the Lord do so to me, and more also, if ought but death part thee and me."[592]

Finally, Naomi agreed to Ruth's wishes, and they returned to Bethlehem. We all go through difficult times in life but it is not a time to abandon people around us who may be going through the same situation. It is the best time to support one another in order to gather strength to survive that season. "Iron sharpeneth iron; so a man sharpeneth the countenance of his friend."[593] "If either of them falls, one can help the other up. But pity anyone who falls and has no one to help them up."[594]

Ruth was able to look beyond her loss, she identified with Naomi who lost three family members. She hung around to sharpen the countenance of her mother-in-law which

---

592 Ruth 1:16-17
593 Proverbs 27:17 KJV
594 Ecclesiastes 4:10

could probably have led to another death due to loneliness or depression. They were able to pick each other up throughout their season of loss.

It is important to know that no good deeds go unrewarded. "For God is not unjust to overlook your work and the love that you have shown for his name in serving the saints, as you still do."[595]

Yes! Ruth got rewarded. God turned her story around, and she was favored and got married again. "Boaz, kindred of Naomi, married Ruth, and God blessed them with a son."[596] Ruth was rewarded for her act of kindness, love, and commitment to someone who was in pain like herself. "Ruth asked why she Boaz showed her favor, and he responded "I have heard about your act of kindness, love and commitment towards my sister, therefore; the Lord reward you."[597]

"Consider it pure joy, my brothers and sisters, whenever you face trials of many kinds, because you know that the testing of your faith produces perseverance. Let perseverance finish its work so that you may be mature and complete, not lacking anything."[598]

Everything about Ruth was tested, but by God's grace she persevered, and it paid off. We must be conscious of the

---

595   Hebrews 6:10
596   Ruth 4:13 Paraphrased
597   Ruth 2:10-12 Paraphrased
598   James 1:2-4

decisions we make during difficult times; it is pivotal to the next line of action and the outcome. It may be tough to make certain decisions sometimes, but with the help of God; we can make the right decisions.

ATTRIBUTES OF RUTH

Kindness: As a people, one of the best gifts we can offer to others around us is kindness. "Be kind to one another, tenderhearted…"[599]

The act of kindness helps take away the pain, and restore hope and love to people who may have suffered a devastating blow in their lives, or those who are currently experiencing hard times in their lives. Ruth was a recipient of one of those blows that life throws; she lost her husband with whom she had no child. More devastating was the loss her mother-in-law suffered, losing two sons and a husband; all in the same household. This must have been a tough season for them, but Ruth decided to help her mother-in-law survive the season.

"And Ruth said, Intreat me not to leave thee, or to return from following after thee: for whither thou goest, I will go; and where thou lodgest, I will lodge: thy people shall be my people, and thy God my God: Where thou diest, will I die, and there will I be buried: the Lord do so to me, and more also, if ought but death part thee and me."[600]

---

599   Ephesians 4:32
600   Ruth 1:16

Most times, our kindness to others helps them believe a change and restoration is still possible because they found a support system. We must ensure we do everything within our God-given capacity to support others who need support emotionally, mentally, physically, or otherwise. People heal quickly when they are shown kindness in their difficult times.

"Carry one another's burden... So then, while we [as individual believers] have the opportunity, let us do good to all people [not only being helpful, but also doing that which promotes their spiritual well-being], and especially [be a blessing] to those of the household of faith (born-again believers)."[601]

"Be completely humble and gentle; be patient, bearing with one another in love. Make every effort to keep the unity of the Spirit through the bond of peace."[602]

Commitment: Commitment to others around us is a display of support for them no matter what they are going through. When people feel supported, they find a sense of belonging which helps them hold and carry on in life no matter what befell them[603]. Most times, people fade away or fall into depression because they have no shoulder to fall on or people to talk to during their difficult times.

---

601   Galatians 6:2, 10
602   Ephesians 4:2-3
603   Esther 1:16-18

Ruth was in a tough season of her life, and so was her mother-in-law, Naomi. I believe she examined the situation, and she concluded that leaving this woman, Naomi, could be catastrophic and anything could happen to her. Knowing fully that she was in the same kind of situation, she decided to stick around. That singular decision made by Ruth altered the course of a negative and bad situation that could have happened. Staying with her mother-in-law helped both of them survive their season of loss and grief. They were available to pull each other up. "If either of them falls down, one can help the other up. But pity anyone who falls and has no one to help them up."[604]

Ruth stood by Naomi even with a bleak future, not knowing what would become of her or her marital destiny. The good news is that whatever good we do comes back to us even when we are not expecting it "A man who is kind benefits himself..."[605]

Love: Love is one of the greatest gifts that we can offer to one another. Genuine love creates an atmosphere of trust, kindness, friendship, selflessness, unity, and peace. The foundation of our lives is love. "For God so loved the world that he gave his one and only Son, that whoever believes in him shall not perish but have eternal life."[606]

---

604   Ecclesiastes 4:10
605   Proverbs 11:17
606   John 3:16

True love looks beyond us but focuses on the needs of others too. Ruth demonstrated the God kind of love; she looked beyond her loss, though painful. She decided to express the most important thing Naomi needed at that time, something she also needed herself. Her act of love for Naomi gave Naomi something to look up to.

Apostle Paul said, "If I give all I possess to the poor and give over my body to hardship that I may boast, but do not have love, I gain nothing."[607] Our actions and activities come to nothing if not done in love. Whatever we do must be anchored on love, because it is what simplifies and beautifies all things.

"And above all these put on love which binds everything together in perfect harmony."[608]

God loved us, and He gave what was precious to Him for our sakes. The same is expected of us, we must ensure we look beyond our needs and circumstances by paying attention to those around us. A simple act of love will help people heal from whatever pain they are going through. Most times, people don't need material things to heal, all they want is someone to love them. However, the whole expression of love starts with us because what we don't have, we cannot give. Loving ourselves empowers us to also show that kind of love to our friends, family, colleagues,

607   1 Corinthians 13:3
608   Colossians 3:14

233

neighbors, community, and society. "Love one another with brotherly affection. Outdo one another in showing honor."[609]

"Dear friends, let us love one another, for love comes from God. Everyone who loves has been born of God and knows God. Whoever does not love does not know God, because God is love. This is how God showed his love among us: He sent his one and only Son into the world that we might live through him."[610]

We must strive to always express genuine love if we want to see a better us, family, community, society, and nation. Even in the season of Ruth's pain, she was able to give love to someone who also needed love. Love is from within, and circumstance cannot alter or change the love of God that was shed in us unless we are not a genuine carriers of that kind of love.

"Who shall separate us from the love of Christ? Shall tribulation, or distress, or persecution, or famine, or nakedness, or peril, or sword? Nay, in all these things we are more than conquerors through him that loved us…For I am persuaded, that neither death, nor life, nor angels, nor principalities, nor powers, nor things present, nor things to come, nor height, nor depth, nor any other creature, shall be able to separate us from the love of God, which is in Christ Jesus our Lord."[611]

---

609 Romans 10:12
610 1 John 4:7-9
611 Romans 8:35, 37-39

234

Genuine love empowers us to live through tough times, while we also help others through their tough moments.

Ruth's determination to remain with Naomi tells us about her character, and her love for her mother-in-law. "A friend loves at all times, and a brother is born for a time of adversity."[612]

"Love is patient, love is kind. It does not envy, it does not boast, it is not proud. It does not dishonor others, it is not self-seeking, it is not easily angered, and it keeps no record of wrongs. Love does not delight in evil but rejoices with the truth. It always protects, always trusts, always hopes, and always perseveres. Love never fails..."[613]

Our demonstration of love must not only be in words but like Ruth, let us show it.

"Dear children, let us not love with words or speech but with actions and in truth."[614]

BENEFITS OF RUTH'S ATTRIBUTES

Kindness: Kindness as a fruit of the Spirit promotes love, joy, peace, patience, goodness, and faithfulness[615] Our expression of kindness to others should be wrapped

---

612   Proverbs 17:17
613   1 Corinthians 13:4-8
614   1 John 3:18
615   Galatians 5:22

in the above-mentioned fruit of the Spirit. Ruth's show of kindness, I believe, served as a pivotal moment that strengthened Naomi's belief that life can still be good to her despite her catastrophic loss[616]. We are a product of our choices, whatever choice we make sets a tone for the outcome we experience. Being kind to others give hope, prevents loss of life, helps to overcome loneliness, and most importantly, restores lost joy and hope in God. Doing this gives us joy in return, and makes us feel fulfilled and challenged to do more because of the change our act of kindness has brought to people.

"Whoever pursues righteousness and kindness will find life, righteousness, and honor."[617]

Our quest to show others kindness will bring us honor, celebration, favor, and blessings.

"Then she fell on her face, and bowed herself to the ground, and said unto him, why have I found grace in thine eyes, that thou shouldest take knowledge of me, seeing I am a stranger? And Boaz answered and said unto her, it hath fully been shewed me, all that thou hast done unto thy mother-in-law since the death of thine husband: and how thou hast left thy father and thy mother, and the land of thy nativity, and art come unto a people which thou knewest

---

616   Ruth 1:11-13
617   Proverbs 21:21

not heretofore. The Lord recompense thy work, and a full reward be given thee of the Lord God of Israel."[618]

Finally, we must remember that whatever we sow as a seed is what we will reap during the harvest seasons.

Commitment: Our commitment to others around us is a demonstration of our love for them. Ruth was committed to her mother-in-law during their difficult times. Her choice to stay with Naomi restored her hope in and trust in God despite her loss.

"Don't call me Naomi" she told them. "Call me Mara, because the Almighty has made my life very bitter, I went away full, but the LORD has brought me back empty. Why call me Naomi? The LORD has afflicted me; the Almighty has brought misfortune upon me."[619]

"But Ruth replied, "Don't urge me to leave you or to turn back from you. Where you go I will go, and where you stay I will stay. Your people will be my people and your God my God. And when she saw that she adamant, she allowed her stay."[620]

Our support for others brings and restores hope. It helps them stay above the situation just as Ruth supported Naomi throughout the journey. Sometimes, our strength

---

618   Ruth 2:10-12
619   Ruth 1:20-21
620   Ruth 1:16

and beauty lie in helping others. Ruth helped Naomi even when she had her own problems, but amid helping Naomi, she got her blessings. She was able to get married again, and through her the lineage of King David came to be[621]

We all go through difficult and tough moments in life, and sometimes amid these uncertainties, our desired change could be tied to committing to helping others. Jesus, our perfect example, knowing fully well He was to die to rescue us from the enemy remained committed despite our unfaithfulness and stubbornness. And yes, Jesus got a reward that no man could ever give. "Going a little farther, he fell with his face to the ground and prayed, "My Father, if it is possible, may this cup be taken from me. Yet not as I will, but as you will.""[622]

"Wherefore God also hath highly exalted him and given him a name which is above every name: That at the name of Jesus every knee should bow, of things in heaven, and things in earth, and things under the earth; And that every tongue should confess that Jesus Christ is Lord, to the glory of God the Father."[623]

We must sometimes learn to look beyond just our circumstances to how we can help others go through their

---

621 Ruth 4:13-22
622 Matthew 26:29
623 Philippians 2:9-11

situation. Remember, we can do all things through Christ who strengthens us[624], and every good deed we do will always be rewarded.

"And lovingkindness is Yours, O Lord, For You recompense a man according to his work."[625]

Prayer: Lord, help me to remain strong in the midst of difficult situations because You are my light and shield. Help me to love and support others in their tough moments.

---

624   Philippians 4:13
625   Psalm 62:12

Chapter 19

SOLOMON

Solomon was a man full of God's wisdom; he was loving, and he demonstrated great strength of leadership during his reign as a king. As a young king, the only thing he wished for was to have a great deal of wisdom to rule God's people in order to discern and give judgment accordingly.

"And now, O LORD my God, thou hast made thy servant king instead of David my father: and I am but a little child: I know not how to go out or come in. And thy servant is amid thy people which thou hast chosen, a great people, that cannot be numbered nor counted for multitude. Give therefore thy servant an understanding heart to judge thy people that I may discern between good and bad: for who is able to judge this thy so great a people?"[626]

---

626   1 Kings 3:7-9

As a result of his sincere heart and genuineness to do what is right as a privileged leader, God gave him wisdom that no man could ever possess or give to Solomon.

"And the speech pleased the Lord, that Solomon had asked this thing. And God said unto him, Because thou hast asked this thing, and hast not asked for thyself long life; neither hast asked riches for thyself, nor hast asked the life of thine enemies; but hast asked for thyself understanding to discern judgment; Behold, I have done according to thy words: lo, I have given thee a wise and an understanding heart; so that there was none like thee before thee, neither after thee shall any arise like unto thee. And I have also given thee that which thou hast not asked, both riches, and honor: so that there shall not be any among the kings like unto thee all thy days."[627]

Just like Solomon, God expects us to love others as we love ourselves regardless of our background, race, gender, color, or beliefs. "My command is this: Love each other as I have loved you. Greater love has no one than this: to lay down one's life for one's friends."[628] As privileged leaders, our goal should be to serve the people in love and truth without partiality or oppression.

Our show and demonstration of love to others shows we are obedient to the instructions of God, as a result, we are

---

627   1 Kings 3:10-13
628   John 15:12-13

blessed by God[629]. Everyone has a need, and amid those needs, we must ensure we include others in our plan.

ATTRIBUTES OF SOLOMON

Wisdom: According to the scriptures, wisdom is the principal thing. Wisdom plays a pivotal role in the outcome of our life and everything around us. The scriptures highlighted four types of wisdom namely earthly, sensual, devilish, and heavenly wisdom. This means these levels of wisdom can be engaged to get different results. The most important of them all is the heavenly wisdom; it sets us apart and makes people wonder at the operations of our hands.

"This wisdom descends not from above, but is earthly, sensual, and devilish. For where envying and strife is, there is confusion and every evil work. But the wisdom that is from above is first pure, then peaceable, gentle, and easy to be entreated, full of mercy and good fruits, without partiality, and without hypocrisy."[630]

Solomon subscribed to the wisdom from above, and that wisdom made him spectacular, he became a showpiece. Many people traveled to see and hear about Solomon's wisdom because of the strange and mighty things that happened in his kingdom.

---

629 Deuteronomy 28:1-12
630 James 3: 15-17

"From all nations people came to listen to Solomon's wisdom, sent by all the kings of the world, who had heard of his wisdom."[631]

This kind of wisdom which is the heavenly one possessed by Solomon had no limit, and it operates beyond normal human capacity because it is the same wisdom that created the entire universe and everything in it.

"By wisdom the LORD laid the earth's foundations, by understanding he set the heavens in place."[632]

The same wisdom is available for us, all we need to do is ask, and when we ask with a good motive like Solomon, God will give it to us.

"If you need wisdom, ask our generous God, and he will give it to you. He will not rebuke you for asking."[633]

"When you ask, you do not receive, because you ask with wrong motives, that you may spend what you get on your pleasures."[634] We must ensure our primary purpose of asking is not just for ourselves, but for the benefit of others as well.

Loving: Genuine love is a fundamental principle that makes everything around us work. When we have and demonstrate

---

631   1 Kings 4:34
632   Proverbs 3:9
633   James 1:5
634   James 4:3

genuine and trustworthy love towards others besides ourselves, we create an atmosphere and environment where people can cohabit peaceably.

"Love is patient, love is kind. It does not envy, it does not boast, it is not proud. It does not dishonor others, it is not self-seeking, it is not easily angered, and it keeps no record of wrongs. Love does not delight in evil but rejoices with the truth. It always protects, always trusts, always hopes, and always perseveres. Love never fails."[635]

Solomon demonstrated a true and genuine sense of love toward God and God's people. He exhibited giving as a lifestyle. His genuine love for others made him ask God for wisdom that will help him facilitate good rulership over the kingdom and his people the right way without being partial or self-seeking. "And Solomon loved the Lord, walking in the statutes of David his father. Give therefore thy servant an understanding heart to judge thy people that I may discern between good and bad."[636]

When we love others, we will respect them, and help them feel comfortable within our capacity. Our act of love must be demonstrated always, and shown to everyone around us, not just to people we know or those within our circle.

"Therefore, as we have opportunity, let us do good to all people..."[637]

---

635 1 Corinthians 13:4-8
636 1 Kings 3:3&9
637 Galatians 6:10

Loving people is loving God. "Whoever claims to love God yet hates a brother or sister is a liar. For whoever does not love their brother and sister, whom they have seen, cannot love God, whom they have not seen."[638]

When God sees that we truly love and demonstrate such love just as He gave us His only son as a ransom, He grants us access to heavenly ideas that no mortal could ever have conceived or imagined. Daniel was a man who loved God, he chose God above everything, even those things that could pitch him against God. "Daniel chose God over material things and sin. As a result, he secured access to heavenly secrets."[639] "Then was the secret revealed unto Daniel..."[640]

Love is a revealer of secrets. Those who genuinely love one another reveal secrets to each other while it is hidden from those who do not belong in that love circle.

"However, as it is written: "What no eye has seen, what no ear has heard, and what no human mind has conceived" -- the things God has prepared for those who love him."[641]

God is always pleased with those who love others regardless of their status, race, or beliefs. "Oh Lord, you have given me a great assignment, but give me an understanding heart

---

638   1 John 4:20
639   Daniel 1:8 Paraphrased
640   Daniel 2:19
641   1 Corinthians 2:9

to please you and your people as I rule over them."[642] And God was pleased with Solomon's request. When we please God, we enjoy supernatural order of peace.

"When a man's ways please the Lord, he makes even his enemies to be at peace with him."[643] "King Solomon said "The Lord has given me rest on every side, so that there is neither adversary nor evil occurrence."[644] These are some of the numerous blessings true lovers of God and God's people enjoy.

Leadership: Leadership is for service and not for titles. We are selected, voted for, or placed in the place of leadership to first and foremost listen to the flowers, help maintain order, solve problems, create opportunities, mentor, and teach others what they need to do. Leadership positions could be earned because of hard work via promotion or attained via a lengthy period of service with results to show, and we could be picked as a leader because of certain traits, qualities, and favor. In all, regardless of how we find our way to the place of leadership, the most important thing is to serve others in trust, openness, and equality without being partial.

642 1 Kings 3:7-10 Paraphrased
643 Proverbs 16:7
644 1 Kings 5:4

Solomon wanted to be a just King (Leader), he wanted to be fair with all his subjects when it came to decision and judgment making; the main reason he asked God for a good and discerning heart[645]

One such account where Solomon exhibited a sound and impartial judgment as a leader was in the case of two mothers and their children. Leaders are there to solve problems in fairness and truth, not in lies or partiality.

"Then came there two women, that were harlots, unto the king, and stood before him. And the one woman said, O my lord, I and this woman dwell in one house; and I was delivered of a child with her in the house. And it came to pass the third day after that I was delivered, that this woman was delivered also: and we were together; there was no stranger with us in the house, save we two in the house. And this woman's child died in the night because she overlaid it. And she arose at midnight, and took my son from beside me, while thine handmaid slept, and laid it in her bosom, and laid her dead child in my bosom. And when I rose in the morning to give my child suck, behold, it was dead: but when I had considered it in the morning, behold, it was not my son, which I did bear. And the other woman said, nay; but the living is my son, and the dead is thy son. And this said, no; but the dead is thy son, and the living is my son. Thus, they spoke before the king. Then

---

645   1 Kings 3:7-9

said the king, the one saith, this is my son that lives, and thy son is the dead: and the other saith, nay; but thy son is the dead, and my son is the living. And the king said, Bring me a sword. And they brought a sword before the king. And the king said, Divide the living child in two, and give half to the one, and half to the other. Then spoke the woman whose the living child was unto the king, for her bowels yearned upon her son, and she said, O my lord, give her the living child, and in no wise slay it. But the other said, let it be neither mine nor thine, but divide it. Then the king answered and said, give her the living child, and in no wise slay it: she is the mother thereof. And all Israel heard of the judgment which the king had judged; and they feared the king: for they saw that the wisdom of God was in him, to do judgment."[646]

As leaders, we must strive to work in wisdom and understanding because people's lives are partially dependent on us, and our actions, words, decisions, or judgment sets a tone for what direction(s) the lives of those we lead go. Being a leader is not an easy task, but we must be willing to be dedicated to serving others in truth, ensuring their well-being, and most importantly, laying a foundation for good examples.

"If a king judges the poor with truth, His throne will be established forever."[647]

---

646 1 Kings 3:16-29
647 Proverbs 29:14

Disobedient: Solomon was loved by God because of his unique desire to lead and judge the people of God right.

"Give therefore thy servant an understanding heart to judge thy people, that I may discern between good and bad: for who is able to judge this thy so great a people? And the speech pleased the Lord, that Solomon had asked this thing."[648]

However, God instructed Solomon to be obedient and observe his commandment in order not to lose his passion for Him. "If thou will walk in my ways, to keep my statutes and commands as your father David, I will give you long life."[649]

Obedience is a guarantor of God's hand upon our lives which confers His blessings over us and our generations unborn. "If they obey and serve me, they will be blessed with prosperity throughout their lives. All their years will be pleasant."[650]

Unfortunately, at a point in Solomon's life, he got carried away and failed in obeying those commandments, and his heart was turned against God because he got himself involved in sin.

---

648   1 Kings 3:9-10
649   1 Kings 3: 14
650   Job 36:11

"And God commanded Solomon concerning this thing… but Solomon did not keep the commandments God gave to him."[651]

God is faithful, He knows that our human nature has the capacity to fail us, which is why He always warned us, to prepare us against situations like this. Apostle Paul reiterated this advice "Be ye not unequally yoked together with unbelievers: for what fellowship hath righteousness with unrighteousness? And what communion hath light with darkness?"[652]

"Walk with the wise and become wise but associate with fools and get into trouble."[653]

Doing this puts us at risk of losing our nature of God to the enemy, and it is detrimental to our relationship with God and the honor bestowed on us. Solomon set himself up for failure, he got himself yoked with the things that turned him away from God; unfortunately, it led to God stripping the throne from their lineage, leaving one tribe for him to rule for the sake of his father's name, David[654]

"But Solomon loved many strange women, including the ones God warned him against. His heart was turned against God to other gods, building houses for these gods."[655]

---

1 Kings 11:10
652 2 Corinthians 6:14
653 Proverbs 13:20
654 1 kings 11:29-31-39
655 1 Kings 11: 1-4 Paraphrased

251

"Wherefore, let him that think he stands, take heed, else he will fall."[656]

It is important we remain steadfast in serving God in obedience because it is the link to continuous connection to God that helps us remain empowered to overcome the wiles of the enemy who is out to destroy and disgrace us. The commandments of God are not to deny us our desires, but to protect us from the enemy who desires to destroy us because He loves us.

"Loving God means keeping his commandments, and his commandments are not burdensome."[657]

This singular act of disobedience by Solomon brought upon him the anger of the Lord.

"And the LORD was angry with Solomon, because his heart was turned from the LORD God"[658]

We must be careful not to incur the anger of God. We risk the chances of losing it all when God is angry with us, just like Solomon lost part of the kingdom to the servant because of his disobedience. A singular act of disobedience can erase all the good we have done in the past. Disobedience is not measured or quantified, it is the action that counts.

---

656   1 Corinthians 10:12
657   1 John 5:3
658   1 Kings 11:9

"Wherefore the LORD said unto Solomon, forasmuch as this is done of thee, and thou hast not kept my covenant and my statutes, which I have commanded thee, I will surely rend the kingdom from thee, and will give it to thy servant."[659]

"If they listen and obey God, they will be blessed with prosperity throughout their lives. All their years will be pleasant."[660] Obedience to God secures posterity for us and our generation unborn, so we must not be careless in our ways with God.

"Their children will be successful everywhere; an entire generation of godly (obedient) people will be blessed."[661]

Like our Father Abraham, we must walk before God blameless. It doesn't come cheap, it takes spiritual commitment, discipline, dedication, determination, and prayer.

Spiritual Carelessness: The scriptures recorded Solomon to be a man who loved and reverenced God. Unfortunately, he was careless in his walk with God, and as a result, he fell to the wiles of the enemy. And a man who once enjoyed honor and glory lost them.

659   1 Kings 11:11
660   Job 36:11
661   Psalm 112:2 Emphasis Added

"Solomon showed his love for the LORD by walking according to the instructions given him by his father David, except that he offered sacrifices and burned incense on the high places."[662]

As a people, we cannot afford to be careless, or else we fall to the tricks of the enemy. The Devil's aim is to damage or soil our reputation with God just as Adam and Eve's relationship with God was damaged due to carelessness by falling for the evil intention of the devil. We must constantly guard our walk with God jealously because the enemy is prowling around to see us fall[663]

"So, if you think you are standing firm, be careful that you don't fall!"[664]

Solomon, unfortunately, was careless and he missed it. "As Solomon grew old, his wives turned his heart after other gods, and his heart was not fully devoted to the LORD his God, as the heart of David his father had been."[665] Our ability to remain steadfast in God is not dependent on our skillsets or intelligence, but on the wisdom of God. Solomon, a great king full of God's wisdom became Solomon full of foolishness because of his carelessness.

We must ensure we remain spiritually alert, tapping into the sufficient grace of God in order not to fall. We must guard

---

662   1 Kings 3:3
663   1 Peter 5:8
664   1 Corinthians 10:12
665   1 Kings 11: 4

our hearts with all our God-given wisdom by surrounding ourselves with things that will keep us connected, committed, and reliant on God.

"Guard your heart above all else, for it determines the course of your life."[666] Our heart is the seat of destiny, it defines what becomes of our lives. Hence, we must watch over it, and secure it in order not to give room to the enemy.

Apostle Paul gave us admonition on ways we could succeed in guarding our life and walk with God without losing it as a result of carelessness.

"Finally, brothers and sisters, whatever is true, whatever is noble, whatever is right, whatever is pure, whatever is lovely, whatever is admirable—if anything is excellent or praiseworthy—think about such things."[667]

These are ways we can overcome spiritual carelessness; by surrounding ourselves with spiritual things that will keep us always connected because the Devil is never at rest. The more we stay connected, the more strength and grace are released to outdo the devices of the enemy.

"Do not be slothful in zeal, be fervent in spirit, serve the Lord. Finally, we must ensure we cut away any weight, or depart from ways that may dampen our spiritual sensitivity."[668]

---

666 Proverbs 4:23
667 Philippians 4:8
668 Romans 12:11

"Therefore, since we are surrounded by such a huge crowd of witnesses to the life of faith, let us strip off every weight that slows us down, especially the sin that so easily trips us up. And let us run with endurance the race God has set before us."[669]

BENEFITS AND DISBENEFITS OF SOLOMON'S ATTRIBUTES

Wisdom: The scriptures allude to the significance of wisdom in our lives. Proverbs 4:7 "Getting wisdom is the wisest thing you can do! And whatever else you do, develop good judgment." The wisdom of God sets us apart from every other free-thinking individual around us. The wisdom of God is not book smart, neither is it human smart, but the ability and the supremeness of God at work. "God gave Solomon wisdom and very great insight, and a breadth of understanding as measureless as the sand on the seashore."[670]

Solomon, being a recipient of this said wisdom, had the world at his attention. They came to hear and see the wisdom at work in him. "From all nations people came to listen to Solomon's wisdom, sent by all the kings of the world, who had heard of his wisdom. His wisdom was so distinct that men marveled and blessed him."[671]

---

669   Hebrews 12:1
670   1 Kings 4:29
671   1 Kings 4:34

God's wisdom distinguishes us among many. The order of report we generate makes men wonder, and take note of us; leaving them with absolutely no choice but to associate with us.

"In fact, his wisdom exceeded that of all the wise men of the East and the wise men of Egypt. He was wiser than anyone else... His fame spread throughout all the surrounding nations. He could speak with authority... And kings from every nation sent their ambassadors to listen to the Wisdom of Solomon."[672]

Wisdom puts us in a place of authority, decorates us as a celebrity, ushers us into our beauty and honor, spreads our fame to the glory of God across the nations of the world, and makes us a household name with our name on every lip. Therefore, it is important to be a man or woman of wisdom; it brings glory to God, and decorates our lives immensely.

"This wisdom is embedded and released in doing the will of God. No creation of God can offer it except God himself. This wisdom is sweet, and it decorates with beauty for those who are privileged to have it; and genuinely operate in it in line with the will of God."[673]

"If any of you lacks wisdom, you should ask God, who gives generously to all without finding fault, and it will be given to you."[674]

---

672 1 Kings 4: 30-34
673 Job 28: 20-28 Paraphrased
674 James 1:5

Leadership: Leadership is a function of responsibility, taking and making the right judgment with the help of God. Decisions of leaders are very important; followers, or subordinates to a large extent rely on the instruction and decisions of their leader to carry out their given task. So, as a leader, we need the help of God. Everyone cannot be a leader of a team, but we are all indirectly leaders of one thing or the other. Some could be leaders of projects, assignments, groups, or households. The one leadership role everyone takes on is the leadership role of our lives. As leaders of our lives, our decisions, moves, results, reports, and successes are dependent on and guided by the decision we make. God is interested in the success of any leadership role we occupy. He testified of Abraham as His friend for being able to lead his children in the right way "For I know him, that he will command his children and his household after him, and they shall keep the way of the LORD… "[675] God is happy and proud of us when we execute our leadership role with responsibility because the destiny of others is dependent on it.

Solomon also demonstrated a good sense of leadership and judgment when he presided over a situation that could either make or destroy the destiny of one of his subjects "Then the king gave his ruling: "Give the living baby to the first woman. Do not kill him; she is his mother."[676] Real

---

675   Genesis 18:19
676   1 Kings 3: 19-27 Paraphrased

leaders demonstrate great judgment and strength in the face of tough situations through the wisdom of God. As a leader, we enjoy the support of our subordinates, we enjoy success, promotion, and victories.

Love: Love is the definition of who God is. The entire ministry of Jesus was encapsulated in love. The Bible recorded that Jesus moved with compassion when He saw people in need.

"When he saw the crowds, he had compassion on them, because they were harassed and helpless, like sheep without a shepherd."[677]

Our lives must always demonstrate the true God, which is love. "Whoever does not love does not know God, because God is love."[678]

The proof of us being a child of God is our display of compassion and love towards others regardless of their language, creed, age, gender, race, or color because God loves everyone. The only thing God dislikes is the sinful acts and not the person. God showed us this example "But God demonstrates his own love for us in this: While we were still sinners, Christ died for us[679] He loved us so much that He sacrificed His only Son for our sakes.

---

677 Matthew 9:36
678 1 John 4:8
679 Romans 5:8

"For God so loved the world that he gave his one and only Son, that whoever believes in him shall not perish but have eternal life."[680]

We must learn to love others around us unconditionally because love makes the world a better place, restores hope in the hopeless, gives joy to the joyless, strengthens the weak, lifts the downtrodden, and above all; opens everyone to the person, and love of God.

Love is everything. When we genuinely love, we are empowered to fulfill the will of God and love everyone around us. "Love does no wrong to others, so love fulfills the requirements of God's law."[681]

1 Corinthians 13: 1-8 paraphrased "If I am everything the world could ever imagined it to be, but do not have love, I have gained nothing, and failed in everything. Love is patient, love is kind. It does not envy, it does not boast, it is not proud. It does not dishonor others, it is not self-seeking, it is not easily angered, and it keeps no record of wrongs. Love does not delight in evil but rejoices with the truth. It always protects, always trusts, always hopes, and always perseveres. Love never fails."

Solomon as a king demonstrated his side of love as a leader in his decision-making. He was not biased, and neither did

---

680 John 3:16
681 Romans 13:10

he favor one person over the other during his decision-making over his subjects. He allowed the genuine love of God to guide him to deliver good judgment.

Carelessness: Spiritual sensitivity is important in our quest to please God, do His will, fulfill purpose, and bring others to the knowledge of God through His acts in our lives.

Solomon was a man who was sensitive in the spirit, he justifiably walked in the counsel of God as taught by his father.

"And Solomon loved the LORD, walking in the statutes of David his father: only he sacrificed and burnt incense in high places."[682]

Solomon's sensitivity and obedience to the statutes of God earned him a place in destiny. As long as we are connected to God in spirit and truth, our beauty and glorious destiny are guaranteed no matter how much the devil tries to derail us. That's why the Bible admonishes that those who must walk with God must do it in spirit and in truth in order not to lose the heavenly signal that guides us per time in our quest to fulfill God's purpose for our lives.

"God is a Spirit: and they that worship him must worship him in spirit and in truth."[683]

---

682 1 Kings 3:3
683 John 4:24

Our consistency in spiritual sensitivity guarantees our continuous connectivity to the flow of revelation and His secrets that preserves and guarantees our security with a wall of defense against the enemy.

Job was a man of the spirit, he tapped into God's frequency always until a point in his life when he got himself disconnected. "Oh, for the days when I was in my prime, when God's intimate friendship blessed my house."[684] Job got disconnected from that frequency as a result of perceived fear. "What I feared has come upon me; what I dreaded has happened to me."[685] Part of the signals God sends to us always is the spirit of sound and perfect mind and not of fear. That is why it is very dangerous to lose signal, it could lead to a lot of damage just as in the case of Job. "For God has not given us a spirit of fear and timidity, but of power, love, and self-discipline."[686]

"So do not fear, for I am with you; do not be dismayed, for I am your God. I will strengthen you and help you; I will uphold you with my righteous right hand."[687] We must ensure we don't lose sight of God has placed around us as a shield. Job lost sight of it, and fear came into his heart.

---

684 Job 29:4
685 Job 3:25
686 2 Timothy 1:7
687 Isaiah 41:10

Everything that disconnects from God's spiritual signal originates from the heart, which is why we must guard our hearts with all diligence.

"But the things that come out of a person's mouth come from the heart, and these defile them. For out of the heart come evil thoughts—murder, adultery, sexual immorality, theft, false testimony, slander."[688]

We must beware of the things that enter our hearts so that we don't lose our spiritual connectivity with God like Solomon lost his when he allowed strange things of this world to disconnect his heart from God, which is the tower of connectivity that receives signals from God[689]

Spiritual carelessness can be costly. It could lead to a loss of spiritual connectivity that guarantees the fulfillment of destiny and God's purpose and blessings for our lives. Solomon destroyed his father's legacy and limited the transgenerational blessing God gave to his lineage because of his father as a result of his carelessness. Therefore, we must beware.

The Lord became angry with Solomon because his heart had turned away from Him. In spite of the warning Solomon got from God about dealing with other gods, Solomon failed to heed the Lord's warning.

---

688   Matthew 15:18-19
689   1 Kings 11:4

So, the Lord said to Solomon, "Since this is your attitude and you have not kept my covenant and my decrees, which I commanded you, I will most certainly tear the kingdom away from you and give it to one of your subordinates. Nevertheless, for the sake of David your father, I will not do it during your lifetime. I will tear it out of the hand of your son. Yet I will not tear the whole kingdom from him but will give him one tribe for the sake of David my servant and for the sake of Jerusalem, which I have chosen"[690]

There are consequences for flouting instructions, and sometimes it could be costly. Solomon cost his lineage honor, respect, and destroyed the legacy of his father. We must be smart in decision-making.

Disobedience: Obedience, the Bible says, is better than sacrifice. Solomon in the early days of his life walked in the statutes of God in obedience. Unfortunately, over the course of his life, he began to gravitate away from the will of God towards the non-will of God. This act of his earned him severe punishment that was extended to generations yet unborn, damaging and ruining the legacy his father built. "And the LORD was angry with Solomon, because his heart was turned from the LORD God. And God commanded Solomon concerning these things… but Solomon did not keep the commandments God gave to him."[691]

---

690   1 Kings 11:9-13
691   1 Kings 11:9-10

Disobedience leads to dishonor, shame, pain, loss, and humiliation.

"But if you will not listen to me and carry out all these commands, and if you reject my decrees and abhor my laws and fail to carry out all my commands and so violate my covenant, 16then I will do this to you: I will bring on you sudden terror, wasting diseases and fever that will destroy your sight and sap your strength. You will plant seed in vain, because your enemies will eat it. I will set my face against you so that you will be defeated by your enemies; those who hate you will rule over you, and you will flee even when no one is pursuing you..." [692]

Prayer: Lord, help me to remain in love with You, obey You, and commit to the advancement of Your kingdom.

---

692 Leviticus 26:14-28

Chapter 20

THOMAS

Thomas Didymus was one of Jesus' twelve disciples[693]. He became famous and known as doubting Thomas as many Bible readers will call him because he doubted the resurrection of Jesus Christ; he wanted physical proof before believing that Jesus had indeed resurrected. Of course, men and women have different levels or degrees of faith which leaves room for more growth in order to graduate from being a seeing-only before believing follower of Christ to those who believe without having the physical proof right before them. That is a whole new level of faith that Christ encouraged because it has the capacity to move the hand of God regardless of unforeseen or unwanted situations.

---

693 Matthew 10: 3

"Jesus said to him, "Because you have seen Me, do you now believe? Blessed [happy, spiritually secure, and favored by God] are they who did not see [Me] and yet believed [in Me]."[694]

Thomas was called as part of the twelve disciples by Jesus into ministry[695]. He was sent on ministerial assignment with other disciples, equipped and empowered with the grace and ability to teach and preach the gospel, heal the sick, and subdue demonic forces.

"And when he had called unto him his twelve disciples, he gave them power against unclean spirits, to cast them out, and to heal all manner of sickness and all manner of disease. Now the names of the twelve apostles are these; The first, Simon, who is called Peter, and Andrew his brother; James the son of Zebedee, and John his brother; Philip, and Bartholomew; Thomas..."[696]

Thomas, as a disciple of Christ, had access to the same spiritual authority as Jesus[697]. Like Thomas, we all have the opportunity to access the same spiritual power possessed by Jesus because we are God's ambassadors, and every ambassador is backed by the governing authority of his country. We are heavenly ambassadors, the reason why access to the power is available to us. "Therefore, we are

694   John 20:29
695   Mark 3:18, Luke 6:13-16
696   Matthew 10:1-3
697   Matthew 10:1

ambassadors for Christ, as though God were making an appeal through us; we beg you on behalf of Christ, be reconciled to God."[698]

"I assure you and most solemnly say to you, anyone who believes in Me [as Savior] will also do the things that I do; and he will do even greater things than these [in extent and outreach], because I am going to the Father."[699]

We must understand that things don't just happen, they are made to happen. So, we have a part to play, and a responsibility to take to access the same spiritual empowerment made available by God through Jesus.

Thomas was not just a random disciple, but one who was prayerfully called into ministry by Jesus[700]. Like Thomas, everyone has a calling on their lives because we have been chosen by Jesus to do His will. Therefore, it is important for each individual to identify his or her calling, and begin to build capacity in order to succeed in that assignment or calling.

"Before I formed you in the womb, I knew you [and approved of you as My chosen instrument], And before you were born I consecrated you [to Myself as My own]; I have appointed you as a prophet to the nations."[701]

---

698   2 Corinthians 5:20
699   John 14: 12
700   Luke 6:12-15
701   Jeremiah 1:5 AMP

"You did not choose me, but I chose you and appointed you so that you might go and bear fruit…"[702]

Therefore, as one chosen of God, we must ensure we grow in our given assignment. Thomas was an anointed and empowered disciple, yet he lacked the authority and audacity to walk in the reality of a daring faith. Despite his casting out the demons, healing the sick, and preaching the gospel, he could not operate in the realm of faith that does not see physical proof to believe. Despite being told by Jesus and other disciples about His death and resurrection and the circumstances surrounding it, Thomas still needed physical proof to believe it was His master, Jesus.

"Now Thomas (also known as Didymus), one of the Twelve, was not with the disciples when Jesus came. So, the other disciples told him, "We have seen the Lord!" But he said to them, "Unless I see the nail marks in his hands and put my finger where the nails were, and put my hand into his side, I will not believe."[703]

Association with someone does not guarantee access to the grace on their lives. It is the thirst and genuine connection that guarantees the release of the same grace. They said of the apostles, there is something different about these men. They are no longer what they used to be, we perceived they have been with Jesus (Acts 4:13). When there is a genuine connection, the grace flows ceaselessly. Thomas,

702   John 15: 16
703   John 20:24- 25

270

though brave, did not build his faith capacity. He was so brave that he encouraged the disciples to go with Jesus to raise Lazarus when they feared being stoned by the Jews. John 11:8 & 16 "Rabbi," they replied, "the Jews just tried to stone You, and You are going back there?" Then Thomas called Didymus said to his fellow disciples, "Let us also go, so that we may die with Him."

We must not only receive our assignment, but we must ensure we build capacity and have mastery of those things that will make us succeed.

ATTRIBUTES OF THOMAS

Had a calling on his life: Every child of God has a calling upon their life. Some are called to be pulpit pastors, preachers of the gospel, evangelists, musicians, athletes, businessmen, and women, and so many more. The most important thing is engaging whatever platform God puts us to propagate the gospel and His kingdom. "For this is what the Lord has commanded us: "'I have made you a light for the Gentiles, that you may bring salvation to the ends of the earth.'"[704]

"And all things are of God, who hath reconciled us to himself by Jesus Christ, and hath given to us the ministry of reconciliation."[705]

---

704   Acts 14:47
705   2 Corinthians 5:18 KJV

Our goal is to fulfill our heavenly assignment by reconciling the unsaved to God through whatever platform God puts us on. Our lives, actions, behaviors, and activities regardless of the kind of calling given to us are ways we can evangelize the kingdom of God.

Nobody was created by God to exist in a vacuum, there is a unique assignment, and a unique goal for all of God's creation. Whatever assignment it is, the plan of God is to see us live by the dictates of the Bible as an example of heaven here on earth, and preach the gospel to the lost through our God-like attributes and characters, while we secure eternity.

Therefore, we must identify that area of calling like Thomas, he was called to be one of the disciples of Jesus.

Fulfilling one's calling is the most beautiful thing that can ever happen to man after salvation where lives are touched, changed, impacted, and lifted. Above all, the feel of joyfulness seeing how the calling has changed the world around us. In the words of Apostle Paul, "I have fought the good fight, I have finished the race, I have kept the faith."[706]

We must not surrender to any life of mediocrity, but rather to a life and purpose God has called us to.

---

706   2 Timothy 4:7

"And the LORD spoke unto Moses, Go unto Pharaoh, and say unto him, Thus saith the LORD, Let my people go, that they may serve me."[707]

Myles Monroe said, "Live out your name, so when you are done with your assignment, your name still speaks for you because of the impact and change you brought to the lives of those around you, and your environment."

Bravery: "For God did not give us a spirit of timidity or cowardice or fear, but [He has given us a spirit] of power and of love and of sound judgment and personal discipline [abilities that result in a calm, well-balanced mind and self-control]."[708]

We have been called to a life of dominion. "Then God said, "Let Us (Father, Son, Holy Spirit) make man in Our image, according to Our likeness [not physical, but a spiritual personality and moral likeness]; and let them have complete authority over the fish of the sea, the birds of the air, the cattle, and over the entire earth, and over everything that creeps and crawls on the earth."[709]

We are a creation of authority, and dominion. No one has ever succeeded in exacting authority or ruling over a people or things in fear. Fear and dominion are contrasts. Fear is

---

707   Exodus 8:1
708   2 Timothy 1:7 AMP
709   Genesis 1:26

described as "False Evidence Appearing Real" It is not real, it's just a tool of deceit from the enemy. We must learn to speak with authority and boldness in order to be in charge of everything God has placed in our hands or on our path.

The apostles demonstrated the spirit of boldness during their ministries even when they were threatened with death. "So they sent for them and commanded them not to speak [as His representatives] or teach at all in the name of Jesus [using Him as their authority] But Peter and John replied to them, "Whether it is right in the sight of God to listen to you and obey you rather than God, you must judge [for yourselves]."[710] This reminds me of Daniel where he was charged not to pray to God, but he refused and decided to place his life on the line for the sake of the gospel Daniel 6:10-28. Men and women with the boldness of Christ at work in them do not fear physical or death threats from the enemy. "Do not be afraid of those who kill the body but cannot kill the soul; but rather be afraid of Him who can destroy both soul and body in hell."[711]

"Whoever finds his life [in this world] will [eventually] lose it [through death], and whoever loses his life [in this world] for My sake will find it [that is, life with Me for all eternity]."[712]

---

710   Acts 4:18-19 AMP
711   Matthew 10:28
712   Matthew 10:39 AMP

Apostle Paul summed up that nothing has the capacity to separate anyone who genuinely loves God from doing God's bidding, not even death[713].

Like Thomas and other apostles, we must never give in to fear because fear will only cripple our dominion power and hold our minds captive.

"Rabbi," they replied, "the Jews just tried to stone You, and You are going back there?" Then Thomas called Didymus said to his fellow disciples, "Let us also go, so that we may die with Him."[714]

The knowledge of who we are in God as a creation of dominance will help us live above fear. It is said that "When you don't know who you are, you will answer to whatever people call you."

"They know not, neither will they understand; they walk on in darkness: all the foundations of the earth are out of course. I have said, Ye are gods; and all of you are children of the most High."[715]

We can discover our true selves from the pages of God's manual of creation and instruction (The Bible). The more we read and meditate on the manual (Bible), the more we discover our worth and operate in it.

---

713 Romans 8:35-39
714 John 11:8, 16
715 Psalm 82:5-6 KJV

"And we all, with unveiled face, continually seeing as in a mirror the glory of the Lord, are progressively being transformed into His image from [one degree of] glory to [even more] glory, which comes from the Lord, [who is] the Spirit."[716]

"Now when the men of the Sanhedrin (Jewish High Court) saw the confidence and boldness of Peter and John and grasped the fact that they were uneducated and untrained [ordinary] men, they were astounded, and began to recognize that they had been with Jesus."[717]

Jesus, our perfect example, showed us the path to take in order to discover ourselves and operate in the reality of that discovery. "Jesus picked of the book (Bible) to read, there He discovered in totality who He was, and what He was created for."[718] The discovery lifted Him into a new level of operation. No one can succeed or attain his or her rightful place in dominion without self-discovery and taking corresponding actions.

Loyalty: There are certain people who we come in contact with as we journey through life, they play a significant role in our lives in our quest to fulfill purpose. Having genuine and trustworthy people around us helps to navigate the waters of life with the assurance that someone is watching our back in case we fall short. No one succeeds alone in the

---

716   2 Corinthians 3:18 AMP
717   Acts 4:13 AMP
718   Luke 4:16-20 Paraphrased

race of life. We will always need people who believe in our course and are willing to stand by us no matter the situation per time.

"If you fall, your friend can help you up. But if you fall without having a friend nearby, you are really in trouble."[719]

We must be humble enough to associate ourselves with others, but it must be done prayerfully and with wisdom in order to select the right people as our support system. Thomas was one of those who were loyal to Jesus during His days of ministry. In our quest to fulfill purpose, many will give up on us, desert us, or even set us up for failure. But true and loyal friends will always support and stand by until the purpose is fulfilled.

"Rabbi," they replied, "the Jews just tried to stone You, and You are going back there?" Then Thomas called Didymus said to his fellow disciples, "Let us also go, so that we may die with Him."[720]

Jesus called 72 disciples to help in the propagation of the gospel, but he had "The 12" who were His support system through the help of the Holy Spirit. Having people around us is key to our success in life, either spiritually, career-wise, or in any other area of our lives.

719 Ecclesiastes 4:10
720 John 11:8 & 16

277

King David was about to be toppled by Absalom, but a loyal servant came to the rescue.

But Ittai answered the king, "As the Lord lives, and as my lord the king lives, wherever my lord the king shall be, whether for death or for life, there also will your servant be."[721]

The King didn't want Ittai to come with him for various reasons, but as a loyal servant, he was committed to the success of King David. Prayerfully, we must identify those who are our co-pilots in the flight and journey of life. Identifying them will make the journey sweet and successful regardless of the turbulences along the way.

In our world today, we have a man called David Abioye, the first vice-president of the Living Faith Church worldwide, a.k.a Winners Chapel. He has been faithfully committed to the life and the God-given vision of Bishop David Oyedepo for over forty years despite mockeries and challenges. In his words, "By the grace of God, I have stayed committed to David Oyedepo's God-given vision over several decades. And by God's grace, I have tasted and experienced the same thing he has enjoyed as a man of God." True commitment brings honor, blessings, and completeness. In our quest to support others, we find our calling or passion being discovered and fulfilled.

---

721 2 Samuel 15:21

Ruth was committed to her mother-in-law despite her problems. As a result of her loyalty, her marital destiny was fulfilled.

"But Ruth replied, "Don't urge me to leave you or to turn back from you. Where you go, I will go, and where you stay, I will stay. Your people will be my people and your God my God."[722]

Lacked growth: The will of God for all His creation is to experience growth. He is interested in our all-round development. Just as we are expected to grow biologically except in a few cases where there is a medical impediment.

"The way of the righteous is like the first gleam of dawn, which shines ever brighter until the full light of day."[723]

"He cuts off every branch in me that bears no fruit, while every branch that does bear fruit he prunes so that it will be even more fruitful."[724]

Our growth is proof that we have the Spirit of God at work in us. Our life is not expected to remain at a status quo, we must exercise our God-given spiritual strength to effect the necessary growth we want in our lives.

God spoke to Abraham to leave his family because his growth in life was impeded. The moment Abraham

---

722 Ruth 1:16
723 Proverbs 4:18
724 John 15:2

responded to the call of God; he experienced growth that he had not experienced in 75 years of his life.

"Get thee out of thy kindred, and I will terminate the plague of limitation, I will cause you to grow exceedingly great."[725]

"Abraham was now very old, and the LORD had blessed him in every way."[726]

Every child of God is expected to grow spiritually, that is proof that we are skilled in the things of God. Thomas could not operate in a greater dimension of faith because he did not grow his faith. Though I want to believe he had some level of faith but did not pursue development. There is always room to grow.

"Brethren building up your most holy faith…"[727]

"The righteous keep moving forward, and those with clean hands become stronger and stronger."[728] We take responsibility for building capacity in every area of our lives because as a creation of God, we are ordained to change levels per time. There is a different level of anointing that can be exploited for those who are willing and ready to take up the challenge[729]

---

725   Genesis 12: 1-2 Paraphrased
726   Genesis 24:1
727   Jude 1:20
728   Job 17:19
729   Ezekiel 47:1-4

Apostle Joshua Selman stated that "The only growth that is automatic is our biological growth. Every other growth must be made to happen."

Thomas may have had a little faith, but did not grow it, the reason why he needed to confirm first before believing it was Jesus. In most cases, the failure we experience is a function of the growth we lack.

"If you falter in a time of trouble, how small is your strength!"[730] Note that strength here could be mental, physical, spiritual, or any other strength a man needs to prevail. It is important to commit ourselves to build capacity in order to grow, have the audacity, and be in charge of everything in our lives. However, failure to grow will impede, delay, or deny our access to what is rightly ours.

"Think of it this way. If a father dies and leaves an inheritance for his young children, those children are not much better off than slaves until they grow up, even though they own everything their father had."[731] In most family communities, parents who leave an inheritance for their children always put an age peg before they can have access to it. So, certain things will not come to us, and neither will we have access to them until we have attained the required growth. In the kingdom of God, growth is not just a function of age, but spiritual capacity.

---

730 Proverbs 24:10
731 Galatians 4: 1

BENEFITS AND DISBENEFITS OF THOMAS ATTRIBUTES

Divine Calling: Every creation of God has a calling (purpose) on their life. Like Thomas, he was called as one of the disciples of Jesus. All through the Bible, we saw how God called men and women, even children to a life of purpose.

"Before I formed you in the womb, I knew you [and approved of you as My chosen instrument], And before you were born I consecrated you [to Myself as My own]; I have appointed you as a prophet to the nations."[732]

It is important we identify our calling and begin to operate in the calling in order to prevent a life of mediocrity. David Abioye said, "When you don't know who you are, people will call you who you are not." That is very dangerous; if care is not taken, you will begin to respond to what others say you are rather than what God has ordained you to be.

"But you are A CHOSEN RACE, A royal PRIESTHOOD, A CONSECRATED NATION, A [special] PEOPLE FOR God's OWN POSSESSION, so that you may proclaim the excellencies [the wonderful deeds and virtues and perfections] of Him who called you out of darkness into His marvelous light."[733]

---

732   Jeremiah 1: 5 AMP
733   1 Peter 2:9 AMP Emphasis Added

There is a calling on our lives, and we must respond to those calling before it's too late.

"Only, let each one live the life which the Lord has assigned him, and to which God has called him [for each person is unique and is accountable for his choices and conduct, let him walk in this way]. This is the rule I make in all the churches."[734]

When we obey our calling, we experience and enjoy the diverse blessings of God, such as unending provisions, preservation, promotion, honor, longevity, fruitfulness, favor, and divine presence among many others.

Provisions: "And He said to them, "When I sent you out without a money belt and [provision] bag and [extra] sandals, did you lack anything?" They answered, "Nothing."[735]

Preservation: "For he shall give his angels charge over thee, to keep thee in all thy ways. They shall bear thee up in their hands, lest thou dash thy foot against a stone… "I will rescue him; I will protect him, for he acknowledges my name."[736]

---

734 1 Corinthians 7:17
735 Luke 22:35 AMP
736 Psalm 91:11-12 & 14

Promotion: "For promotion cometh neither from the east, nor from the west, nor from the south... But God puts down one and promotes another."[737]

Longevity: "With long life I will satisfy him..."[738]

Honor: When we obey and do His bidding, we are honored. "Because he loves me," says the Lord, "I will rescue him; I will protect him, for he acknowledges my name... and honor him."[739] "...I will fulfill the number of your days."[740]

Fruitfulness: Obedience to one's calling will always secure heaven's order of provisions. "But seek first the kingdom of God and his righteousness, and all these things will be added to you."[741]

Favor: Unreserved commitment to our assignment secures heaven's order of favor. "Thou shalt arise and have mercy upon Zion: for the time to favor her, yea, the set time, is come. For thy servants take pleasure in her stones and favor the dust thereof."[742]

---

737   Psalm 75:6-7 KJV
738   Psalm 91:16
739   Psalms 91:14-15
740   Exodus 23:26
741   Matthew 6:33
742   Psalms 102:13-14 KJV

Divine presence: "And they went forth, and preached everywhere, the Lord working with them, and confirming the word with signs following. Amen."[743]

In all, we must pray to God to help us identify or discover our purpose; while we also seek to understand what it entails in order to pursue it accordingly. If we are not conscious or understand why we were created by God, abuse of our calling and destiny is inevitable.

Dr. Myles Munroe said, "When the purpose of a thing is not known abuse is inevitable."

Loyalty: A life of loyalty is needed in order to commit ourselves genuinely to the course of others. Thomas displayed a level of loyalty to God among the other disciples when they were faced with some level of unwanted situations. Many in the same situation as Thomas would have agreed with other disciples to back out. Our proof of loyalty to others in a difficult situation is a demonstration of our love for them and their course. "Rabbi," they replied, "the Jews just tried to stone You, and You are going back there?" Then Thomas called Didymus said to his fellow disciples, "Let us also go, so that we may die with Him."[744]

Ruth said to Naomi (paraphrased), "Your situation or mine regardless, I am totally committed to your course."

---

743   Mark 16:20 KJV
744   John 11:8, 16

"But Ruth replied, "Don't urge me to leave you or to turn back from you. Where you go I will go, and where you stay I will stay. Your people will be my people and your God my God.""[745]

Loyalty brings us into a realm of honor, love, bond, trust, favor, and blessings.

"Because he set his love on Me, therefore I will save him; I will set him [securely] on high, because he knows My name [he confidently trusts and relies on Me, knowing I will never abandon him, no, never]. "He will call upon Me, and I will answer him; I will be with him in trouble; I will rescue him and honor him. "With a long life I will satisfy him And I will let him see My salvation."[746]

Bravery: Every child of God has a gene of bravery in them. Our father "God" is a lion, He is called the Lion of the tribe of Judah. By redemption, we have been adopted into that spiritual family, and that is why we must demonstrate our roots. Thomas was not afraid to act his root when other disciples were concerned about what could befall them if Jesus embarked on a journey back to where their lives were initially threatened.

If we truly know who we are, we will dominate the world regardless of the enemy's threat. "Moses sent the few individuals to check out the land God has promised them,

---

745 Ruth 1:16
746 Psalms 91: 14-16 AMP

but they returned with fear that it will be impossible for them to take the land."[747] Our minds are very powerful, whatever seed of thought we sow in there is what will dominate and determine the course of our lives. We must beware.

Bishop David Oyedepo said, "A kind will always produce after its kind". Therefore, we must operate with this understanding. He said further "It will only take those with a lion's heart to take their lion's share." Remember, you and I belong to a Lionic root.

The spies came back with a negative report about the land, but Caleb saw it differently. He spoke and acted according to his root, not what he saw.

"Then Caleb silenced the people before Moses and said, "We should go up and take possession of the land, for we can certainly do it."[748]

Our act of bravery will always put us in a place of dominion, honor, promotion, and blessings.

The three Hebrew boys were brave enough to stand for God, and they enjoyed honor, promotion, riches, fame, protection, and many others.

"Shadrach, Meshach, and Abednego, answered and said to the king, O Nebuchadnezzar, we are not careful to answer thee in this matter.

---

747 Numbers 13:1-33 Paraphrased
748 Numbers 13:30

If it be so, our God whom we serve is able to deliver us from the burning fiery furnace, and he will deliver us out of thine hand, O king. But if not, be it known unto thee, O king that we will not serve thy gods, nor worship the golden image which thou hast set up… Then the king promoted Shadrach, Meshach, and Abednego, in the province of Babylon."[749]

We must learn to behave like our roots because that is what guarantees our lion share and dominance, not what the environment presents.

Lack of growth - stagnation: Lack of right human growth in areas necessary will lead to stagnation. Stagnation robs us of our true identity, delays the fulfillment of destiny, limits the impact we were ordained to make, and it will also rob others whose destinies are tied to us for purpose fulfillment.

Thomas was a follower of Christ, but his faith level was stunted, the reason why he asked to put his fingers in Jesus' wound to ascertain whether it was really Jesus.

"But Thomas, one of the twelve, called Didymus, was not with them when Jesus came. The other disciples therefore said unto him, we have seen the Lord. But he said unto them, except I shall see in his hands the print of the nails and put my finger into the print of the nails, and thrust my hand into his side, I will not believe."[750]

---

749 Daniel 3:16-18, 30
750 John 20:24-25

Though Jesus called everyone to Himself as they were, He does not expect us to remain the way we came to Him. Growth is very important, it ushers in lots of positive vibes into our lives. When we came to Jesus, we came with an un-renewed mind, but He expects us to transform our minds in other to enjoy the blessings.

"And be not conformed to this world: but be ye transformed by the renewing of your mind..."[751] Those who pursue after development are marked out for double honor[752]

As children of God, we must strive to grow in every area of our spiritual lives in order to fulfill destiny in grand style. Failure to subscribe to development will limit our access to that inheritance.

"What I am saying is that as long as an heir is underage, he is no different from a slave, although he owns the whole estate."[753]

This growth or development is not a function of age, or how long you and I have been involved in one activity or the other, but it is the mental development and the largeness of the thought of our heart.

Chris Oyakhilome said, "Strive not to be a mental hobo who only subscribes to what others have created, and is not willing to engage his or her own mind to create something.

---

751 Romans 12:2
752 1 Timothy 5:17
753 Galatians 4:1

Many wear designer shoes, colognes, bags, etc.; but have never strived to design something of their own."

Growth is a function of personal development; we must ensure we subscribe to relevant resources that will help us grow. I believe Thomas did not subscribe to self-development in the area of his faith which is why he needed proof before he could believe. But the Bible tells us that blessed are those who do not see, yet they believe.

"Jesus saith unto him, Thomas, because thou hast seen me, thou hast believed: blessed are they that have not seen, and yet have believed."[754]

No one gets to the described level of faith by accident, it requires self-development. "So then faith cometh by hearing, and hearing by the word of God."[755]

Growth is part of the life cycle, anyone not growing needs either spiritual or medical attention. The only growth that is automatic is our biological growth, every other growth is made to happen.

Prayer: Lord, grant me the grace to remain faithful in my walk with You even as I strive to build upon the foundation You laid for me.

---

754   John 20:29 KJV
755   Romans 10:17 KJV

Chapter 21

UZZIAH

U zziah was the tenth king of Judah, he ascended the
throne at the age of sixteen and reigned for about
fifty-two years. His reign was prosperous. During his reign,
king Uzziah positioned himself under the influence of
the prophet Zechariah, a man who understood the ways
of God. Uzziah was faithful to God and did that which
was right in the eyes of the Lord. As a result, God blessed
him[756]

When we seek God with all our hearts, we enjoy the glory
and presence of God that guarantees the fulfillment of
destiny in grand style and all-round rest.

"They entered into a covenant to seek the Lord, the God of their

---

ancestors, with all their heart and soul. ...They sought God eagerly, and he was found by them. So, the Lord gave them rest on every side."[757]

King Uzziah was a great king, his trust was in God, and it secured for him the help of God[758]. Securing the help of God delivers from any form of unwanted and enemy-planned attack. God is our only source of help because the help of God is without limits, while that of men is limited to their God-given ability. It is important to put our trust in God concerning everything.

"Help us defeat our enemies! No one else can rescue us."[759]

"I lift my eyes to the mountains where does my help come from? My help comes from the Lord, the Maker of heaven and earth because He is my defense against all form of satanic and human assault."[760]

Uzziah was so helped by God that he designed and made machines designed by skillful men for use on the towers and on the corner defenses to shoot arrows and hurl large stones. He was victorious in battle, became very famous, and was blessed with gifts[761]

A wise man once said, "Give God the best of your time, and

---

757 2 Chronicles 15:12, 15
758 2 Chronicles 26:7
759 Psalm 108:12
760 Psalm 121:1-8 Paraphrased
761 2 Chronicles 26:8-15

not the leftover." Just like King Uzziah, if we can make time for God first, He will put us at the forefront of His agenda. "I know you are in need of all these earthly necessities that others have decided to make their priority before they think of Me, you don't worry; make me the priority, and all those things will be added to you cheaply."[762]

In our walk with God, we must learn to prioritize, that way we are able to plan and give God the quality time that will secure His hand over our lives. It is also important to know that the enemy will not rest when he sees the glory of God around us, therefore we must remain steadfast and connected to God in order not to fall prey to the enemy.

Despite his greatness and successes, Uzziah made one mistake every one of us could possibly make if care is not taken after we have received the help of God, and we have all round success. Uzziah allowed all the fame, riches, accolades, and success to get into his heart, and he turned against God. What a tragedy! It led to pride, then his pride led to his downfall.

"But when he was strong, his heart was lifted up to his destruction: for he transgressed against the LORD his God and went into the temple of the LORD to burn incense upon the altar of incense."[763]

---

762   Matthew 6:32-33 Paraphrased

763   2 Chronicles 26:16

In the end, Uzziah who enjoyed the help of God due to his love for God ended up in shame and reproach. We must beware of pride, and self-adulation, it destroys and brings shame. It is said that pride brings destruction[764]. Beware!

"Then Uzziah was wroth and had a censer in his hand to burn incense: and while he was wroth with the priests, the leprosy even rose up in his forehead before the priests in the house of the LORD, from beside the incense altar. And Azariah the chief priest, and all the priests, looked upon him, and behold, he was leprous in his forehead, and they thrust him out from thence; yea, himself hasted also to go out, because the LORD had smitten him. And Uzziah the king was a leper unto the day of his death, and dwelt in a several house, being a leper; for he was cut off from the house of the LORD..."[765]

Uzziah the great became Uzziah the leper. What a sad way to end a fulfilling and glorious destiny!

We must always remember that without God, we are nothing, and we must never allow our success to get into our heads so that we now take the glory of God. It is dangerous and can destroy all that we have built. Remember, there is nothing that we have not received from God.

---

764 Proverbs 16:18
765 2 Chronicles 26:19-21

"For who makes you different from anyone else? What do you have that you did not receive? And if you did receive it, why do you boast as though you did not?"[766]

"I am the vine, ye are the branches: He that abideth in me, and I in him, the same bringeth forth much fruit: for without me ye can do nothing."[767]

A writer said, "Never share the glory of God with him, it is poisonous." The story of king Nebuchadnezzar who gave himself the glory for his achievements but ended up in disgrace is an example:

"Twelve months later, as the king was walking on the roof of the royal palace of Babylon, he said, "Is not this the great Babylon I have built as the royal residence, by my mighty power and for the glory of my majesty?" Even as the words were on his lips, a voice came from heaven, "This is what is decreed for you, King Nebuchadnezzar: Your royal authority has been taken from you. 32You will be driven away from people and will live with the wild animals; you will eat grass like the ox. Seven times will pass by for you until you acknowledge that the Most High is sovereign over all kingdoms on earth and gives them to anyone he wishes." Immediately what had been said about Nebuchadnezzar was fulfilled. He was driven away from people and

---

766   1 Corinthians 4:7
767   John 15:5 KJV

ate grass like the ox. His body was drenched with the dew of heaven until his hair grew like the feathers of an eagle and his nails like the claws of a bird."[768]

ATTRIBUTES OF UZZIAH

Love of God: Uzziah was a young king who demonstrated his love for God by following in the steps of his father, Amaziah; obeying the commandments of God, and doing the will of God.

"And he did that which was right in the sight of the LORD, according to all that his father Amaziah did. And he sought God in the days of Zechariah, who had understanding in the visions of God: and as long as he sought the LORD...."[769]

When we genuinely love God, our hearts will pant after him regardless of our titles, position, or socioeconomic status. When we love God, we abase ourselves before Him, and God in turn will lift us in honor just like Uzziah enjoyed.

"Whoever has my commands and keeps them is the one who loves me. The one who loves me will be loved by my Father, and I too will love them and show myself to them."[770]

---

768   Daniel 4:29-33
769   2 Chronicles 26:4-5
770   John 14:21

Our love for God is proof that we believe in His personality, and this is what guarantees God's divine presence in our lives.

"Because he set his love on Me, therefore I will save him; I will set him [securely] on high, because he knows My name [he confidently trusts and relies on Me, knowing I will never abandon him, no, never]."[771]

If we are to enjoy the presence of God that guarantees an all-round fulfillment, we must engage the secret traded by Uzziah. The secret is genuine love and thirst for the things of God. No wonder Apostle Paul said his life is all about Christ, same as in death because that is what brings him gain and fulfillment[772] Apostle Paul's love for God made him the greatest of the disciples even though he never met Jesus physically. It's not too late for you and me, we can ask the Holy Spirit to ignite that fire, passion, and love that will propel us to greater heights. Remember, the secret of God is with them that love Him[773] Those secrets are our tickets to the world of exploits just like Uzziah who became a genius and an inventor of weapons of war "And he made in Jerusalem engines… for he was marvelously helped, till he was strong."[774]

---

771   Psalms 91:14 AMP
772   Philippians 1:21
773   Psalm 25:14
774   2 Chronicles 26:15

Diligence: In the race of life, diligence is key to everyone's success. The absence of diligence will keep a man in the same state, or possibly retrogress.

"Seest thou a man diligent in his business? He shall stand before kings; he shall not stand before mean men."[775]

"Diligent hands will rule, but laziness ends as a slave."[776]

Uzziah was a diligent individual, he did not allow his office or his status as a king to deter him from getting his hands dirty. He was always engaged with one assignment or the other. Those who commit to true and clean labor will always end a wonder among men.

"He built Eloth, and restored it to Judah... And he went forth and warred against the Philistines, and brake down the wall of Gath, and the wall of Jabneh, and the wall of Ashdod, and built cities about Ashdod, and among the Philistines. And God helped him against the Philistines, and against the Arabians that dwelt in Gurbaal, and the Mehunims. Moreover, Uzziah built towers in Jerusalem at the corner gate, and at the valley gate, and at the turning of the wall, and fortified them. Also, he built towers in the desert, and digged many wells: for he had many cattle, both in the low country, and in the plains: husbandmen also, and vine dressers in the mountains, and in Carmel: for he loved husbandry."[777]

---

775   Proverbs 22:29
776   Proverbs 12:24
777   2 Chronicles 26:2, 6, 9-10

Diligence in any God-led chosen field of life will always end up in sweet victory and success if we don't give up. "Let us not become weary in doing good, for at the proper time we will reap a harvest if we do not give up."[778] We must remain committed to that assignment in diligence because when the cloud of hard work and diligence is full, it will give its rain.

"If the clouds be full of rain, they empty themselves upon the earth."[779]

Skillful: God gave every one of us a gift, and those gifts are meant for our profiting. However, it will take you identifying that gift, and putting it to work to enjoy its profiting.

"Every good gift and every perfect gift is from above, coming down from the Father of lights with whom there is no variation or shadow due to change."[780]

"As each has received a gift, use it to serve one another, as good stewards of God's varied grace."[781]

We are to engage our gifts to promote the kingdom of God as His ambassadors here on earth, no one's gift should lie dormant. We must engage the use of that gift to the benefit of mankind. Jesus admonished that we don't relent, but

778 Galatians 6:9
779 Ecclesiastes 11:3
780 James 1:17
781 1 Peter 4:10

get busy with those gifts until He comes. And when He returns, only those who have engaged are entitled to the blessings associated with those gifts.

"So he called ten of his servants, delivered to them ten minas, and said to them, 'Do business till I come.'"[782]

"… The worker deserves his wages."[783]

"Behold, I come quickly; and my reward is with me, to render to each man according as his work is."[784]

Our access to some of the blessings of God is tied to putting our gifts or talents to work. Uzziah engaged his gifts; he built engines, engaged his God-given leadership skills to lead his men to war, built pieces of machinery, and he also engaged in husbandry[785]. All these he did as a king. The life of a king is demanding but Uzziah never allowed that to limit his ability to engage his God-given gift. No wonder his fame was spread abroad.

"and his name spread abroad even to the entering in of Egypt; for he strengthened himself exceedingly… And his name spread far abroad; for he was marvelously helped, till he was strong."[786]

---

782   Luke 19:13
783   1 Timothy 5:18
784   Revelation 22:12
785   2 Chronicles 26: 6-15
786   2 Chronicles 26: 8, 15

To enjoy fame to the glory of God, and to be marvelously helped by God as Uzziah enjoyed, we must subscribe to consistent and diligent use of our God-given talent positively.

"A man's gift makes room for him and brings him before the great."[787]

Wealth: As children of God, one of God's desires for us is to be blessed. However, the blessings of God don't just fall on people's lap, there is always what to do to provoke the release of heavenly wealth.

"Beloved, I pray that in every way you may succeed and prosper..."[788]

From the above scripture, we can see that it was only a wish from God, there is a part we have to play to secure the release. God will only release the blessings on those He knows are diligent and responsible enough to effectively put the blessing to good use. According to the word of a wise man, as received by God, "God's prosperity plan does not answer to prayer and fasting, it only answers to covenant practice." No level of prayer and fasting will make anyone wealthy. Everyone who desires to be wealthy must subscribe to the covenant of seed time and harvest time.

"While the earth remains, seedtime and harvest, and cold and heat, and summer and winter, and day and night shall not cease."[789]

787 Proverbs 18:16
788 3 John 1:2
789 Genesis 8:22

301

Any farmer who failed to plant his or her seed during the planting season will never have anything to harvest during the harvest season.

We can engage the mystery of seed time and harvest time in various ways. We can sow the following as a seed with the confidence that our harvest is guaranteed if they were sown in the right and good ground. This includes our time, our talent, and our resources, either monetary or non-monetary.

Uzziah was a man who sowed his love for God as a seed, his time and gift to the benefit of his people.

"And he sought God in the days of Zechariah, who had understanding in the visions of God: and as long as he sought the LORD, God made him to prosper. Moreover, Uzziah built towers in Jerusalem at the corner gate, and at the valley gate, and at the turning of the wall, and fortified them. Also, he built towers in the desert, and digged many wells: for he had many cattle, both in the low country, and in the plains: husbandmen also, and vine dressers in the mountains, and in Carmel: for he loved husbandry."[790]

No one has ever labored in vain; as long as they are being led by God, the returns are guaranteed.

"The LORD will open the heavens, the storehouse of his bounty, to send rain on your land in season and to bless all the work of your

---

790   2 Chronicles 26:5, 9-10

hands. You will lend to many nations but will borrow from none."[791]
Only those who give seeds to the earth will have something to harvest.
"Give, and it will be given to you..."[792]

Pride: Pride is one of the fastest ways to bring a man down from his high places. We are quick to forget that everything we have, or who we are couldn't have happened without God.

"John replied, "No one can receive anything unless God gives it from heaven."[793]

Uzziah became a victim of pride after all his success. He allowed pride to set in, and it ended in disgrace for him. "But when he was strong, his heart was lifted up to his destruction: for he transgressed against the LORD his God... leprosy even rose up in his forehead before the priests in the house of the LORD... and they thrust him out from thence; yea, himself hasted also to go out, because the LORD had smitten him."[794]

"Whoever exalts himself shall be humbled; and whoever humbles himself shall be raised to honor."[795]

A man who was once great now became a joke; and was

---

791   Deuteronomy 28:12
792   Luke 6:38
793   John 3:7
794   2 Chronicles 26:16
795   Matthew 23:12

mocked as a leper. Pride will always make mockery of those who subscribe to it. "When pride comes, then comes disgrace."[796]

All through the scriptures, we saw men whose hearts were lifted against God in pride, and they were either disgraced or destroyed. King Nebuchadnezzar[797], Herod[798], Hezekiah[799]

We must beware of the spirit of pride, or else we lose the presence of God that guarantees our beauty and lifting.

"But he gives us more grace. That is why Scripture says: "God opposes the proud but shows favor to the humble."[800]

"Humble yourselves before the Lord, and he will lift you up."[801]

BENEFITS AND DISBENEFITS OF UZZIAH ATTRIBUTES

Love of God: Love is the bedrock of our entire existence, without love, we are limited in fulfilling purpose and making an impact here on earth. God speaking said, "For without

---

796 Proverbs 11:12
797 Daniel 4:30-33
798 Acts 12:22-23
799 2 Chronicles 32:25
800 James 4:6
801 James 4:10

me ye can do nothing"[802] In other words, God is love, and the absence of God in our lives creates a vacuum, and that vacuum can be filled with terrible issues in life.

"Beloved, let us love one another, for love is from God, and whoever loves has been born of God and knows God. Anyone who does not love does not know God, because God is love."[803]

We can have the best of everything, but once we lack genuine love of God, life is empty.

Uzziah was a man who loved God, his father taught him the way of the Lord. Even after the death of his father, Amaziah, he continued on the path of loving God because he understood that God is the only way to destiny fulfillment.

"And he did that which was right in the sight of the LORD, according to all that his father Amaziah did. And he sought God in the days of Zechariah, who had understanding in the visions of God: and as long as he sought the LORD, God made him to prosper... And his name spread far abroad; for he was marvelously helped, till he was strong."[804]

Love is a catalyst to the realm of the supernatural where the secrets of God to a life of exploits are hidden. If we

802 John 15:15 KJV
803 1 John 4:7-8
804 2 Chronicles 26:4-5, 15

desire to be marvelously helped like Uzziah in life, we must subscribe to loving God because that is our access to what eyes have never seen or any mind conceived. The secret of God gives us leverage above every other creation of God. A lover will only reveal his or her secret to a fellow lover.

"However, as it is written: "What no eye has seen, what no ear has heard, and what no human mind has conceived" — the things God has prepared for those who love him."[805]

Daniel, Joseph, and Paul are other examples of people who subscribed to the love and the things of God, this made them a wonder to behold by many during their time and ministry on earth.

"...but the people that do know (love) their God shall be strong and do exploits."[806]

Joseph said, "How then could I do such a wicked thing and sin against God?"[807]

Apostle Paul affirmed, "Who shall separate us from the love of Christ? Shall tribulation, or distress, or persecution, or famine, or nakedness, or peril, or sword? ... Nay, in all these things we are more than conquerors through him that loved us. For I am persuaded, that neither death, nor life, nor angels, nor principalities, nor powers, nor things

---

805   2 Corinthians 2:9
806   Daniel 11:32 Emphasis Added
807   Genesis 39:9

present, nor things to come, Nor height, nor depth, nor any other creature, shall be able to separate us from the love of God, which is in Christ Jesus our Lord."[808]

These men were ardent lovers of God and they all enjoyed the help of God through divine secrets which made them a force to be reckoned with during their days[809]

Our access to the help of God that secures for us undeniable feats and testimonies is anchored on the love of God. Remember that the absence of love equals the absence of God in our life because God is love.

"If I speak in the tongues of men or of angels, but do not have love (God), I am only a resounding gong or a clanging cymbal. If I have the gift of prophecy and can fathom all mysteries and all knowledge, and if I have a faith that can move mountains, but do not have (God) love, I am nothing. If I give all I possess to the poor and give over my body to hardship that I may boast, but do not have (God) love, I gain nothing."[810]

Diligence: The Bible says those who walk with the wise, shall be wise, and those who keep company with fools shall be destroyed[811]. Uzziah was a wise man, he walked with God, and his life was a testimony to everyone around him[812]

---

808   Romans 8:35, 37-39
809   Daniel 2:19, Colossians 1:25–28, Job 29:4
810   1 Corinthians 13:1-3 (Emphasis Added)
811   Proverbs 13:20
812   2 Chronicles 26:4-5

We must be smart like Uzziah by pitching our tent with God so that the grace of God and His person can rob off on us. God was very diligent with His assignment, there was no room for slack and or idle moments. Jesus testified of this, and He encouraged us to do the same because diligence is the gateway to a life of exploits.

"But Jesus answered them, "My Father has been working until now [He has never ceased working], and I too am working."[813]

We must commit ourselves to diligence if we must enjoy the good things God has packaged for us here on earth. Being diligent gives us the platform to blaze the trail, set the pace, and do the things that others find difficult to do.

"The hand of the diligent shall bear rule: but the slothful shall be under tribute."[814]

"See thou a man diligent in his business? he shall stand before kings; he shall not stand before mean men."[815]

If we subscribe to diligence like Uzziah and other great men in the Bible, our lives will be decorated beyond human comprehension.

813   John 5:17 AMP
814   Proverbs 12:24
815   Proverbs 22:29

"Moreover Uzziah built towers in Jerusalem at the corner gate, and at the valley gate, and at the turning of the wall, and fortified them. Also, he built towers in the desert, and digged many wells: for he had many cattle, both in the low country, and in the plains: husbandmen also, and vine dressers in the mountains, and in Carmel: for he loved husbandry… And he made in Jerusalem engines, invented by cunning men, to be on the towers and upon the bulwarks, to shoot arrows and great stones withal. And his name spread far abroad; for he was marvelously helped, till he was strong."[816]

Diligence confers on us successes, blessings of God, favor, promotion, wealth, and excellence[817]

"The soul of the sluggard craves and gets nothing, while the soul of the diligent is richly supplied."[818]

"The plans of the diligent lead surely to abundance…"[819]

Remember, there is dignity, beauty, honor, and fulfillment in labor.

Skill: "In his grace, God has given us different gifts for doing certain things well. So, if God has given you the ability to prophesy, speak out with as much faith as God has given you. If your gift is serving others, serve them well. If you are a teacher, teach well. If your gift is to encourage others,

---

816 2 Chronicles 26:9-10, 15
817 Proverbs 10:4, Proverbs 14:23, Proverbs 12:27, 2 Peter 3:4
818 Proverbs 13:4
819 Proverbs 21:5

be encouraging. If it is giving, give generously. If God has given you leadership ability, take the responsibility seriously. And if you have a gift for showing kindness to others, do it gladly."[820]

No creation of God was designed to be without skill. God in His wisdom gave everyone a gift or multiple gifts for our profiting[821] His desire is that we have a fulfilled life, and those skills (gifts) are one of the tools that will get us closer to our place of fulfillment[822] Uzziah was a man who exercised his God-given gift to the point of profiting and fulfillment.

"...Uzziah built towers in Jerusalem at the corner gate, and at the valley gate, and at the turning of the wall, and fortified them. Also, he built towers in the desert, and digged many wells: for he had many cattle, both in the low country, and in the plains: husbandmen also, and vine dressers in the mountains, and in Carmel: for he loved husbandry. And he made in Jerusalem engines... And his name spread far abroad."[823]

We must take cognizance of those God-given skills (gift), develop them, hone them, and bless humanity with them. Nobody profits or experiences fulfillment by just sitting around with his or her God-given gift.

---

820   Romans 12:6-8
821   1 Corinthians 12:4-11
822   Jeremiah 29:11
823   2 Chronicles 26:9-10, 15

Dr. Myles Monroe said, "The wealthiest place is the cemetery, not the Silicon Valley, Wall Street, and other great places in the society." According to him, it is so because many people died and were buried with the wealth of gifts and skills God gave to them without putting them to work. Books not written, businesses not started, songs not composed, mechanical and scientifically inclined devices not invented, and many more. We must come to the point where we have given all that God gave us as a gift to impact the world.

Apostle Paul said, "I have finished my race..."[824] It will only take a man who pursued and engaged each of his God-given abilities to change the world to make such a profound and daring statement. Can you and I say the same? It is possible if we commit to it?

Dr. Myles Munroe said that his greatest achievement would be to die empty, having dished out everything God deposited in him to bless mankind. The use of our God-given gifts ushers in profiting, honor, fame, fulfillment, trans-generational blessings, and most importantly puts our name in the hearts of men forever even when we are long gone. We must understand that our talent, skill, gift, or whatever term we decide to use was given to bring glory

---

824   2 Timothy 4:7

to God and the human race. It is time to make the impact God designed us for, and change the world. The world is waiting for our exploits and manifestation.

"For the earnest expectation of the creation eagerly waits for the revealing of the sons of God."[825]

Wealth: One of God's desires is that we live a wealthy and prosperous life[826] We may have been born into poverty, but God made a provision for us to never remain in poverty, but live a life of abundance and riches.

"For you know the grace of our Lord Jesus Christ that though he was rich, yet for your sake he became poor, so that you through his poverty might become rich."[827] However, wealth and prosperity do not Jump on people, there is a demand that must be met in order to enjoy and experience the reality of God's true riches.

Uzziah was a young king who loved God, and as a result he was helped by God until he became great[828] When we love God genuinely with all our hearts, He reveals His secrets that will make us a point of reference in all areas of our

---

825 Romans 8:19
826 3 John 2
827 2 Corinthians 8:9
828 2 Chronicles 26:1-15

lives. Job testified of how the secrets of God were with him, and how he traded the secrets to be the richest in the Far East in his days[829]

Our loving God opens to us His vault of wealth. This wealth is also given not just for us, but to propagate the gospel of Jesus Christ and to bless humanity. All through the scriptures, we had men who triggered the heavenly vault to release heavenly wealth because of their love for God. David, Solomon, Abraham, Nehemiah, Daniel, The three Hebrew boys (Shadrach, Meshach and Abednego). Loving God and doing his will is our access to wealth and riches[830]

God's given wealth helps us to propagate his gospel and bless humanity. Doing this will usher us into honor, fame, and an abundance of transgenerational wealth and blessings.

"Give therefore thy servant an understanding heart to judge thy people that I may discern between good and bad: for who is able to judge this thy so great a people? And the speech pleased the Lord, that Solomon had asked this thing. And God said unto him, Because thou hast asked this thing, and hast not asked for thyself long life; neither hast asked riches for thyself, nor hast asked the life of thine enemies; but hast asked for thyself understanding to discern judgment; Behold, I have done according to thy words: lo, I have given thee a wise and

---

829   Job 29:4-20
830   Deuteronomy 28:1-13, Job 36:11

an understanding heart; so that there was none like thee before thee, neither after thee shall any arise like unto thee. And I have also given thee that which thou hast not asked, both riches, and honor: so that there shall not be any among the kings like unto thee all thy days."[831]

He touched the heart of God, and God opened unto Solomon the vault of heaven. We can also enjoy the same if our hearts can align only with the things that God values and loves.

Pride: Pride is a limiter and destroyer of destiny. All through the scriptures, we saw great men who God had lifted reduced to nothing because of pride. Pride keeps God out of our reach, and when God is out of our reach, we lose His presence. It is God's presence that makes difference in our lives[832]

"But he giveth more grace. Wherefore he saith, God resist the proud, but giveth grace unto the humble."[833]

Pride bears the following fruits; absence of God, shame, reproach, insignificance, loneliness, and many others. King Uzziah became a victim of pride, and his end was humiliating. Shame and disgrace became his story despite his great feats.

---

831   1 Kings 3:9-13
832   Psalm 124:1-8
833   James 4:6

"But when he was strong, his heart was lifted up to his destruction: for he transgressed against the LORD his God... while he was wroth with the priests, the leprosy even rose up in his forehead before the priests in the house of the LORD, from beside the incense altar... And behold, he was leprous in his forehead, and they thrust him out from thence; yea, himself hasted also to go out, because the LORD had smitten him. And Uzziah the king was a leper unto the day of his death, and dwelt in a several house, being a leper; for he was cut off from the house of the LORD..."[834]

His act of pride reduced him from being a renowned and great king to an ordinary leper rejected by God and his people. He could not live his house due to shame and reproach. Nebuchadnezzar and Herod are other examples of individuals that were disgraced because of their pride[835]

There is nothing beneficial in pride, it is a destroyer of destiny. Like Moses, let us be humble in everything in order to experience and secure God's hand always because He is the one who makes all things possible.

"Now the man Moses was very meek, above all the men which were upon the face of the earth"[836] Moses' meek nature secured him God's help, and he fulfilled destiny in honor and dignity. We must remember

834 2 Chronicles 26:16, 19-21
835 Daniel 4:30-33, Acts 12:21-23
836 Numbers 12:23

that only the meek will God guide, and it will only take His Guidance to arrive at every of our pre-ordained destinations in fulfillment'[837]

"Blessed are the meek, for they shall inherit the earth."[838]

Prayer: Lord, shed Your love afresh in my heart by the Holy Spirit.

---

837 Psalms 25:9
838 Matthew 5:5

Chapter 22

VASHTI

Vashti, a queen in the land of Persia, the wife of King Ahasuerus who reigned from India unto Ethiopia. She was a woman in place of authority, beautiful and privileged to be the wife of the king.

Vashti lived a royal life, a life that not everyone would be desirous of because of the good things that come with being a queen and royalty. Royalty comes with decency, comportment, elegance, and firmness. I believe all these characterized the life of Vashti as the wife of the number 1 citizen of the land of Persia in order not to bring disrepute to the palace of the king. We all are God's creation, born into royalty, therefore we must carry and present ourselves as one so that we can project and carry the name of God in good light. Our speech, actions, behavior, and how we relate with others must be decent because we belong to a decent and honorable lineage.

"But you are A CHOSEN RACE, A royal PRIESTHOOD, A CONSECRATED NATION, A [special] PEOPLE FOR God's OWN POSSESSION, so that you may proclaim the excellencies [the wonderful deeds and virtues and perfections] of Him who called you out of darkness into His marvelous light."[839]

Royalty comes with authority, that is why everyone in such a position must represent the office with dignity and respect because they were placed there by God for a purpose. How we conduct ourselves when occupying the office will determine how the followers will respond to our leadership.

"Where the word of a king is, there is power; and who may say to him, "What are you doing?"[840]

Even though God has instructed that people respect and be obedient to those in the position of authority, leaders cannot afford to get carried away by the position they occupy or become careless.

"Everyone must submit to governing authorities. For all authority comes from God, and those in positions of authority have been placed there by God."[841]

---

839   1 Peter 2:9 AMP
840   Ecclesiastes 8:4
841   Romans 13:1-2

It is important to note that anyone in a place of authority is privileged to be there, and they are not expected to use their position to oppress others.

"He who oppresses the poor taunts his Maker, but he who is gracious to the needy honors Him."[842]

Vashti, despite being in a place of authority, was still subject to a higher authority; in her case, the king her husband was the higher authority over her. She was instructed by the king to appear before his visitors with her royal crown, however, she refused because the request did not go down well with her. According to historians, the call for Vashti by the king was a call to appear nude with her crown on her head before strangers and friends of the king. I believe this was humiliating and embarrassing for her, and she refused to appear before the king's friends nor obey the instruction.

"To bring Vashti the queen before the king with the crown royal, to shew the people and the princes her beauty: for she was fair to look on."[843]

It is not right to disregard instructions given by a superior authority, doing that may incur a strict and severe consequences. However, when instructions given desecrates our values, it is okay to respectfully decline to carry out the instructions because our values are our assets, and no

---

842 Proverbs 14:31
843 Esther 1:11

one should trample on them because they are in authority. When the wife of Potiphar tried to use her position to desecrate Joseph, Joseph respectfully declined because he treasured more his God-instilled values regardless of the consequence that came with the refusal[844]. He did not bow to pressure but sought to please God. Likewise, we should not succumb to the pressure of doing wrong things because the result is never good.

Vashti's move not to appear before the king was a move of modesty; though she acted in disobedience to the demand of the King which could send bad precedence to all other people in Shushan to disobey the order of the king. She found herself in a tough situation beyond her ability, and the only way she thought she could handle the situation was to disobey. This led to the loss of her queenship. People may threaten to take away our status, position, or title but we must never allow them to take away our self-worth and dignity. Nobody should lose their honor, dignity, and respect for something dishonorable. Just like Joseph refused to trample upon his honor for a few minutes' pleasure[845]

"But the queen Vashti refused to come at the king's commandment by his chamberlains: therefore, was the king very wroth, and his anger burned in him."[846]

---

844 Genesis 39:7-11
845 Genesis 39:9
846 Esther 1:12

We must remember that we were fearfully and wonderfully made in the image of God, nobody should trample upon our God-given beauty. We must know our self-worth as a child of God, and our royal lineage. We should never dishonor or bring disrepute to God, ourselves, our family, and society.

"I will praise thee; for I am fearfully and wonderfully made: marvelous are thy works; and that my soul knoweth right well."[847]

ATTRIBUTES OF VASHTI

Royalty: "And hast made us unto our God kings (Queens) and priests: and we shall reign on the earth."[848]

We all belong to the family of God, a royal family. We were ordained by God to reign in over all things, we must have a mentality of royalty in order to discharge our royal duties with honor and dignity. Remember we live in a world where everything is accepted as good even when they are not. Therefore, as royalties, we must know where to draw the line. Apostle Paul said, "All things are lawful, but not all things are good for royalties."[849] When we honor ourselves in everything, we bring honor to our lineage and not disgrace. Vashti was a daughter of King Belshazzar[850] and a granddaughter of King Nebuchadnezzar. She was

---

847 Psalms 139:14
848 Revelation 5:10 Emphasis Added
849 1 Corinthians 6:12 Paraphrased
850 Daniel 5:1

born into royalty, and she knew how to behave like royalty. We must never allow anyone to manipulate or take away from us our self-worth and dignity for their selfish interest.

"But you are a chosen people, a royal priesthood, a holy nation, God's special possession, that you may declare the praises of him who called you out of darkness into his wonderful light."[851]

This is our real identity, and we must protect it with everything in us.

Modesty: "Your beauty should not come from outward adornment, such as elaborate hairstyles and the wearing of gold jewelry or fine clothes. Rather, it should be that of your inner self, the unfading beauty of a gentle and quiet spirit, which is of great worth in God's sight."[852]

Like Vashti, our honor, beauty, and elegance should not be dependent on our outward appearance or look and the beautiful things around us, but our inner beauty and self-worth which is able to empower us to stand against anything that disrespects or demean who we are as royalty. Vashti was not going to allow anyone to bring disrepute to her or her self-worth. It is important we know our values, our precious we are, and importantly set boundaries, and stand by them. We must never succumb to any threat that will bring us disrepute.

---

851 1 Peter 2: 9
852 1 Peter 3:3-4

There is a saying, "If you cannot beat them, join them." From a biblical perspective, it is never okay to join them if you cannot beat them. If men are doing wrong things that displease God, rather than succumb to joining them because you have been outnumbered, quit the activity or leave the environment to save your destiny. Doing this secures God's presence in our lives, and brings honor and beauty.

"Blessed [fortunate, prosperous, and favored by God] is the man who does not walk in the counsel of the wicked [following their advice and example], nor stand in the path of sinners, nor sit [down to rest] in the seat of [b]scoffers (ridiculers). But his delight is in the law of the LORD, and on His law [His precepts and teachings] he [habitually] meditates day and night. And he will be like a tree firmly planted [and fed] by streams of water, which yields its fruit in its season; Its leaf does not wither; And in whatever he does, he prospers [and comes to maturity]."[853]

Daniel chose not to join in the feast of the king, though it was appealing and fun[854]. He chose to do God's desire, and his action secured him greatness, honor, and wealth in the land of Babylon. This is what a man and woman of modesty should do; go for God, and forsake the enticing words or temporary beautiful things men offer.

---

853 Psalms 1:1-3 AMP
854 Daniel 1:8

Disobedience: This is kicking or going against laid down rules, instructions, or commands. The effect of it may result in consequences that could be costly and painful. Vashti as a queen was punished for being disobedient; she was relieved of her position as a queen. However, her disobedience was to protect her dignity. In this stance, it is okay to walk away from anything that will bring us disrepute or dishonor.

David Oyedepo said, "I will rather sink with God than shine with men (refusing to subscribe to the dirty tricks and manipulative ways of man)"

We must always know when to stand our ground or walk away, and it is better to obey God and disobey men. However, it is also necessary and important to obey those in place of authority in order to have orderliness and also accord them the necessary honor as long as they are doing what is right. Even when we spot wrongdoings by our leaders, it is not our duty to discipline them, but those who placed them in place of authority.

The consequences of disobedience are always painful. However, it has two sides to it. Disobeying to do what is right and disobeying not to do what is right. The first act of obedience reels in peace of mind knowing that you did not engage in anything dirty, while the latter form of disobedience will always deal a deadly blow in the end. The choice is ours to make.

Joseph chose to disobey the demands of the king's wife, and he got punished for it, but he ended up being celebrated as a hero[855]

"Pharaoh said to Joseph, "I hereby put you in charge of the entire land of Egypt."[856]

The three Hebrew boys (Shadrach, Meshach, and Abed-Nego) chose to disobey the wrong order of the king, and chose to abide by the command of God; they ended up as heroes.

"... Then the king promoted Shadrach, Meshach, and Abed-Nego in the province of Babylon."[857]

Throughout the scriptures, we have men who disobeyed direct orders to do the right thing, and they were honored in return. As a people, we must know when to draw the line between what is good and not. A final example is the disciples of Jesus; they were told not to preach the gospel, but they chose to disobey a direct order to do what is right.

"Then they called them in again and commanded them not to speak or teach at all in the name of Jesus. But Peter and John replied,

---

855   Genesis 39:9-23
856   Genesis 41:41
857   Daniel 3:30

325

"Which is right in God's eyes: to listen to you, or to him? You be the judges! As for us, we cannot help speaking about what we have seen and heard." [858]

Remember, disobedience is in two forms, we must know when to engage and not to engage.

BENEFITS AND DISBENEFITS OF VASHTI'S ATTRIBUTES

Royalty: We were all made in the image of God. This makes us royalty; our Father (God) is the King of all kings, and we are joint heirs with Jesus Christ.

"and if children, then heirs — heirs of God and joint heirs with Christ, if so it be that we suffer with Him, that we may be also glorified together." [859]

"And on His robe and on His thigh, He has a name written, "King of kings…" [860]

Therefore, it is important to know and behave our roots and lineage. In some parts of the world, people are selected, coronated, or installed as King or Queen over cities, provinces, or countries to oversee and ensure the culture, and tradition of their cities are being upheld by the people, and most importantly bring prosperity to the city and the

---

858   Acts 4:18-20
859   Romans 8:17
860   Revelation 19:16

people by making sound decisions. They are expected to be good examples to society, while they conduct themselves in a respectful manner, with dignity, and honor. A perfect example will be the royal family of the United Kingdom.

As heirs of the heavenly throne, we are expected to carry ourselves with uttermost honor, respect, dignity, and protect the values and integrity of our kingdom. We are the example to the world, their mirror to live a beautiful and better life.

Every royalty is adorned with beautiful things of life, honor, respect, and riches as long as we maintain our status. Vashti enjoyed the honor of royalty and riches while she was the queen; she had everything at her disposal to host an elaborate feast for her guests.

"Where were white, green, and blue, hangings, fastened with cords of fine linen and purple to silver rings and pillars of marble: the beds were of gold and silver, upon a pavement of red, and blue, and white, and black, marble. And they gave them drink in vessels of gold, (the vessels being diverse one from another,) and royal wine in abundance, according to the state of the king. Also, Vashti the queen made a feast for the women in the royal house which belonged to king Ahasuerus."[861]

We can imagine how blessed we are to have the King of all as our Father. The entire world and everything in it belong

---

861   Esther 1:6-7, 9

to our Father, and what belongs to our Father belongs to us. You can imagine how beautiful it is to be a co-owner of the entire world, with the power to dictate how things work, not at the detriment of others but to promote the will of our Father concerning others who are yet to identify as members of the heavenly royalty.

"The earth is the Lord's, and the fullness thereof; the world, and they that dwell therein."[862] *"The silver is Mine, and the gold is Mine,' says the Lord of hosts."*[863]

We are beneficiaries of the inheritances as sons and daughters of the King of all the earth. However, we must behave and represent heaven wherever we find ourselves in order to keep enjoying the blessings of royalty.

Modesty: It is described as a behavior, manner, or appearance intended to avoid impropriety or indecency. This should be a way of life, not just because we want people to see what we want them to believe about us. Our lives must be Christ-like, living and behaving like God daily. We must remember that people may be fooled by our false appearance of good behavior and character, but there is one person we can never deceive, God, our Father. People may celebrate and applaud us with our physical and false

---

862 Psalm 24:1 KJV
863 Haggai 2:8

presentation, but our father (GOD) will not because He is core interest in our heart appearance that dictates the external behavior.

"But the Lord said to Samuel, "Do not look at his appearance or at the height of his stature, because I have rejected him. For the Lord sees not as man sees; for man looks at the outward appearance, but the Lord looks at the heart."[864]

Therefore, the state of our hearts should be our priority and not our outward appearance. Being modest reflects in having manners, and behavior both in action and words, while we strive to be decent in our appearance both in private and public.

A modest man and woman will always enjoy honor, respect, and celebration both from his or her family and society like Vashti who refused to bring disrepute to her lineage of royalty by not condoning the disrespectful and demeaning request of the king[865] Daniel and Joseph and many others chose modesty over the temporary pleasure that could wreck their destinies and bring disrepute to their respectful family[866]

We live in a world where indecency has become normal, and

---

864 1 Samuel 16:7
865 Esther 1:12
866 Daniel 1:8, Genesis 39:7-9

people are comfortable living it. You and me have a choice to make, either good or bad. Today, bad things have been wrapped in good wrappers to make them appear good. We must be vigilant in order not to fall to the wiles and deceit of the world[867] As children of God, we also are free-willed, with the liberty to make choices. Our Father chose not to impose His will on us but gave us the liberty to make a good and sound decision in order to keep enjoying the very good things He has packaged for us from creation.

"I call heaven and earth as witnesses against you today, that I have set before you life and death, the blessing and the curse; therefore, you shall choose life in order that you may live, you and your descendants."[868]

Disobedience: It is willfully going against a set of laid down rules or direct command. It comes with regrettable consequences. When we disobey, we get punished for it. Vashti willfully disobeyed the king's order for a reason best known to her. However, regardless of the reason for disobedience, there is always a consequence and we must be ready to live with the consequence.

"But the queen Vashti refused to come at the king's commandment by his chamberlains: therefore, was the king very wroth, and his anger burned in him. If it please the king, let there go a royal commandment from him, and let it be written among the laws of the Persians and the

---

867 Matthew 10:16
868 Deuteronomy 30:19 AMP

Medes, that it be not altered, That Vashti come no more before king Ahasuerus; and let the king give her royal estate unto another that is better than she.'[869]

Our decision to go against a set rule or instruction must be processed before embarking on it because of the consequences it carries. Some consequences could be short-lived, while some could be generational.

"All these curses will come on you. They will pursue you and overtake you until you are destroyed, because you did not obey the Lord your God and observe the commands and decrees, he gave you. They will be a sign and a wonder to you and your descendants forever. Because you did not serve the Lord your God joyfully and gladly in the time of prosperity, therefore in hunger and thirst, in nakedness and dire poverty, you will serve the enemies the Lord sends against you. He will put an iron yoke on your neck until he has destroyed you.'[870]

However, if our decision to disobey a set of rules or instructions is because we desire to do what is right, we may eventually escape the consequence of disobeying those rules, and then enjoy honor, beauty, respect, promotion, and blessings.

Daniel, Joseph, the three Hebrew boys (Meshach, Shadrach, and Abednego), Peter, and John are a few examples of those

---

869 Esther 1:12, 17&19
870 Deuteronomy 28:45-48

who disobeyed direct instructions to do what is right[871] Though there were consequences for their action(s), in the end, God honored them. This is the only time we get a pat on the back from God for disobeying because our choice of disobedience was to please God and not the evil works of men.

Prayer: Lord, help me to live a modest life to the glory of Your name.

871   Daniel 6:6-28, Genesis 39:9, Genesis 41:37-44, Daniel 3:1-30 and Acts, 4:20

Chapter 23

"In the beginning was the Word, and the Word was with God, and the Word was God. He was with God in the beginning. Through him all things were made; without him nothing was made that has been made. In him was life, and that life was the light of all mankind. The light shines in the darkness, and the darkness has not overcome it."[872]

Words are letters of the Alphabet coined or merged to pass information from one person to the other. It could be verbal or nonverbal (written). Words have meaning, are powerful, and can create, recreate or destroy.

The Word had been in existence before the creation, and it is the same Word that created the entire universe. The

---

872   John 1:1-5

Word is GOD, and by it everything was made. Simply put, the Word is a person with spirit and life. "The words I have spoken to you—they are full of the Spirit and life."[873]

"In the beginning was the Word, and the Word was with God, and the Word was God."[874]

Every man or woman is as good as his or her spoken or written word. People will take, believe, and hold us by our word. For example, when the law enforcement picks up anyone, they say to them, "Whatever you say may be used against you..." Indirectly, they are saying to the individual that he is a representation of his words. That is why we must be careful and truthful with every word that proceeds from our mouth because those confessions have the capacity to make or alter the course of our lives. That's why we were admonished that we should not make guile with our mouth[875] and that we should be careful and not cause our mouth to destroy us, then we say before an angel it is an error[876]

"Let what you say be simply 'Yes' or 'No'; anything more than this comes from the devil"[877] *(The father of lies*[878]*).*

---

873 John 6:63b
874 John 1:1
875 Psalm 34: 13b
876 Ecclesiastes 5:6.
877 Matthew 5:37
878 John 8:44

God, our Father, who is the origin of the Word became our perfect example with His words; no lies in Him, and whatever he says He will do, He does. We saw from the beginning when He spoke and the entire universe and everything in it into existence. He did not renege on His word. He said it and stood by it.

"So shall my word be that goes forth out of my mouth: it shall not return unto me void, but it shall accomplish that which I please, and it shall prosper in the thing whereto I sent it."[879]

We should borrow a leaf from God, our Father by not letting our words jump to the ground whenever we relate with others. People should be able to trust and vouch for us because of our trustworthiness. All through the scriptures, we saw the testament of God upholding His Word. God gave His word of protection and presence in and over our lives.

"When you pass through the waters, I will be with you; and when you pass through the rivers, they will not sweep over you. When you walk through the fire, you will not be burned; the flames will not set you ablaze"[880]

Indeed, He stood by His Word, and still stands by it today. Prophet Jeremiah attested to this:

---

879   Isaiah 55:11
880   Isaiah 43:2

"Because of the LORD's great love, we are not consumed, for his compassions never fails"[881]

We must strive to let our words be a true representation of our lives and who we are, and not the opposite.

"These are the things which you should do: speak the truth to one another; judge with truth and judgment for peace in your gates."[882]

"Therefore, laying aside falsehood, speak truth each one of you with his neighbor, for we are members of one another."[883]

"He who speaks truth tells what is right, But a false witness, deceit."[884]

In our words lies our honor, creativity, integrity, relevance and promotion. We must ensure we live a life worthy of emulation by our words so that when we are long gone; we are still being referenced. God vouched for Abraham, and He did the same for Job. We can also be added to that list, but it will take us being truthful and trustworthy always regardless of the pressure to do the opposite.

"Then the LORD said to Satan, "Have you considered my servant Job? There is no one on earth like him; he is blameless and upright, a man who fears God and shuns evil."[885]

---

881   Lamentations 2:23
882   Zechariah 8:16
883   Ephesians 4:25
884   Proverbs 12:17
885   Job 1:8

ATTRIBUTES OF THE WORD

Creative: The Word is creative. It was the Word that created the entire universe and everything that is in today. Therefore, we can create the world we want by our words, but those words must be infused with trust and belief that whatever we declare in faith in line with God's Word will surely happen no matter how long it takes. "Through him all things were made; without him nothing was made that has been made."[886]

God did not like what He saw in the beginning, the universe was null and void without any beauty. God wanted something different, He engaged the creativeness of His Word, and what He wanted happened by the creative power of His spoken Word.

Our words have the same capacity and ability to create what we want. Words are powerful, they have life in them, and they give life to whatever we send them to do. "The words that I speak unto you, they are spirit, and they are life."[887]

The life we want can easily be created by what we speak. We must not be careless with our words if we desire good things to happen around us. No matter the negative circumstances surrounding us, our word must always be positive.

---

886   John 1:3
887   John 6:63

"Suffer not thy mouth to cause thy flesh to sin; neither say thou before the angel, that it was an error: wherefore should God be angry at thy voice, and destroy the work of thine hands?"[888]

"For, "Whoever would love life and see good days must keep their tongue from evil and their lips from deceitful speech."[889]

"Keep your tongue from evil and your lips from deceitful speech."[890]

We must be conscious of how we engage every word that proceeds from our mouth, they can either make us or ground us. It is imperative that we confess or declare positivity in the face of negative or contrary situation. "When they cast thee down, thou shalt say, there is lifting up; and the humble person he will save."[891] Abraham our father was faced with a negative situation, but he chose to speak those words that will create the kind of world he wanted to live in. The world of parenthood, and indeed, it happened.

"As it is written, "I have made you the father of many nations"—in the presence of the God in whom he believed, who gives life to the dead and calls into existence the things that do not exist." [892]

---

888 Ecclesiastes 5:6
889 1 Peter 3:10
890 Psalms 34:13
891 Job 22:29
892 Romans 4:17 (Emphasis Added)

This is the kind of attitude we need to put on no matter the contrary situation. Life happens sometimes which can result in the following; loss of job, loss of investments, loss of home, sickness in the body, rejection by people, hopelessness, hunger, being beaten and battered, etc. All these are a reminder of what Jesus foretold in the scriptures that in this world we will have troubles, but victory is guaranteed. We must engage the power of the Word to change things because that is our weapon to effect change. "… declare thou, that thou mayest be justified"[893]

Truly I tell you, if anyone says to this mountain, 'Go, throw yourself into the sea,' and does not doubt in their heart but believes that what they say will happen, it will be done for them."[894] .

It is imperative we find the inner strength to remain positive in all situations because the positive mentality is what keeps our thought process intact in order to create a way out. Jesus admonished us to remain cheerful in the midst of all these negative situations because that is the key that secures God's presence (the creative Word) to intervene and turn situations around[895]

"Consider it pure joy, my brothers, and sisters, a whenever you face trials of many kinds, because you know that the testing of your faith

---

893   Isaiah 43:26b KJV
894   Mark 11:23
895   John 16:33

produces perseverance. Let perseverance finish its work so that you may be mature and complete, not lacking anything[896]

The moment we decide to remain steadfast amid the situation by taking the rod which is the Word of God in our hand or mouth, victory is guaranteed.

"And thou shalt take this rod in thine hand, wherewith thou shalt do signs."[897]

The rod is the word of God, and with it we can change situations like it did for the Israelites in Egypt. We must remember that God is the Word Himself, and every time we speak it in faith and truth, we are indirectly calling God into the situation and committing God's integrity. He is the truth. "Sanctify them in the truth; your word is truth."[898]

"For thou hast magnified thy word above all thy name."[899]

Honorable: "Those who honor me I will honor, but those who despise me will be disdained."[900] Our words can bring us honor, and they can also bring us shame and reproach. In the above verse of scripture, God declares that those who honor Him will be honored. How do we honor God? Simply by being obedient to the Word and doing the Word

---

896   James 1:2-4
897   Exodus 4:17 KJV
898   John17:17
899   Psalm 138:2 KJV
900   1 Samuel 2:30

of God. If God says we should depart from a lying tongue, doing that brings us into a place of obedience to God and brings our way honor.

"The remnant of Israel shall not do iniquity, nor speak lies; neither shall a deceitful tongue be found in their mouth: for they shall feed and lie down, and none shall make them afraid."[901]

"Keep thy tongue from evil, and thy lips from speaking guile."[902]

This is what God expects us to do, and when we subscribe to doing His will, we get honored in return. God has wired us with the ability and capacity to keep away from lying because we were made in His image, and there are no lies in Him.

"God is not human, that he should lie, not a human being, that he should change his mind. Does he speak and then not act? Does he promise and not fulfill?"[903]

"So God has given both his promise and his oath. These two things are unchangeable because it is impossible for God to lie."[904]

You and I must cultivate and activate the nature and character of God on our inside if we desire to enjoy the honor that comes with keeping our words in truth. The

---

901   Zephaniah 3:13
902   Psalm 34:13
903   Numbers 23:19
904   Hebrews 6:18

Bible talked about a group of people that were saved from the earth and were in heaven because they were blameless, and no lies were found in them.

"No lie was found in their mouths; they are blameless."[905]

"The LORD detests lying lips, but he delights in people who are trustworthy."[906]

When God takes delight in you and me, He bestows beauty, honor, and blessings on us.

Promotion: "Righteousness [moral and spiritual integrity and virtuous character] exalts a nation, but sin is a disgrace to any people."[907]

What is righteousness? It is doing what is right in the eyes of God and those around us without any form of deception or lying words. When we stay true to our words, we get acknowledged for it by God and those around us. No matter the level of impact we try to make on people if God does not approve us; men and women around us will never notice us.

"Study to shew thyself approved unto God, a workman that needs not to be ashamed, rightly dividing the word of truth."[908]

---

905   Revelation 14:5
906   Proverbs 12:22
907   Proverbs 14:34 AMP
908   2 Timothy 2:15 KJV

Our approval by men will only be sanctioned by God when He has found us faithful as worthy ambassadors for His kingdom. No matter the effort we put into it, when God is not in it; it will fail in the end. Our focus should be pleasing God by doing the right thing, and when God promotes; man has no choice but to promote us because the glory of the Lord is all round us.

"For promotion cometh neither from the east, nor from the west, nor from the south. But God is the judge: he puts down one and sets up another."[909]

"And Jesus kept increasing in wisdom and stature, and in favor with God and people."[910]

Though society is filled with waywardness and corruption, we must ensure we don't join the train because the end is always disastrous. It may look appealing and sweet in the beginning but the end of it is never appealing. We saw how Judas ended his journey on earth because of unrighteousness[911]

We must never at any point in life allow ourselves to become a victim of wrong living that could destroy us, or our lineage.

"

---

909   Psalms 75:6-7
910   Luke 2: 52
911   Matthew 26:15-16; 48-49, Matthew 27:3-5

The way of the righteous [those in right-standing with God—living in moral and spiritual integrity] is smooth and level...[912]

"In the way of righteousness is life; and in the pathway thereof there is no death."[913]

"For the LORD knows and fully approves the way of the righteous, but the way of the wicked shall perish."[914]

If we desire God's approval for a change of levels or promotion, we must at all costs subscribe to righteous living no matter the temptation that comes our way.

Relevance: "But Daniel purposed in his heart that he would not defile himself with the portion of the king's meat, nor with the wine which he drank: therefore, he requested of the prince of the eunuchs that he might not defile himself."[915]

Every time we choose to stand for God, we set ourselves apart for honor and beauty. We were admonished by James to be a doer of God's Word, and not just a hearer because that's the major way to demonstrate our love for God. Every genuine lover of God will always end up a celebrity no matter the opposition[916]

---

912 Isaiah 26:7 AMP
913 Proverbs 12:28
914 Psalm 1:16
915 Daniel 1:8
916 Deuteronomy 28:1-13

"He that loves me not keeps not my sayings: and the word which ye hear is not mine, but the Father's which sent me."[917]

Doing the will of God is exemplifying His ways in the presence of all and sundry without any iota of shame, regret, or remorse. We must never back down in representing God regardless of the backlash that may come with it. Daniel chose to stand for God, and he remained relevant for four governments. Daniel's skills never got diminished, he got recommended to leaders of different governments as power was changed.

"There is a man in thy kingdom, in whom is the spirit of the holy gods; and in the days of thy father light and understanding and wisdom, like the wisdom of the gods, was found in him; whom the king Nebuchadnezzar thy father, the king, I say, thy father, made master of the magicians, astrologers, Chaldeans, and soothsayers."[918]

Standing with God will always make us relevant now and when we are no longer alive. Our names will forever be written on the hearts of men for the good we did and how we loved and reverenced God. Today, we still talk about the disciples of Jesus and the martyrs, most importantly, Apostle Paul; the greatest of them all. In our contemporary world today, we have women and men like Kathryn

---

917 John 14:24
918 Daniel 5:11

Kuhlman, Myles Munroe, Smith Wigglesworth, Billy Graham, Kenneth E. Hagin, Benson Idahosa, Reinhard Bonnke, David Yonggi Cho, and many more.

Our names can also be added to this list if we make a choice to stand for God and not for the deceitful, manipulative, and power-drunk nature of men.

BENEFITS OF THE WORD'S ATTRIBUTES

Creativity: Creativity is a function of ideas that no one has ever thought of or imagined. And when one is creative, he or she is able to proffer solutions, innovate, and most importantly, change the status quo.

The world today is looking for men and women who are innovative, to do what has never been done before or improve and take what has been done before to a whole new level.

To be on this pedestal, there is a need for a different level of thinking and wisdom. Nothing happens by chance, either good or bad. They are all made to happen by those who dared to take responsibility, not minding the mountain-like limitation facing them. The good news is that we can fit into this category if we subscribe to the service and the will of God. He is the giver of all things, and he is able to release in our direction what it takes as long as we are willing and ready to commit to his leading.

Solomon was a recipient of God's different level of wisdom

that no one ever had, as a result; he was marvelously blessed. His distinct wisdom was bestowed on him by God because he had the heart to see change happen by doing the will of God.

"God gave Solomon wisdom and very great insight, and a breadth of understanding as measureless as the sand on the seashore. Solomon's wisdom was greater than the wisdom of all the people of the East, and greater than all the wisdom of Egypt. He was wiser than anyone else, including Ethan the Ezrahite—wiser than Heman, Kalkol and Darda, the sons of Mahol. And his fame spread to all the surrounding nations... From all nations people came to listen to Solomon's wisdom, sent by all the kings of the world, who had heard of his wisdom."[919]

Being creative comes with a different level of wisdom, and it confers fame, relevance blessings and riches like Solomon enjoyed. We also have Daniel in Babylon whose wisdom was unmatchable[920]. Joseph is another example, he operated at a different frequency from others, and that set him apart for beauty, honor, relevance, and promotion in a foreign land.

"And Pharaoh said unto Joseph, Forasmuch as God hath shewed thee all this, there is none as discreet and wise as thou art: Thou shalt be over my house, and according unto thy word shall all my people be ruled: only in the throne will I be greater than thou. And Pharaoh

919   1 Kings 4:29-31, 34
920   Daniel 5:13-15 & 29

said unto Joseph, See, I have set thee over all the land of Egypt. And Pharaoh took off his ring from his hand, and put it upon Joseph's hand, and arrayed him in vestures of fine linen, and put a gold chain about his neck; And he made him to ride in the second chariot which he had; and they cried before him, Bow the knee: and he made him ruler over all the land of Egypt. And Pharaoh said unto Joseph, I am Pharaoh, and without thee shall no man lift up his hand or foot in all the land of Egypt."[921]

The good news is that we also have the same chance as Daniel and Joseph if we are willing and ready to pay the price.

"If any of you lack wisdom, let him ask of God, that giveth to all men liberally, and upbraids not; and it shall be given him."[922]

Part of the price we pay is taking spiritual responsibility and loving God in righteousness among other things. This wisdom is the secret of God, and they are only revealed to lovers, just like Daniel and Joseph and many others enjoyed. Who qualifies as a lover of God? Those who do his will without any reservation.

"But as it is written, Eye hath not seen, nor ear heard, neither have entered into the heart of man, the things which God hath prepared for them that love him."[923]

---

921   Genesis 41:39-44 KJV
922   James 1:5
923   1 Corinthians 2:9

"Whoever has my commands and keeps them is the one who loves me. The one who loves me will be loved by my Father, and I too will love them and show myself to them."[924]

We cannot but take a peep at Job; he enjoyed honor, relevance, and riches because he chose to do what was right, and abode in the will of God despite his challenges. As a result, he had access to the secrets of God.

"In the land of Uz there lived a man whose name was Job. This man was blameless and upright; he feared God and shunned evil... As I was in the days of my youth, when the secret of God was upon my tabernacle."[925]

Honor: It is a product of diligence, commitment, and impact. Those who enjoy honor have one way or the other made an impact. Honor confers on people recognition, change of status, and blessings. All through the scripture, those who enjoyed honor from God did because of their commitment to Him. Our perfect example is Jesus. He gave himself wholly to the will of God despite the difficult and tough situation. Sometimes, it may appear tough, but if we can subscribe to a life of sacrifice in our walk with God, and our work for God – while we also make a meaningful impact around our environment or in the life of people – we will enjoy honor.

---

924   John 14:21
925   Job 1:1; 29:4

"saying, "Father, if Thou be willing, remove this cup from Me; nevertheless, not My will, but Thine be done."[926]

"For this reason also [because He obeyed and so completely humbled Himself], God has highly exalted Him and bestowed on Him (Honor) the name which is above every name."[927]

If we can genuinely commit ourselves to the things of God, we will enjoy honor and the blessings that comes with it.

"I (God) know you need a lot of things. Don't worry, let others keeping running around the circles to get them until their strength fail the, but as for you, just commit yourself to whatever I (God) instructed, and all those things will be added to you without you having to do anything to get them."[928]

Promotion: God has ordained our lives to keep enjoying promotion because it is one of the ways we can remain relevant, change status, and enjoy increase and respect.

"But the path of the just is as the shining light, that shines more and more unto the perfect day."[929]

God is committed to advancing our lives if we are committed to doing His will. He understands the importance of growth and change because they come with a new level

---

926   Luke 22:42 KJV
927   Philippians 2:9 AMP
928   Matthew 6:32-33 Paraphrased
929   Proverbs 4:18

of freshness, increase, beauty and blessings. That is why we were admonished that staying too long in a place is detrimental to our next level of beauty and glory. "You have circled this mountain long enough, turn northward. Turn northward means "go up"[930]

"Arise and depart, for this is not your rest; because it is defiled, it shall destroy, Yes, with utter destruction."[931]

"The Lord our God said to us at Horeb, "You have stayed long enough at this mountain. Break camp and advance into the hill country of the Amorites; go to all the neighboring peoples in the Arabah, in the mountains, in the western foothills, in the Negev and along the coast, to the land of the Canaanites and to Lebanon, as far as the great river, the Euphrates. See, I have given you this land. Go in and take possession of the land the Lord swore he would give to your fathers—to Abraham, Isaac and Jacob—and to their descendants after them."[932]

If you and I will enjoy the beauty that comes with a promotion in our lives, we must remain committed to the things of God, and build ourselves up by subscribing to relevant knowledge and materials.

---

930 Deuteronomy 2:3
931 Micah 2:10
932 Deuteronomy 1:6-8

A wise man said, "The only growth (promotion) that is automatic is our biological growth, except when there are some medical impediments. Every other growth is made to happen."

Relevance: It puts us in a class of our own where we cannot be forgotten because of the impact we have made whether we are still alive or not. We can't strive to make ourselves relevant through our strengths because our personal strength has limitations and cannot keep us on the journey of relevance. However, if we can pitch our tent with God, He will keep us relevant without having to exact too much strength of our own.

"He will guard the feet of his faithful servants, but the wicked will be silenced in the place of darkness. "It is not by strength that one prevails. "[933]

"Then he answered and spoke unto me, saying, this is the word of the LORD unto Zerubbabel, saying, not by might, nor by power, but by my spirit, saith the LORD of hosts. "[934]

Relevance secures us posterity; even when we are gone, our names and works still live on, and they will continue to change and impact lives. Abraham subscribed to doing the will of God throughout his lifetime, and he bagged the badge of relevance from God. Today, we still talk about

---

933 1 Samuel 2:9
934 Zechariah 4:6

Abraham the father of faith. You and I can also secure the badge of eternal relevance if we can simply do the works of Abraham as admonished in the scriptures.

"Abraham is our father," they answered. "If you were Abraham's children," said Jesus, "then you would do what Abraham did."[935]

"And said, By myself have I sworn, saith the LORD, for because thou hast done this thing, and hast not withheld thy son, thine only son: That in blessing I will bless thee, and in multiplying I will multiply thy seed as the stars of the heaven, and as the sand which is upon the sea shore; and thy seed shall possess the gate of his enemies; And in thy seed shall all the nations of the earth be blessed; because thou hast obeyed my voice."[936]

Finally, we must not stop at just hearing or reading the word but continue to do it.

"But he who looks carefully into the perfect law, the law of liberty, and faithfully abides by it, not having become a [careless] listener who forgets but an active doer [who obeys], he will be blessed and favored by God in what he does [in his life of obedience]."[937]

Prayer: Lord, open my eyes to the power behind Your word and empower me to engage it.

---

935   John 8:39
936   Genesis 22:16-18 KJV
937   James 1:25 AMP

Chapter 24

XERXES (AHASUERUS)

+◇◇◉◇◇+

Xerxes, also known as (Ahasuerus) was a king who reigned from India even unto Ethiopia, over a hundred and twenty-seven provinces. He was the number 1 citizen of his kingdom (leader), which was in Shushan. At some point during his reign, he exhibited his inability to make a sound judgment which he later regretted[938]. He was selfish and blinded to the needs and feelings of others, and possibly had anger issues[939]. His actions were only to satisfy his desires and please his friends to the detriment of other people's feelings[940]. The king hosted his friends and demanded that the queen please his friends without putting the queen's feelings into consideration. It is never okay to

---

938   Esther 2:1
939   Esther 1:12
940   Esther 1:10-12

kick against the instruction of a leader; at the same time, a leader should holistically consider the feelings and emotions of others before making their judgment. Remember the law says, love your neighbor as yourself[941], we should never inflict on others what we cannot do to ourselves.

"On the seventh day, when the heart of the king was merry with wine, he commanded Mehuman, Biztha, Harbona, Bigtha, and Abagtha, Zethar, and Carcas, the seven chamberlains that served in the presence of Ahasuerus the king, To bring Vashti the queen before the king with the crown royal, to shew the people and the princes her beauty: for she was fair to look on."[942]

Leaders should never use their positions to satisfy their selfish needs, rather they should use their platforms to serve and lift others around them. It is always good to reason through situations before making a judgment as a leader. King Solomon demonstrated a quality of sound judgment as a leader when he was confronted with a rift between two women over the ownership of a child. Rather than use his leadership platform to satisfy his need, he demonstrated selflessness toward serving others with equality and fairness. He thought through and made a sound decision[943] Our decision as a man or woman in place of authority could either make or destroy lives, we must be very careful.

---

941 Mark 12:31
942 Esther 1:10-11
943 1 Kings 3:16-28

Just like Xerxes, leaders are privileged to occupy place(s) of authority. They must demonstrate good qualities of a leader by managing people well, making sound decisions, and most importantly; being humble. We are the kings and leaders of our lives, and our lives are largely a function of the decisions or choices we have made at some point in the past. As kings and leaders, we have authority over our lives, and we must handle it with the uttermost care.

"I call heaven and earth to record this day against you, that I have set before you life and death, blessing and cursing: therefore choose life that both thou and thy seed may live:"[944]

Ecclesiastes 8:4 "Where the word of a king is, there is power: and who may say unto him, what doest thou?"

The story of the prodigal son teaches the importance of making the right decision in life because our decisions will not only impact our lives but those God has placed around us. His choice and decision to depart from where God placed him for honor, beauty and wealth brought upon him devastation, but the moment he realized he had made a mistake, he made amends. It is never late for anyone to make a U-turn when on the wrong lane to avoid disaster. In his case, he suffered the effect of his decision but luckily got a second chance. Beware, not everyone will or may get that second chance, so use wisely the first chance God has

---

944 Deuteronomy 30:19

placed before you. Wrong decisions have the capacity to humiliate, destroy, ground, and delay one's progress and success in life.

ATTRIBUTES OF XERXES

King: Xerxes was king over a kingdom, which was in Shushan. He was taxed with ensuring the prosperity of his kingdom, the protection, and preservation of lives and properties. This means he had a great deal of responsibility. Therefore, his approach and attitude toward his position will determine if his kingdom prospers or not. The same is true for you and me; we were made kings and queens to rule and take dominion over all things. However, our dominion will not just happen on its own, we must make it happen.

"And hast made us unto our God kings and priests: and we shall reign on the earth."[945]

The success of our reign is contingent on how we approach life, either lackadaisically, or with passion, determination, commitment, fervency, and many other good distinctive factors.

---

945   Revelation 5:10 KJV

"The plans of the diligent lead surely to abundance, but everyone who is hasty comes to poverty."[946]

We are the king of our lives; therefore, we must not live carelessly. We are the salt and light of the world, a city set upon the hills to do amazing things[947]. Doing amazing things is not child's play, it involves taking responsibility regardless of the negative vibes or unwanted happenings around us. Our goal should be how to make our lights shine. Those who are focused become the focus (center of attraction). It is said that those who make news rarely watch the news.

Apostle Paul after discovering destiny pursued it doggedly. He was never ready to look back but to catch up with the years he lost in ignorance. Many of us have lost time and seasons due to carelessness and ignorance. But like Apostle Paul, we must be focused in order to gain speed for the remaining race ahead.

"let us lay aside every weight, and the sin which doth so easily beset us, and let us run with patience the race that is set before us."[948]

We must be focused more than ever to reach the finish tape. God has promised to do a new thing, the negative or failed past regardless. We must show enthusiasm towards the remaining race of our lives as kings and queens. And

946 Proverbs 21:15
947 Matthew 5:13-14
948 Hebrews 12:1

for those who are just starting the race of life, be wise in all your doings, and acknowledge God because He is the key to a successful race no matter the number of hurdles on the way[949]

"Remember not the former things, nor consider the things of old. Behold, I am doing a new thing; now it springs forth, do you not perceive it? I will make a way in the wilderness and rivers in the desert."[950]

As kings and Queens, we have the sole responsibility, with the help of God, to determine the outcomes of our lives. The seat of our glorious destiny in God is in our hearts. Whatever we conceive in our hearts determines the outcome of our lives and happenings around us. "…For as he thinks in his heart, so is he."[951]

Hence, wisdom is profitable in all that we do. We must watch over our lives as a watchman in order to keep the enemy away from destroying us. In the same vein, as the captain of our lives. We must be knowledgeable enough about the map of our lives as designed by God in order to navigate through life gloriously even in the midst of the storm[952]

---

949 Proverbs 3:5-6
950 Isaiah 43:18-19
951 Proverbs 23:7
952 Joshua 1:8

"But if you look carefully into the perfect law that sets you free, and if you do what it says and don't forget what you heard, then God will bless you for doing it."[953]

Blind Bartimaeus knew he was the captain of his life; he was tired of living life as a blind man. He knew he had the sole responsibility to initiate the outcome of whatever he desired. He heard Jesus passing by, immediately he started shouting for help; many tried to keep him quiet. Guess what! He shouted the more, and Jesus noticed him. In the end, his eyes were restored[954]. Many of us find ourselves in Bartimaeus' position, but we do nothing. I believe he was not the only blind man in the city, but he wanted to take charge of his life. Persistence, eagerness, belief, and hard work are a few of the many keys that help us take charge of our lives as kings. What you and I believe is what we become if we take corresponding actions.

David Oyedepo said, "Life is not fanfare, but warfare, and it will take a lion heart to take the lion share."

It is time to dominate, rule and let our lights shine because the destinies of some individuals are tied to the fulfilment of ours.

---

953   James 1:25
954   Mark 10:46-52

"Let your light so shine before men, that they may see your good works, and glorify your Father which is in heaven."[955]

Decision-making: Xerxes as a king (leader) displayed some level of irresponsibility during his reign. He was deficient in decision-making. His ego, anger, and selfish nature took precedence whenever a decision was made. When the queen refused to appear before him, he got angry, and rather than assess the situation, he allowed his councilmen to guide him manipulatively into making a decision[956]. Another account of his delinquency in decision-making happened later, Haman was able to manipulate him into making a wrong decision[957]

Decision-making is one of the core strengths of a leader. He or she must be able to assess situations critically, and project possible positive or negative outcomes if a decision is reached because so many things are at stake.

"On the seventh day, when the heart of the king was merry with wine, he commanded his council men to bring Vashti the queen before the king with the crown royal, to shew the people and the princes her beauty: for she was fair to look on. But the queen Vashti refused to come at the king's commandment by his chamberlains: therefore was the king very wroth, and his anger burned in him. Then

---

955 Matthew 5:16
956 Esther1:13-21
957 Esther 3: 8-11

the king said to the wise men, which knew the times, (for so was the king's manner toward all that knew law and judgment: And his council men saw the anger in the king's face. What shall we do unto the queen Vashti according to law, because she hath not performed the commandment of the king Ahasuerus by the chamberlains? If it please the king, let there go a royal commandment from him, and let it be written among the laws of the Persians and the Medes, that it be not altered, That Vashti come no more before king Ahasuerus; and let the king give her royal estate unto another that is better than she. And the saying pleased the king and the princes; and the king did according to the word of Memucan:"[958]

Anytime we are in a position of leadership, we must never allow our ego to cloud our judgment, we must ensure we assess situations before making decisions. Decision-making is powerful, it could make or destroy people or things around us.

King Xerxes' inability to bring his anger and ego under control gave him up to the manipulative scheme of his councilmen who advised him to make a decree[959] Note that as a leader, it is very okay to consult subordinates or team members regarding a situation before making a decision. This gives the opportunity to review and assess situations before making a conclusion. What is not okay is

---

958 Esther 1:10-15, 19, 21 Paraphrased
959 Esther 1:13-21

to allow anger or retaliation to be the reason why we make decisions. Leaders have the sole responsibility to make a final judgment call on situations because the outcome of that decision will be on them.

Finally, as leaders and kings of our lives, we must be careful before we make decisions that could alter the course of our lives (destiny). It is important to take a deep breath or take a step back from the situation in order to assess the situation before making that decision. It is very okay to seek counsel from trusted family members, colleagues, or spiritual leaders; however, every given counsel must be weighed, examined, and thought through before any decision is made.

Jesus asked the disciples for their opinion when the multitude was hungry. As a leader, he asked His subordinates for counsel that could help the situation, but at the end of the day; he made the right call that solved the problem[960]

Selfishness: As God's creation, we possess a gene of selflessness. We have been called to a life of sacrifice, giving all to see others happy and fulfilled.

Xerxes was the opposite of this. He was majorly concerned about his wealth, party, drunkenness, and elite friends. He

---

960   John 6:5-14

failed to consider that others may be going through hard times. Rather, his egoistic and self-centered nature wanted pleasure to the detriment of others.

During his reign as a king, he summoned his queen to appear before his drunken self and friend to show her beauty like she was merchandise on display. Out of modesty, the queen refused, his ego was bruised and because of his selfish nature he agreed to remove the queen from her position.

"In the third year of his reign, he made a feast unto all his princes and his servants; the power of Persia and Media, the nobles and princes of the provinces. He shewed the riches of his glorious kingdom and the honor of his excellent majesty. The king made a feast unto all the people that were present in Shushan the palace, both unto great and small with beautiful things, drinks in vessels of gold, and royal wine in abundance, according to the state of the king. On the seventh day, when the heart of the king was merry with wine, he commanded his council members to bring Vashti the queen before the king with the crown royal, to shew the people and the princes her beauty: for she was fair to look on. But the queen Vashti refused to come at the king's commandment by his chamberlains: therefore, was the king very wroth, and his anger burned in him."[961]

As decent, loving, and kind people; we must never trample upon the dignity, honor, and respect of others no matter

---

961   Esther 1:3-12 Paraphrased

the position we occupy. As children of God, our goal must be to love others like ourselves because we are all brothers and sisters, family and friends made in the image of God regardless of our background, color, race, societal status, or wealth. We are all the same in the eyes of the Lord.

"There is neither Jew nor Greek, there is neither bond nor free, there is neither male nor female: for ye are all one in Christ Jesus."[962]

Job demonstrated what it means to be considerate of others,

"I rescued the poor who cried for help, and the fatherless who had none to assist them… I made the widow's heart sing… I was eyes to the blind and feet to the lame. I was a father to the needy; I took up the case of the stranger. I broke the fangs of the wicked and snatched the victims from their teeth."[963]

Our lives must be dedicated to serving others around us. The scriptures remind us that no one can deceive God, whatever we sow we will reap.

"Be not deceived; God is not mocked: for whatsoever a man so that shall he also reap. For he that sow to his flesh shall of the flesh reap corruption; but he that sow to the Spirit shall of the Spirit reap life everlasting. And let us not be weary in well doing for in due season we shall reap, if we faint not."[964]

---

962 Galatians 3:28
963 Job 29:12-19
964 Galatians 6:7-9

No farmer sows corn during the planting season, then reaps peanuts during the harvest time. Whatever was placed into the soil will be the product for harvest. In the same vein, if we sow love, care, concern for others, joy, and happiness into the lives of others, we will reap the same in return.

We must not emulate the selfish nature of Xerxes and others who may have such nature around us, but the loving nature of God that Jesus taught us.

"Then shall the King say unto them on his right hand, Come, ye blessed of my Father, inherit the kingdom prepared for you from the foundation of the world: For I was hungry, and ye gave me meat: I was thirsty, and ye gave me drink: I was a stranger, and ye took me in: Naked, and ye clothed me: I was sick, and ye visited me: I was in prison, and ye came unto me. Then shall the righteous answer him, saying, Lord, when saw we thee hungry, and fed thee? Or thirsty, and gave thee drink? When saw we thee a stranger, and took thee in? Or naked, and clothed thee? Or when saw we thee sick, or in prison, and came unto thee? And the King shall answer and say unto them, Verily I say unto you, inasmuch as ye have done it unto one of the least of these my brethren, ye have done it unto me."[965]

This should be our lifestyle towards everyone around us in words and in actions if we truly love and claim we know Jesus.

---

965 Matthew 25:34-40 KJV

"If someone says, "I love God," but hates a fellow believer, that person is a liar; for if we don't love people we can see, how can we love God, whom we cannot see?"[966]

BENEFITS AND DISBENEFITS OF XERXES ATTRIBUTES

King: Kings are royalty installed or chosen to oversee the affairs of a given kingdom or province and the residents. Kings are leaders, and as a result, they are accorded honor, reverence, adulations, and celebrations with lots of blessings, riches and wealth. As joint heirs with Jesus, we are also heirs to the heavenly throne of our Father in heaven. "Now if we are children, then we are heirs—heirs of God and co-heirs with Christ."[967]

As kings and queens, we are ordained to enjoy the same honor, riches, wealth, and celebrations of our Father (God) because we are His children.

"They know not, neither will they understand; they walk on in darkness: all the foundations of the earth are out of course. I have said, Ye are gods; and all of you are children of the most High."[968]

We must operate with the consciousness of being a king and a queen in order to enjoy the blessings and honor that comes with it. Kings and Queens occupy a place of reverence,

---

966 1 John 4:20
967 Romans 8:17
968 Psalms 82:5-6

authority, honor, and beauty. Therefore, we must carry ourselves as kings in order to be honored and reverenced by those around us. Kings and Queens don't appear or behave anyhow, they carry themselves with uttermost finesse and reverence. Why? Because they occupy a place of honor and beauty, and they serve as good examples to those around them. As kings and queens over our lives, when we carry the only life God gave to us in honor and dignity; men will also honor us. There is a saying that goes thus, "The way you are dressed is the way you are addressed." This is not limited to dressing our bodies in beautiful robes only, but our character, behavior, actions, and words are invisible dresses we wear and others around us can see them.

"But the Lord said to Samuel, "Do not look on his appearance or on the height of his stature, because I have rejected him. For the Lord sees not as man sees: man looks on the outward appearance, but the Lord looks on the heart."[969]

Decision-making: At creation, God taxed the first man with decision-making in order to have orderliness, peace and prosperity. This decision-making task was passed down to generations after.

---

969   1 Samuel 16:7

"Now the Lord God had planted a garden in the east, in Eden; and there he put the man he had formed… The Lord God took the man and put him in the Garden of Eden to work it and take care of it."[970]

"I call heaven and earth to record this day against you, that I have set before you life and death, blessing and cursing: therefore, choose life that both thou and thy seed may live:"[971]

Decision-making is vital in our day-to-day life activities. The decisions we make can make or destroy us, the people around us and things as well. However, when sound decisions are made, peace, progress, breakthroughs, success and many more good stuff become the order of the day.

We must strive to be sound in making decisions. However, we cannot do it by ourselves, we should always ask God to guide us in all things because He knows the outcome or result of every situation.

"Trust in the Lord with all your heart and lean not on your own understanding; in all your ways submit to him, and he will make your paths straight."[972]

Though we are creations of choice, we must not be too

---

970   Genesis 2:8, 15
971   Deuteronomy 30:19
972   Proverbs 3:5-6

proud to seek guidance before making decisions. This is because the outcome of our decisions will determine the temporary or permanent trajectory of our lives or that of others.

David was a man very skilled and sound in decision making but he will always seek God's opinion before he makes any life-changing decision[973]

He enjoyed victories and peace because he sought the opinion of God before making his decisions. We can also borrow a leaf from David, though we are the king over our lives, we must learn to seek guidance in order not to make wrong decisions.

Selfishness: Life is not just about us alone but everyone around us. We must learn to be good to those God has placed in our lives, along our path, and those we may not even be in a relationship with. Xerxes at a point during his reign cared only about his affluence, party, drinks and wealth, and failed to consider the emotion of one person he called his wife; queen Vashti[974]

Being considerate and good to others make them feel loved and cared about. When people feel loved and cared about, there is this natural joy and peace all-round them. When

---

973   1 Samuel 23:3-4; 30:8, 2 Samuel 2:1; 5:19; 5:23; 21:1
974   Esther 1:3-12

we refuse to take on evil or unpleasant things that can hurt others, but choose the path of Jesus, which is a life of love support and care, our lives and the lives of others is filled with joy unspeakable, rest of mind, and togetherness. Choosing to be selfish and blind to the needs of others will always create room for hatred, bigotry, division, and so many other negative vibes.

Whatever choice we make, either an act of kindness or selfishness is a seed and it will grow and yield the harvest. We must be wise as admonished by the scriptures.

"I said, 'Plant the good seeds of righteousness, and you will harvest a crop of love'"[975]

"He who sows injustice will reap disaster, and the rod of his fury will be destroyed. A generous man will be blessed, for he shares his bread with the poor."[976]

If we desire good things, we must strive to sow a seed of good things into the soil (life) of others.

Prayer: Lord, help me to live a responsible life as I work towards the fulfillment of my purpose.

---

975 Hosea 10:12
976 Proverbs 22:8-9

Chapter 25

YESHUA

Yeshua in Hebrew is a verbal derivative from "to rescue," "to deliver" It is the alternate name for Jesus, with the meaning "Savior."

Yeshua is the son of God, the Creator of heaven and earth[977] The One sent by God to deliver the world from their troubles by laying down His life to reconcile and reconnect us back to our heavenly Father – God – and the throne we lost through the first man, Adam.

"And she will bring forth a Son, and you shall call His name JESUS, for He will save His people from their sins."[978]

---

977   1 Peter 1:3
978   Matthew 1:21

"All this is from God, who through Christ reconciled us to himself and gave us the ministry of reconciliation..."[979]

We are all children of God like Jesus, and we are joint heirs with Him to the heavenly throne, reason why He came to restore us to our rightful place[980]

"For you are all sons of God through faith in Christ Jesus."[981]

Jesus also had an earthly father and mother, just like us; their names were Joseph and Mary. "Jacob was the father of Joseph the husband of Mary, by whom Jesus was born, who is called the Messiah (Christ)."[982] Our earthly parents were positioned by our Father in heaven to guide, provide, protect, love, watch, and keep us in His (God's) ways in order for us to fulfil the purpose God had for our lives[983]

Yeshua, as the Jews will call Him was born for a mission, and a purpose just like you and I were born for a purpose. His birth and purpose were prophesied and told to His father. "She will give birth to a son, and you will call him Jesus, because He will save His people from sin"[984]

Yeshua's primary assignment was to bring the children of

---

979   2 Corinthians 5:18
980   2 Corinthians 6:18, Romans 8:14, Galatians 4:7
981   Galatians 3:6
982   Matthew 1:16
983   I Timothy 5:8, Deuteronomy 11:18-19, Deuteronomy 4:9, Proverbs 22:6
984   Matthew 1:21

God back to God from their sinful ways. God so much loved us that He decided to give Yeshua as the platform for our restoration by allowing Him die on the cross for our sakes. Our brother Yeshua sacrificed Himself for us, we must not allow His death and sacrifice be in vain. We must begin to do and behave everything He died for, to show our appreciation for His sacrifice, but also making our Father in heaven rejoice because His action and decision to give our brother for our sake was not in vain.

"And since we are His children, we are His heirs, and together with Christ we are heirs of His glory."[985]

As mentioned earlier, like Yeshua we all have a purpose and the discovery of that purpose is what sets the pace for fulfilment of destiny by taking corresponding, relevant, and responsive actions towards actualization like Jesus fulfilled His. "Before I formed you in the womb, I knew you; before you were born, I sanctified you; I ordained you a prophet to the nations."[986]

"And when Yeshua saw His purpose has been fulfilled according to the scriptures, He said it is finished..."[987]

Yeshua was able to fulfil His purpose because He discovered it, pursued, and was passionate about it. His passion led

---

985 Romans 8:17
986 Jeremiah 1:5
987 John 19:28-30 paraphrased

Him to search books, pray, fast, and importantly, take responsibility. A wise man said, "Everyone is responsible for the outcome of their life, and every faith that makes God hundred percent responsible for the outcome of his or her life is an irresponsible faith." Everyone has a role to play, until that role is played, purpose, vision, and mission may not be realized. Among other things, Yeshua was and still is a very compassionate, loving, kind, and humble individual.

ATTRIBUTES OF YESHUA

Purpose driven: Only those who are passionate and diligent about their choice of assignment are guaranteed to succeed and attain greater heights no matter the obstacles.

"Seest thou a man diligent in his business? he shall stand before kings; he shall not stand before mean men."[988]

Jesus was very passionate about His assignment, was very dedicated and not willing to allow anything stand in His way. Only those who remain focused on their journey arrive at their destination without succumbing to any distraction along the way. The power of focus was well illustrated in the Scripture, "The eye is the lamp of the body; so if your eye is clear [spiritually perceptive], your whole body will be full of light [benefiting from God's precepts]."[989]

---

988   Proverbs 22:29
989   Matthew 6:22 AMP

When we refuse to look around but remain focused, no devil can succeed in distracting us. Apostle Paul shared with us how he was determined not to be ensnared by distractions, but pressed towards his goals, forgetting those things that may distract him because he had a mission. Men and women on mission are forever focused, they don't have time for distractors. They set their eyes on the trophy.

"Therefore, since we also have such a large cloud of witnesses surrounding us, let us lay aside every hindrance and the sin that so easily ensnares us. Let us run with endurance the race that lies before us… keeping our eyes on Jesus, A t he pioneer and perfecter of our faith. For the joy that lay before him."[990]

"No, dear brothers and sisters, I have not achieved it, but I focus on this one thing: Forgetting the past and looking forward to what lies ahead."[991]

Everyone who desires to arrive at their God destination must be self-disciplined in order not to fall victim to distractions. Distractions can come in different ways, it could be what we love, friends, associations, environment, and sometimes family. All these things may be good for us, but sometimes serve as distractions. It is important to do a review of everything around and along our part to shed off any distractions.

990   Hebrews 12:1-2
991   Philippians 3:13

When God called Abraham, he was instructed to leave his family, environment, and livelihood if he was to fulfilll purpose and arrive at his God-ordained destination. Abraham moved, and in the end, he arrived at his destination. It may be difficult to leave behind those things, but it is more beneficial when we move on.

"The Lord had said to Abram, "Go from your country, your people, and your father's household to the land I will show you. I will make you into a great nation, and I will bless you; I will make your name great, and you will be a blessing. I will bless those who bless you, and whoever curses you I will curse; and all peoples on earth will be blessed through you." So Abram went, as the Lord had told him... Now Abraham was old, [well] advanced in age; and the LORD had blessed Abraham in all things."[992]

Abraham arrived at the point where he was blessed all round only because he moved, and was focused. Jesus, a perfect example, at age 12 began to explore ways He could possibly fulfill purpose without allowing any form of distraction, not even His own family.

"When he was twelve years old, they went up to the festival, according to the custom. After the festival was over, while his parents were returning home, the boy Jesus stayed behind in Jerusalem, but they were unaware of it. Thinking he was in their company, they traveled on for a day. Then they began looking for him among their relatives and friends. When they did not find him; they went back to Jerusalem

---

992 Genesis 12:1-4; 24:1

to look for him. After three days they found him in the temple courts, sitting among the teachers, listening to them, and asking them questions. Everyone who heard him was amazed at his understanding and his answers. When his parents saw him, they were astonished. His mother said to him, "Son, why have you treated us like this? Your father and I have been anxiously searching for you." "Why were you searching for me?" he asked. "Didn't you know I had to be in my father's house?" But they did not understand what he was saying to them."[993]

The latter part of the passage said Jesus' parents did not understand Him. Everyone does not need to understand where you are heading, just focus and refuse distractions. The result will announce you to everyone around you.

Reader: Reading is key to any level of growth and development that any man or woman desires. Reading gives access to information that will inform, transform, and move individuals from form level of glory to another level. The difference between a successful man, and woman, and the unsuccessful ones is the set of information they have accessed and applied. Daniel expressed how reading gave him access to information that brought about change. "During the first year of his reign, I, Daniel, learned from reading the word of the LORD."[994]

---

993 Luke 2:42-50
994 Daniel 9:2

Accessing and reading relevant materials is always the first step that initiates the change that a man or woman desires. The moment relevant information is accessed, the mind which is the seat of destiny becomes fertile to become productive and yield results. "Do not be conformed to this age but be transformed by the renewing of your mind."[995]

Yeshua was a man who devoted time to reading because He understood that reading, studying, and meditating is key to seeing a vision fulfilled. His reading lifestyle led to the discovery of His purpose. Until a search is carried out, a discovery cannot be made. At age 12, Yeshua dedicated himself to reading; in the process, purpose was discovered.

"He went to Nazareth, where he had been brought up, and on the Sabbath day he went into the synagogue, as was his custom. He stood up to read, and the scroll of the prophet Isaiah was handed to him. Unrolling it, he found the place where it is written... Then he rolled up the scroll, gave it back to the attendant and sat down. The eyes of everyone in the synagogue were fastened on him. He began by saying to them, "Today this scripture is fulfilled in your hearing."[996]

Nobody fulfills their purpose by accident, a discovery must be made to experience the reality and the fulfillment of the purpose. Commitment to reading, especially relevant materials sets us on the pedestal of discovery, and when

---

995 Romans 12:2
996 Luke 4:16, 20-21

the discovery is made; it fuels and drives the passion to see purpose actualized, regardless of barriers or hindrances.

"Your word is a lamp to my feet and a light to my path."[997]

"After three days they found him in the temple courts, sitting among the teachers, listening to them and asking them questions."[998]

If we must fulfill purpose as declared by God, we must commit ourselves to reading and thorough search like in the above scriptures where Yeshua committed to reading, and at another time sat down to ask questions. Remember, only those who ask questions get answers. In the quest to fulfill our purpose, it is vital that we ask questions whenever we feel any form of limitation or restriction. When we do so, we get clarity which enables us to progress.

"There are people who have achieved and fulfilled their purpose, in humility, reach out to them and ask for guidance."[999]

Prayer: All through the scriptures, we saw prophets, disciples, and people of God commit themselves to prayer. Prayer was a vital part of their lives because that was one of the ways they communicated with God. Yeshua is a perfect example for all of us, He gave himself to prayer because it was not just a platform to commune with God

---

997 Psalm 119:105
998 Luke 2:46
999 Jeremiah 6:16 Paraphrased

but an avenue to engage God to intervene and change situations for the best, and also a place of empowerment and revelation.

"And He withdrew Himself into the wilderness and prayed"[1000]

"Then Jesus went with his disciples to a place called Gethsemane, and he said to them, "Sit here while I go over there and pray.""[1001]

He did not just do it alone, He taught His disciples to pray. Every time He prayed, there were encounters, empowerment, and release of fresh grace. Praying was His lifestyle, and it became a tool that helped him throughout His ministry days.

"As he was praying, the appearance of his face changed, and his clothes became as bright as a flash of lightning."[1002]

Scripture admonishes that we pray and not faint, and likewise, pray all time and everywhere[1003]. David, despite his busy life as a king, created time to pray to God because he understood the significance and the benefits that come with it.

1000   Luke 5:16
1001   Matthew 26:36
1002   Mark 9:29
1003   Luke 18:1, 1 Thessalonians 5:17

"Evening, and morning, and at noon, will I pray, and cry aloud: and he shall hear my voice."[1004]

If we desire to fulfill purpose like Jesus, we must also give ourselves to a life of prayer because every greatness and path that leads to it are lined with oppositions, barriers, hindrances, and. As a scriptural fact, the greater the door, the more the enemy.

"Because there is a wonderful opportunity for me to do some work here. But there are also many people who are against me."[1005]

It will take commitment and diligence on the prayer altar which will empower us to overcome hindrances without giving up. The devil tried to stand in the way of Jesus after He returned from 40 days and 40 nights of prayer and fasting, however, He was able to subdue every attempt of the devil because of the empowerment He secured while on the prayer altar[1006]

"When I cry (Pray) unto thee, then shall mine enemies turn back: this I know; for God is for me."[1007]

Fasting: Today, scientists acknowledged that fasting is beneficial to human health. Among numerous benefits that come with fasting, it is researched that it helps with weight

---

1004   Psalms 55:17
1005   1 Corinthians 16:9 CEV
1006   Luke 4:1-14
1007   Psalms 56:9 Emphasis Added

loss, and improve blood sugar control, heart health, and brain function. It is abstaining from food for a period. Fasting has been observed centuries back by religious people. This act helps them put their body under subjection, by submitting themselves to spiritual exercise that will open them up to a new dimension of empowerment. Fasting, scripturally, is beneficial to the spirit of man. It helps one focus and connects to the spirit realm forsaking any or all physical appearance that can limit access to God for spiritual empowerment.

"For just as the body without the spirit is dead, so also faith without works is dead."[1008]

"The spirit of a man can endures his sickness, but as for a broken spirit who can bear it?"[1009]

Yeshua lived a fasted life, He taught us to fast because it is an avenue to subject the flesh and build spiritual capacity that will enable us to operate beyond the natural strength and human capacity. Though we have a body, it is the spirit in the body that keeps the body functional. The reason we need to keep our spirits empowered, or else the physical body may collapse. Yeshua embarked on a fast of forty days and forty nights, and as a result; he returned empowered for fulfilment of purpose[1010]

1008   James 2:26
1009   Proverbs 18:14
1010   Luke 4:1-2 and Matthew 4:2

"Jesus returned to Galilee in the power of the Spirit, and news about him spread through the whole countryside."[1011] A life of power is required to take charge and dominate, if not we will be at the mercy of the enemy. Fasting will not only empower us, it will also help us destroy any form of hindrances that may be in our way. How will that happen? When we fast, we separate ourselves unto God, and in the process, God is showing us what to do via revelation that will lead to breakthroughs.

"Is not this the kind of fasting I have chosen: to lose the chains of injustice and untie the cords of the yoke, to set the oppressed free and break every yoke? ... Then your light will break forth like the dawn, and your healing will quickly appear."[1012]

We stand to benefit both spiritually and health-wise when we engage it. The disciples of Jesus were cautioned that it was important for them to build fasting capacity because a time in their lives will come when they will have to do it on their own to get results. Remember, no one can fast for you like yourself, just as no one can eat, sleep, or drink for anybody.

"But the time will come when the bridegroom will be taken from them; in those days they will fast."[1013]

1011 Luke 4:14
1012 Isaiah 58: 6, 8
1013 Luke 5:35

All through the scriptures, we saw men and women engaged in fast to secure their desires, receive directions, defeat oppositions, and got empowered[1014]

Moses: "Moses was there with the LORD forty days and forty nights without eating bread or drinking water. And he wrote on the tablets the words of the covenant—the Ten Commandments"[1015]

Jehoshaphat: "Then Jehoshaphat was afraid and set himself determinedly, as his vital need] to seek the LORD; and he proclaimed a fast throughout all Judah."[1016]

Elijah: "He arose, and ate and drank, and went in the strength of that food forty days and forty nights to Horeb, God's Mountain."[1017]

"There was also a prophet, Anna, the daughter of Penuel, of the tribe of Asher. She was very old; she had lived with her husband seven years after her marriage, and then was a widow until she was eighty-four. She never left the temple but worshiped night and day, fasting and praying."[1018]

All these individuals and many more from the scriptures engaged fasting as a lifestyle with results and rewards to

---

1014 Esther 4:16, 2 Chronicles 20:3-25, Daniel 1:8 and Isaiah 58:6-11
1015 Exodus 34: 28
1016 2 Chronicles 20:3
1017 1 Kings 19:8
1018 Luke 2:36-37

show for their engagement. There is no exemption when it comes to spiritual things that secures heaven's connection and guarantees the release of heavenly benefits that are associated with fasting. If those men in the past were successful at it, we can also do it. God has wired us with the strength to do it, all we need is to make up our minds and take responsibility. It is also important to note that whenever we decide to engage in fasting, we must also apply wisdom to it. Everyone is wired by God differently, but we all have the opportunity to access the same resource depending on our level of engagement. Everyone can always engage in a fast as they deemed fit and at their level; what is important is that we engage in spiritual exercise whenever we are fasting by praying, reading and meditating on the Word of God. Fasting in the spiritual sense of it is not just going without food but engaging in the above-mentioned exercise because they are what give meaning to fasting. Fasting without engaging any of these things is going on hunger strike just like some men did just because they wanted to destroy Apostle Paul.

"The next morning some Jews formed a conspiracy and bound themselves with an oath not to eat or drink until they had killed Paul."[1019]

Compassionate: The word compassion is from the Latin root word 'Pati' meaning suffer and the prefix 'com' which

---

1019   Acts 23:12

means with. Compati as a word means suffer with. It means identifying with other people when they are going through certain situations, putting ourselves in their shoes, and doing what we can within our capacity to support them.

Yeshua demonstrated the act of compassion many times during His ministry, He identified with people who suffered one affliction or the other; while He also showed them love and did everything within His God-given capacity to provide succor.

"When he saw the crowds, he had compassion on them, because they were harassed and helpless, like sheep without a shepherd."[1020]

"Jesus called his disciples to him and said, "I have compassion for these people; they have already been with me three days and have nothing to eat. I do not want to send them away hungry, or they may collapse on the way.""[1021]

We have been called to a life of compassion, caring and supporting one another in good and bad times regardless of our socio-economic, religious, ethnic, race or political background. Showing and having compassion for one another makes the world a better place and the people in it. It is important to note that without genuine love for one another, showing or having compassion for others like Yeshua did will be far-fetched.

1020 Matthew 9:36
1021 Matthew 15:32

"Therefore, as God's chosen people, holy and dearly loved, clothe yourselves with compassion, kindness, humility, gentleness and patience."[1022]

"Finally, be ye all of one mind, having compassion one of another, love as brethren, be pitiful, and be courteous."[1023]

If we claim we truly love people, then we will not discriminate, bully, enslave, or rob them of their rights. Many times, we claim we love God, but our inhumane actions show that we don't really love God. If we do, then we will let true love ooze out of us toward others.

"Whoever claims to love God yet hates a brother or sister is a liar. For whoever does not love their brother and sister, whom they have seen, cannot love God, whom they have not seen."[1024]

God said to us that if He will truly deal with us according to our behaviors, no one will get a pass mark. However, because of His love and compassion for us, our imperfect ways are overlooked by Him. So, He expects us to do the same to others around us.

1022　Colossians 3:12
1023　1 Peter 3:8
1024　1 John 4:20

"If You, LORD, should keep an account of our sins and treat us accordingly, O Lord, who could stand [before you in judgment and claim innocence?"[1025]

The acid test of our love for God is a world filled with peace, tolerance, compassion, empathy, and care towards Him and those around us regardless of their background, beliefs, language, religion, race, or gender.

BENEFITS OF YESHUA'S ATTRIBUTES

Purpose-Driven: Everyone is born for a purpose. However, fulfilling that purpose rides on the wings of discovery. What is not discovered cannot be explored. Everything of value were researched, discovered, and worked upon to arrive at its finest place of value. Precious gifts are never found on the surface, a search is conducted before discovery is made, then leads to transformation. To fulfill purpose, everyone must carry out the search in the Creator's manual (Bible) to discover the individual assignment with a pursuit to see fulfillment.

Yeshua did a search, found it, pursued it, and he fulfilled its purpose. If the first Son of God had to engage the process, then neither of us is left out.

"And there was delivered unto him the book of the prophet Esaias. And when he had opened the book, he found the place where it was

---

written, The Spirit of the Lord is upon me, because he hath anointed me to preach the gospel to the poor; he hath sent me to heal the brokenhearted, to preach deliverance to the captives, and recovering of sight to the blind, to set at liberty them that are bruised, To preach the acceptable year of the Lord. And he closed the book, and he gave it again to the minister, and sat down. And the eyes of all of them that were in the synagogue were fastened on him. And he began to say unto them, this day is this scripture fulfilled in your ears."[1026]

When we discover purpose and pursue it, we enjoy divine presence, provisions, protection, success, guidance, and fulfilment[1027]

"After this the Lord appointed seventy-two and other and sent them two by two ahead of him to every town and place where he was about to go... The seventy-two returned with joy and said, "Lord, even the demons submit to us in your name."[1028]

God will never leave a genuine purpose-driven individual alone, it doesn't matter the challenges they may face along the line, He will always stand by them to guide them to fulfilment[1029]

"The one who sent me is with me; he has not left me alone, for I always do what pleases him."[1030]

1026   Luke 4:17-21
1027   Luke 10:1-17
1028   Luke 10: 1, 17
1029   Isaiah 43:2
1030   John 8:29

Everything we need to fulfill our purpose has been made available by God, all we need is to make the discovery, move in faith, and God will play His own part.

"He said to them, "Go into all the world and preach the gospel to all creation… Then the disciples went out and preached everywhere, and the Lord worked with them and confirmed his word by the signs that accompanied it."[1031]

Our success is guaranteed if we can take up that responsibility to search for our individual assignment, while we pursue to see it fulfilled. Note, God will never leave anyone stranded in the pursuit of their given assignment so long they are connected to His leading by doing what He has instructed, and not what they want for themselves. Learning not to lean on our own understanding but totally depending on God while we play our required role is what guarantees arrival at the place of glory in pursuit of divine purpose.

"Trust in the LORD with all thine heart; and lean not unto thine own understanding. In all thy ways acknowledge him, and he shall direct thy paths."[1032]

Reader: Our quest for fulfilment is anchored on purpose discovery. Discovery doesn't just happen; it is made to happen by intentionally engaging a search. Reading is one

---

1031   Mark 16:15, 20

1032   Proverbs 3:5-6 KJV

of the ways we can discover purpose. We saw how Jesus gave Himself to reading, and purpose was discovered.

"He went to Nazareth, where he had been brought up, and on the Sabbath day he went into the synagogue, as was his custom. He stood up to read, and the scroll of the prophet Isaiah was handed to him. Unrolling it, he found the place where it is written "The Spirit of the Lord is on me, because he has anointed me to proclaim good news to the poor. He has sent me to proclaim freedom for the prisoners and recovery of sight for the blind, to set the oppressed free, to proclaim the year of the Lord's favor." Then he rolled up the scroll, gave it back to the attendant and sat down. The eyes of everyone in the synagogue were fastened on him. He began by saying to them, "Today this scripture is fulfilled in your hearing."[1033]

When purpose is discovered, the drive to its actualization is engaged. Yeshua began to put His discovery to practice. As a result, His fame was spread through the city.

"In the synagogue there was a man possessed by a demon, an impure spirit. He cried out at the top of his voice, "Go away! What do you want with us, Jesus of Nazareth? Have you come to destroy us? I know who you are—the Holy One of God!" "Be quiet!" Jesus said sternly. "Come out of him!" Then the demon threw the man down before them all and came out without injuring him. And they were all amazed, ... And the fame of him went out into every place of the country round about."[1034]

1033 Luke 4:16-21
1034 Luke 4:33-37

Reading brings us to a world of discoveries that engenders fulfilment, honor, blessings, and relevance. Shortly after Yeshua discovered His purpose, He began to work it out; and as a result, He became the toast of the people. Many were amazed and intrigued by His ability and prowess[1035] When we impact the lives of others, we bring them relief, in turn we are celebrated, blessed, honored, and lifted.

"But whoever looks intently into the perfect law that gives freedom and continues in it—not forgetting what they have heard but doing it—they will be blessed in what they do."[1036]

Those who commit to a life of reading set themselves apart for great things because their commitment to reading will not only help them discover things but also enhances their ability in their chosen field or pursuit.

Apostle Paul, in his quest to fulfill purpose, gave himself to reading at every given opportunity, as a result; he became better than his predecessors. At a point in his life, men could not hold back their thoughts about Paul's crave for reading, and knowledge.

"When you come, be sure to bring the coat I left with Carpus at Troas. Also bring my books, and especially my papers."[1037]

1035 Luke 4:36-37
1036 James 1:25
1037 2 Timothy 4:13

"At this point Festus interrupted Paul's defense. "You are out of your mind, Paul!" he shouted. "Your great learning is driving you insane.""[1038]

Note, learning doesn't make you mad, it builds your capacity, moves you away from the level you were previously with others to a greater dimension. Festus thought Paul was mad because of his knowledge, unfortunately for him, Paul's knowledge only transformed his thought process, and took him beyond Festus level of comprehension. That is what reading or learning does.

Hence, we must always strive to grow, but the only way to make that happen is to learn to grow.

"Study to shew thyself approved unto God, a workman that needs not to be ashamed, rightly dividing the word of truth.""[1039]

Prayer: Prayer is a form of communication system that helps us convey our thoughts, concerns and desires to God. It avails us the opportunity to rob minds with God about issues of our lives.

"Produce your cause, saith the LORD; bring forth your strong reasons, saith the King of Jacob.""[1040]

1038   Acts 26:24
1039   2 Timothy 2:15
1040   Isaiah 42:21

"Come now, and let us reason together, saith the LORD: though your sins be as scarlet, they shall be as white as snow; though they be red like crimson, they shall be as wool."[1041]

In the process of praying, we are able to secure the hand of God or His intervention in our situation. When we pray, we remind God of His words concerning our lives, and our victory is established[1042]

Hannah had a situation, she decided to go to God in Prayer and at the end; the situation was resolved.

"Hannah prayed to the Lord... So, in the course of time Hannah became pregnant and gave birth to a son. She named him Samuel, saying, "Because I asked the Lord for him."[1043]

When we pray in faith, we remind God, and God moves to confirm His words in our lives. Remember, when we ask in prayer for a righteous reason, God will always give to us what we requested because anyone who asks will always receive so far it is in the will of God for us.

"Ask, and it shall be given you; seek, and ye. shall find; knock, and it shall be opened unto you: For every one that asks receives; and he that seeks. finds; and to him that knocks it shall be opened."[1044]

1041   Isaiah 1:18
1042   1 Samuel 1: 6-20
1043   1 Samuel 1:10, 20
1044   Matthew 7:7-8

"Therefore I tell you, whatever you ask for in prayer, believe that you have received it, and it will be yours."[1045]

No matter how long it takes, God will grant us our desires because those things are for a set time and a season just like Hannah got hers when the time came.

There are times when we may not receive those things from God, it is not because He doesn't have them, it may be that it is not yet time to have them, or they are harmful to our lives, or our sinful way of life, or maybe we asked for selfish reasons.

"You ask [God for something] and do not receive it, because you ask with wrong motives [out of selfishness or with an unrighteous agenda], so that [when you get what you want] you may spend it on your [hedonistic] desires."[1046]

Therefore, it is important to ensure we ask for the right reasons in order not to be denied. Yeshua showed us an example and gave a confirmation that God will always answer our requests if we do it right.

"So they took away the stone. Then Jesus looked up and said, "Father, I thank you that you have heard me. I knew that you always hear me..."[1047]

1045   Mark 11:24
1046   John 4:3 AMP
1047   John 11:41-42

God is not partial, He gives the same opportunity to everyone who is willing to do it right and abide by all the laid down principles

"Surely the arm of the Lord is not too short to save, nor his ear too dull to hear..."[1048]

Praying helps us secure the hand of God that will initiate change, deliverance, advancement, and ultimately secure victory.

"But in my distress, I cried out to the LORD; yes, I prayed to my God for help. He heard me from his sanctuary; my cry to him reached his ears."[1049]

Fast: According to the scriptures, fasting is a spiritual platform to enhance spiritual capacity and empowerment. Yeshua engaged this platform throughout his ministry, and it secured for Him results, enhanced his spiritual capacity which placed him in a supernatural realm.

"After fasting forty days and forty nights, he was hungry."[1050]

1048   Isaiah 59:1
1049   Psalm 18:6
1050   Matthew 4:2

"And Jesus being full of the Holy Ghost returned from Jordan, and was led by the Spirit into the wilderness, being forty days tempted of the devil. And in those days, he did eat nothing: and when they were ended, he afterward hungered."[1051]

Fasting puts you in charge of situations; it helps you dominate as a result of the revelation contracted on the mountain. We enjoy spiritual rejuvenation, enthronement and distinction because of the change of power received from the altar of fasting. The scripture recorded that Yeshua's fame went abroad on His return from the journey of 40 days and 40 nights.

"And Jesus returned in the power of the Spirit into Galilee: and there went out a fame of him through all the region round about."[1052]

Everyone who genuinely embarks on a session of fasting never returns the same, transformation will always happen. It is that transformation that launches us into a new realm of glory.

"Is not this the kind of fasting I have chosen: to loose the chains of injustice and untie the cords of the yoke, to set the oppressed free and break every yoke? Then your light will break forth like the dawn, and your healing will quickly appear..."[1053]

1051 Luke 4:1-2
1052 Luke 4:14
1053 Isaiah 58:6, 8

Among other things, fasting secures freedom for the oppressed, restores health, and changes stories. Fasting is a spiritual exercise, and when approached as such, the benefits are reaped.

Judah was in a dire situation, and to overcome their fear, they fasted in order to effect their rescue. Revelation broke forth during the proclaimed fast, and as they engaged the revelation; the rescue was established[1054].

"And Jehoshaphat feared, and set himself to seek the LORD, and proclaimed a fast throughout all Judah. 4And Judah gathered themselves together, to ask help of the LORD: even out of all the cities of Judah they came to seek the LORD."[1055]

The above situation shows that fasting can indeed turn things around to our favor. It doesn't matter the circumstances we find ourselves in, as long as we are willing to commit or engage in fasting as a spiritual tool, victory is guaranteed.

Compassionate: Life is full of ups and downs. No one wants or likes to live a life filled with constant breakdowns, troubles, and pain. We all want a life of peace filled with

---

1054 2 Chronicles 20:1-24
1055 2 Chronicles 20:3-4

love. This kind of life will only come when we live a life of compassion towards one another regardless of our background or beliefs.

Yeshua, throughout His time on earth, taught us the importance of compassion.

"Jesus called his disciples to him and said, "I have compassion for these people; they have already been with me three days and have nothing to eat. I do not want to send them away hungry, or they may collapse on the way."[1056]

We must strive to show love to everyone around us. True love promotes unity, peace, innovation, progress, stability, growth, and abundance. When we intentionally decide not to hurt one another, or do anything negative or foolish towards our neighbor, peace and love is established and it becomes a way of life. God is love, and those who claim to love Him must express the same towards their neighbors.

Everyone is entangled in one unwanted situation or the other, but if we can be kind, respectful and loving to one another; our world will definitely be a better place.

"Finally, be ye all of one mind, having compassion one of another, love as brethren, be pitiful, and be courteous."[1057]

1056   Matthew 15:32
1057   1 Peter 3:8

When we empathize with others, we put ourselves in their shoes, identifying with their pain. Doing this makes the recipient accepted, loved, and cared for. No one ever repays bad with good, except a person who has been taken over by the spirit of wickedness.

"For our struggle is not against flesh and blood [contending only with physical opponents], but against the rulers, against the powers, against the world forces of this [present] darkness, against the spiritual forces of wickedness in the heavenly (supernatural) places."[1058]

Note, we only reap what we sow, and time will always catch up with our deeds[1059]

Prayer: Heavenly Father, I pray for grace, wisdom, strength, and guidance for the fulfilment of destiny.

1058 Ephesians 6:12 AMP
1059 Galatians 6:7

Chapter 26

ZECHARIAH
————— ✦◇◇◉◇◇✦ —————

Zechariah was a priest in the house of God. He was married to Elizabeth, the mother of John the Baptist. They were both righteous and devoted to the things of God. Zechariah and his wife lived an obedient life. They conducted their affairs after the dictates and commands of God, and it was recorded that they lived a sanctified life void of sin because they loved God and reverenced Him[1060]

It is the expectation of God that every of His creation, and all who are called by His name live a life of sanctification because that is the foundation of our access to Him. He is a holy God, and He cannot behold iniquity. Everyone who desires to see God or have a relationship with Him must be willing to pay the price of holiness. Nothing of great value

---

1060 Luke 1:6

comes free or cheap, a heavy price must be paid. So, anyone who desires to have that father and child relationship with Him must be willing and ready to pay the ultimate price.

"Speak to all the congregation of the people of Israel and say to them, you shall be holy, for I the LORD your God am holy."[1061]

"Surely the arm of the Lord is not too short to save, nor his ear too dull to hear. But your iniquities have separated you from your God; your sins have hidden his face from you, so that he will not hear."[1062]

As a priest, Zechariah served in the house of God. He was fervent, reliable, and joyful about it. Despite having a life situation that was not favorable, he remained committed to the God in his duties. The same is what God expects of us, to be committed to our God-given assignments regardless of life situations. God will always come through for us, and every situation we go through in life is only meant to refine and prepare us for the greatness ahead. Precious gifts like gold, diamonds, etc. all go through a lot of beating and refining before coming out precious. The refining moments are not meant to kill or destroy us, but to shape us for the beauty ahead.

"And let us not be weary in well doing: for in due season, we shall reap if we faint not."[1063]

1061 Leviticus 19:2
1062 Isaiah 59:1-2
1063 Galatians 6:9

We must never be tired of seeking first the kingdom of God because the beauty and the successes of our lives are anchored on it. "But seek ye first the kingdom of God, and his righteousness; and all these things shall be added unto you."[1064]

When we commit ourselves to promoting God's kingdom, we set ourselves up for His blessings. "When you commit yourselves to making my kingdom a priority, and in righteousness; I "God" will supply all your needs and be your defense."[1065]   It is important to know that life will always happen, and sometimes not go the way we want it to. It is our approach toward life that determines what we get out of it. Nobody who succumbs to worries has ever been productive. Rather than worry, commit your ways unto God in cheerfulness because in your cheerfulness is when He will communicate the way out.

"I have told you these things, so that in Me you may have [perfect] peace. In the world you have tribulation and distress and suffering, but be courageous [be confident, be undaunted, be filled with joy]; I have overcome the world." [My conquest is accomplished, My victory abiding.]"[1066]

Zechariah was diligent at his duty to God; he never allowed the delay in childbearing take his peace or joy. Despite this

---

1064   Matthew 6:33
1065   Exodus 23:25-26 Paraphrased
1066   John 16:33 AMP

delay, he remained committed to carrying out His duties as a priest. Remember, the moment we allow the enemy, the devil, convince us into losing our peace and joy, we have set ourselves up for a roller coaster of emotional breakdown and distress. This is a risky place to be because it may lead to depression. We must guard our joy and peace jealously because it is our access to our next level and change of situation.

"Even though the fig trees have no blossoms, and there are no grapes on the vines; even though the olive crop fails, and the fields lie empty and barren; even though the flocks die in the fields, and the cattle barns are empty, yet I will rejoice in the LORD! I will be joyful in the God of my salvation! The Sovereign LORD is my strength! He makes me as surefooted as a deer, able to tread upon the heights."[1067]

It is important to note that our commitment to God is a great asset that secures the presence and the hand of God over our lives. This gets the enemy angry, and they will do everything in their capacity to disrupt God's plan for us. The devil tried this with Job but Job passed the test.

"So, the LORD blessed Job in the second half of his life even more than in the beginning. For now, he had 14,000 sheep, 6,000 camels, 1,000 teams of oxen, and 1,000 female donkeys."[1068]

1067 Habakkuk 3:17-19
1068 Job 42:12

We must beware of the scheme of the enemy to distract and take our focus off God; our focus should never shift. There may be grave consequences if the enemy succeeds at it. No matter the situation, we must stay connected to our source. Note, God has a backup plan to checkmate the enemy, allow God to play the game while you enjoy the victory that has been established by Jesus[1069] The enemy was excited thinking they had crucified Jesus, unknown to them, they only helped God deliver the plan[1070] It was all in the plan, our glory destination is sure if we don't faint or give up. It may look tough sometimes, but we must ensure we surround ourselves with positive things that will keep our mind focused[1071]

If we refuse to be distracted and commit ourselves to God, He will show us the way out like He did to Zechariah.

"And it came to pass, that while he executed the priest's office before God in order of his course… there appeared unto him, an angel of the Lord… But the angel said unto Zechariah fear not for God has seen your service and heard your prayer, and your wife Elizabeth will have a son, and your household will be full of joy."[1072]

Zechariah's testimony was delivered at the right time. God is never late; He will always show up at the right and due

---

1069 John 16:33
1070 1Corinthians 2:8
1071 Philippians 4:4-8
1072 Luke 1:8-15 Paraphrased

season. We must remain steadfast like Zechariah, void of distraction in order not to miss our time of visitation.

"The eye is the lamp of the body; so, if your eye is clear [spiritually perceptive], your whole body will be full of light [benefiting from God's precepts]."[1073]

"For His anger is but for a moment, His favor is for a lifetime. Weeping may endure for a night, but a shout of joy comes in the morning."[1074]

Zechariah's trouble was synonymous to the night season, but his joy came in the morning. God is always working behind the scenes, all we need is to trust and be patient, and taking responsibility like Zechariah who continued his daily routine as a priest in God's house without putting his life on hold. Doing this guarantees the full delivery of God's package for us.

"So do not throw away your confidence; it will be richly rewarded. You need to persevere so that when you have done the will of God, you will receive what he has promised. For, "In just a little while, he who is coming will come and will not delay."[1075]

1073   Matthew 6:22 AMP
1074   Psalms 30:5
1075   Hebrews 10:35-36

ATTRIBUTES OF ZECHARIAH

Honest and Righteous: A life of honesty dignifies and sets pace for a peace of mind. Those who live a life of honesty have nothing to hide or be afraid of. Their lives are void of pressure to cover up lies or bad behaviors. "The wicked (dishonest & unrighteous) flee when no one pursues them, but the righteous are as bold as a lion."[1076]

Zechariah was a man of integrity, no wonder the angel of the Lord was able to share the honest and righteous nature of Zechariah[1077]. Having an angel talk of one's good behavior does not happen by accident; such testimony is triggered by our way of life in line with God's will and plans embedded in His commandment. This was the same way God vouched for Abraham[1078] and Job[1079] We can also join the list if we make up our mind to flee all forms of discrepancies like lying, stealing, harboring hate for others, promiscuity, and many more.

"Don't you realize that those who do wrong will not inherit the Kingdom of God? Don't fool yourselves. Those who indulge in sexual sin, or who worship idols, or commit adultery, or are male prostitutes, or practice homosexuality,

---

1076   Proverbs 28:1
1077   Luke 1:5-6
1078   Genesis 18:19
1079   Job 1:8

or are thieves, or greedy people, or drunkards, or are abusive, or cheat people—none of these will inherit the Kingdom of God"[1080]

Zechariah made a choice, and it earned him a good name with God. We can also make the same choice because we are all creation of choice[1081]

His honest and righteous nature gave him the boldness to appear every day at his job, while he served and provided the priestly duty his job required without any fear or malpractice[1082]

Prophet Samuel further proved that confidence is an offshoot of honesty.

"Here I stand. Testify against me in the presence of the Lord and his anointed. Whose ox have I taken? Whose donkey have I taken? Whom have I cheated? Whom have I oppressed? From whose hand have I accepted a bribe to make me shut my eyes? If I have done any of these things, I will make it right." You have not cheated or oppressed us," they replied. "You have not taken anything from anyone's hand."[1083]

1080 1 Corinthians 6:9-10
1081 Deuteronomy 30:19
1082 Luke 1:8-10
1083 1 Samuel 3:3-4

This is the kind of life God expects from all of his creations, to live before Him and all men in righteousness and integrity because it will bring glory to Him, and in turn we secure a good name.

"Providing for honest things, not only in the sight of the Lord, but also in the sight of men."[1084]

Dedication: A life of dedication is a life of commitment. In our quest to attain certain heights in life, we must engage a diligent search on the path that God has prepared for us and follow that path with all zeal and tenacity no matter the barriers along the way. Zechariah was a man who dedicated himself to his God-given assignment despite his challenges. We will recall that himself and his wife, Elizabeth were without a child (barren).

"There was in the days of Herod, the king of Judaea, a certain priest named Zacharias, and his wife, Elisabeth..., they were both righteous before God, had no child. But he executed the priest's office before God in the order of his course, according to the custom of the priest's office, his lot was to burn incense when he went into the temple of the Lord."[1085]

He did not allow his situation to deter him for carrying out his duties. Note that worrying would never solve a problem, rather it will further complicate the life of a man. So, for

---

1084   2 Corinthians 8:21
1085   Luke 1:5-9 Paraphrased

411

Zechariah, neglecting his duties was not an option for him, instead he focused on his assignment in order not to allow the enemy to rob him of the benefits that came with the Job, or even lose his job like any of us could if we lose focus. However, he continued with zest and joy, delivering his duties. Everyone who engages in labor is worthy of his wages (salary), especially when it is unto God. God will always reward everyone for their labor. We must be careful and not allow the troubles of life derail our focus from God who is the only solution to all issues of life.

"Therefore, my dear brothers and sisters, stand firm. Let nothing move you. Always give yourselves fully to the work of the Lord, because you know that your labor in the Lord is not in vain."[1086]

"God is not unjust; he will not forget your work and the love you have shown him as you have helped his people and continue to help them."[1087]

Our employers may forget to pay our salary, or deny us our benefits, but God will never forget. The benefits due to us will always come at the right pay period. Everyone who serves God with a genuine heart is entitled to a pay, the only parameter of payment with God is that we are paid according to the level of labor, not by age, religion,

---

1086 1 Corinthians 15:18
1087 Hebrews 6:10

and status. When Zechariah's pay for his labor came, it was massive. He did not just get a gift of a child, but one of a kind that will bring honor and blessings to his household[1088]

"Look, I am coming soon! My reward is with me, and I will give to each person according to what they have done."[1089]

Dedication will always lead to success and breakthroughs.

Focused: Anyone who desires to arrive at his or her destination must be ready to do away with distraction(s). Distraction is subtle in nature, it has the capacity to take man's eyes off the set goal, and that could be detrimental to a man's vision and quest.

Apostle Paul during his ministry was the least of all the disciples, but he became the greatest of them all. He did not get there by accident, he disciplined himself by remaining focused.

"Therefore, since we are surrounded by such a huge crowd of witnesses to the life of faith, let us strip off every weight that slows us down, especially the sin that so easily trips us up. And let us run with endurance the race God has set before us."[1090]

1088   Luke 1:13-17
1089   Revelation 22:12
1090   Hebrews 12:1

Zechariah operated on that same frequency, he did not allow their inability to conceive and have a child hinder him from executing his priestly duties. He remained righteous and honest before God, committed to his priesthood assignment, and serving others according to his job description[1091]

Many of us, sometimes, allow the weight of life to overshadow us, derail and distract to the point where we miss the good things around us. A wise man said "Nobody cries and sees clearly at the same time." Is it wrong to cry? No! But we must remain focused in order not to miss our time and season of visitation.

Zechariah's focused nature made him catch the wind of God's angels when they came visiting. If he had allowed his situation to distract him, he probably would have had to wait for another season of visitation again. Note, not everyone who misses a season is privileged to see the next, reason why carelessness is not an option.

"And there appeared unto him an angel of the Lord standing on the right side of the altar of incense. And when Zacharias saw him, he was troubled, and fear fell upon him."[1092]

"And they will level you to the ground, you [Jerusalem] and your children within you. They will not leave in you one stone on another, all

---

1091 Luke 1:5-10
1092 Luke 1:11-12

because you did not [come progressively to] recognize [from observation and personal experience] the time of your visitation [when God was gracious toward you and offered you salvation]."[1093]

We live in a world full of distractions, and if care is not taken; we may lose out on God's plan for us and fall a victim to the enemy. We must be the watchman of our lives day and night because this is the only way we can remain positioned and catch His appearance when our time of visitation comes.

Jacob experienced both worlds of focus and distraction. He realized the danger of not paying attention, and he made up his mind to stay focused.

"When Jacob awoke from his sleep, he thought, "Surely the LORD is in this place, and I was not aware of it."[1094]

"So Jacob was left alone, and a man wrestled with him till daybreak. When the man saw that he could not overpower him, he touched the socket of Jacob's hip so that his hip was wrenched as he wrestled with the man. Then the man said, "Let me go, for it is daybreak." But Jacob replied, "I will not let you go unless you bless me." The man asked him, "What is your name?" "Jacob," he answered. Then the man said, "Your name will no longer be Jacob, but Israel, e because you have struggled with God and with humans and have overcome."[1095]

1093   Luke 19:44 AMP
1094   Genesis 28:16
1095   Genesis 32:24-28

In all, staying focused is beneficial to our progress and success in life.

"Do you not know that in a race all the runners run, but only one gets the prize? Run in such a way as to get the prize. Therefore, I do not run like someone running aimlessly; I do not fight like a boxer beating the air. No, I strike a blow to my body and make it my slave so that after I have preached to others, I myself will not be disqualified for the prize."[1096]

Kingdom-oriented: Being kingdom-oriented is being God-oriented. The commitment to the things of God is what demonstrate our love for His kingdom. He will commit Himself also to our needs.

People run after so many things like fame, riches, success, and other good things of life, neglecting the things of God. However, God said that we should make Him the priority, and all those things that others are running after will be added to us.

Zechariah lived a kingdom-oriented life. He was sold out to the things of God, and as a result, God added to Him what he needed[1097] Neglecting the ways of God can be detrimental to our lives, and the consequences could have

---

1096   1 Corinthians 9:24, 25-27
1097   Luke 1:5-14

a lasting effect because we are no more under the security of God. We saw the consequences of abandoning God for our own personal desires and goals;

"This is what the Lord Almighty says: "These people say, 'The time has not yet come to rebuild the Lord's house.' Then the word of the Lord came through the prophet Haggai: 'Is it a time for you yourselves to be living in your paneled houses, while My house remains a ruin?" Now this is what the Lord Almighty says: "Give careful thought to your ways. You have planted much but harvested little. You eat, but never have enough. You drink, but never have your fill. You put on clothes but are not warm. You earn wages, only to put them in a purse with holes in it." This is what the Lord Almighty says: "Give careful thought to your ways. Go up into the mountains and bring down timber and build my house, so that I may take pleasure in it and be honored," says the Lord. "You expected much, but see, it turned out to be little. What you brought home; I blew away. Why?" declares the Lord Almighty. "Because of my house, which remains a ruin, while each of you is busy with your own house. Therefore, because of you the heavens have withheld their dew and the earth its crops. I called for a drought on the fields and the mountains, on the grain, the new wine, the olive oil and everything else the ground produces, on people and livestock, and on all the labor of your hands."[1098]

We must understand that everything we desire will only come from God, whatever man offers is temporal, and man is limited in capacity.

1098   Haggai 1: 2-11

"Every good gift and every perfect gift is from above, and cometh down from the father of lights, with whom is no variableness, neither shadow of turning."[1099]

"John replied, "No one can receive anything unless God gives it from heaven."[1100]

Our focus should be how we can serve God with our lives. There are so many ways we can serve God; we can serve God spiritually by praying for His kingdom, the people of God, evangelizing, and committing ourselves to physical stewardship by engaging our God-given talent or gift to promote His kingdom. We can serve God with our resources to ensure the propagation of the gospel[1101]

Our service to God secures divine provisions, preservation, longevity, and fruitfulness. All through the scriptures we saw men and women who dedicated themselves to the work of God, and they were blessed in return. David, Solomon, Hannah the prophetess, Elijah, Elisha, The disciples, and many more[1102]

There is joy in serving God, and when we have joy, we have everything because joy is what we use to draw whatever belongs to us from God.

1099   James 1:17
1100   John 3:27
1101   Exodus 23:25-26, Zechariah 1:17
1102   Exodus 23:25-26

BENEFITS OF ZECHARIAH'S ATTRIBUTES

Honesty and Righteousness: Honesty is the bedrock of greatness. Everyone who commits to a life of honesty and integrity secures for himself or herself a good name[1103] According to scriptures, a good name is better than riches. We must understand that our lives are not only lived for ourselves, but also our family, friends, and society. We must do everything within our power to give our family a good name. Doing this brings glory to God.

Zechariah and his wife's honest way of life could not be overlooked. The angel of the Lord could not hold back his observation[1104] A good attestation was made of the couple, and I believe the same attestation would have come from their neighbors and friends. Note, we are not to live our lives because we want some accolades from those around us, but we do it because we fear and love God. Men will always have their opinion whether what you are doing is right or wrong. Our motivaton for doing righteous deeds should be God.

Living a life integrity earns us respect, honor, dignity, and most importantly confidence. We are able to defend ourselves because our hands and ways are clean. If anyone

---

1103   Proverbs 22:1
1104   Luke 1:5-6

desires to see God, a clean and clear conscience is needed. "Whoever walks in integrity walks securely, but whoever takes crooked paths will be found out."[1105]

"Who may ascend onto the [c]mountain of the LORD? And who may stand in His holy place? He who has clean hands and a pure heart, who has not lifted his soul to what is false, nor has sworn [oaths] deceitfully. He shall receive a blessing from the LORD."[1106]

God is the source of all things, and if we desire to receive all that we desire from Him, we must live a holy and honest life because no one can experience God without being honest[1107]

Finally, living an honest and righteous life is a catalyst to a world of promotion, but dishonesty brings shame.

"Righteousness [moral and spiritual integrity and virtuous character] exalts a nation, But sin is a disgrace to any people."[1108]

Dedication: Dedication is an acid test that we are desirous of a particular level of success, change, or victory. Those who dedicate themselves to their God-ordained assignment or cause always end up a force to be reckoned with. They leave their name on the sand of time, even when they are gone; their work still speaks for them.

1105   Proverbs10:9
1106   Psalms 24:3-5 AMP
1107   Matthew 5:8
1108   Proverbs 14:24

"Therefore, my dear brothers and sisters, stand firm. Let nothing move you. Always give yourselves fully to the work of the Lord, because you know that your labor in the Lord is not in vain."[1109]

Zechariah committed himself to his God-given assignment, he did not allow his unwanted but present situation to deter him. He did what was expected of him daily, and God who sees in the secret rewarded him in the open.

"And they had no child, because that Elisabeth was barren, and they both were now well stricken in years. And it came to pass, that while he executed the priest's office before God in the order of his course, according to the custom of the priest's office, his lot was to burn incense when he went into the temple of the Lord. And the whole multitude of the people were praying without at the time of incense. But the angel said unto him, Fear not, Zacharias: for thy prayer is heard; and thy wife Elisabeth shall bear thee a son, and thou shalt call his name John."[1110]

If we must experience the reality of the beauty, victories, and testimonies associated with our assignment; we must remain committed to it, the negative or unwanted situation notwithstanding.

Dedication keeps us focused and helps channel our minds to God and not the situation. It could be tough sometimes because the situation is staring us in the face, but it is riskier

---

1109   1 Corinthians 15:58
1110   Luke 1:7-10&13

when we give in to worries rather than surround ourselves with things that could help overcome the situation. Many have slipped into a depression that ended their lives, while some eventually find the strength to come out.

"Finally, brethren, whatsoever things are true, whatsoever things are honest, whatsoever things are just, whatsoever things are pure, whatsoever things are lovely, whatsoever things are of good report; if there be any virtue, and if there be any praise, think on these things. Those things, which ye have both learned, and received, and heard, and seen in me, do: and the God of peace shall be with you."[1111]

I believe Zechariah saw his priestly office and wife as an avenue to remain focused on God. This helped him fight distracting voices that may have constantly reminded him of his failure to have children, and in the end, he laughed. Hannah gave in to an unhappy mood as a distraction due to her childlessness but the moment she decided to change her approach, God visited her with her testimony.

"Hannah said, "Let your maidservant find grace and favor in your sight." So, the woman went on her way and ate, and her face was no longer sad… and the Lord remembered her."[1112]

No matter what we are going through, we must not give room to idleness, it could lead us further down a bitter

---

1111   Philippians 4:8-9
1112   1 Samuel 1:8, 15, 19

path. Being dedicated will not only help us stay strong but become victorious with sounds of joy, testimonies, peace of mind, and achievements.

"Brethren, I count not myself to have apprehended: but this one thing I do, forgetting those things which are behind, and reaching forth unto those things which are before, I press toward the mark for the prize of the high calling of God in Christ Jesus."[1113]

That is the antidote to lack of success, limitation, or unwanted situations. Everyone who broke through in the Bible days, and in our contemporary world today, remained steadfast in their quest to fulfil their goal despite confrontations, hindrances, and rejections. Their dedication kept their mind focused, and they broke through in the long run.

Apostle Paul, and other great men and women in the Bible such as David, Daniel, the three Hebrew boys (Meshach, Shedrach, Abednego), Abraham, Esther, Ruth, and many more all had situations they never bargained for. However, they all had one common denominator - "dedication" and they all came out victorious. Today, we still talk about them, and engage their theories and principles because of their proven results. If they had given up, we would not be talking about or referencing them today. Anyone who cares to defy the negative odds with steadfastness while heeding to the leading of God can also be enlisted as part of those who through diligence and patience obtained the prize.

1113 Philippians 3:13-14

Passion is key in overcoming any obstacle that may arise at anytime in our lives while we pursue purpose because passion is a driver of success. Those who are passionate about real and genuine things never lack testimonies.

Jesus advised His disciples on the need to remain dedicated to their cause the unwanted situation regardless because those things are only distractions, and they cannot stand the test of time because it will end for them in songs of joy.

"Then He said to them, "Nation will rise against nation, and kingdom against kingdom. And there will be great earthquakes in various places, and famines and pestilences; and there will be fearful sights and great signs from heaven. But before all these things, they will lay their hands on you and persecute you, delivering you up to the synagogues and prisons. You will be brought before kings and rulers for My name's sake. But it will turn out for you as an occasion for testimony."[1114]

Focused: One of the easiest ways to fizzle out of one's assignment is to entertain distraction. We live in the world where there are so many distractions that are detrimental to our victories and successes. Distraction could be internal or external. Whichever way it comes, we must be prepared to tackle it. External distractions are those external noises, images, voices, and the things we can feel that constantly take our time and shift our focus from the real purpose.

1114 Luke 21:10-13

While internal distractions are the noises from within. It is interesting and deceptive to feel and think that just staying in a very quiet place connotes a state of serene or quietness. It may seem that way; but sometimes not. We can be in a room alone and still be distracted because our mind is pacing up and down with so many thoughts. The main tool for quietness that will guarantee and enable focus is a focused heart (mind). When silence in your mind is mastered, the ability to focus will improve. You will be able to think more clearly, and enjoy increase in comprehension of things going on around.

"Let not your heart be troubled: ye believe in God, believe also in me."[1115]

When we remain focused, we can discern the right time to make the victory move. Being focused helps us achieve a lot, become a better person, experience better productivity, and do quality work with results.

Apostle Paul said,

"I do all this for the sake of the gospel that I may share in its blessings. Do you not know that in a race all the runners run, but only one gets the prize? Run in such a way as to get the prize. Everyone who competes in the games goes into strict training. They do it to get a crown that will not last, but we do it to get a crown that will last forever. Therefore, I do not run like someone running aimlessly; I do

---

1115   John 14:1

not fight like a boxer beating the air. No, I strike a blow to my body and make it my slave so that after I have preached to others, I myself will not be disqualified for the prize."[1116]

If we must get to the tape like Zechariah got to his own tape of having a son after many years, we must remain focused, trusting in God for the grace and strength to reach our own tape. We all have our different races, and the only way we can finish is to remain focused.

"I have fought the good fight, I have finished the race, and I have remained faithful."[1117]

Kingdom-oriented: Our primary call is the call to service, and that service is to God. Every other form of service is secondary. In the book of Exodus, God emphatically stated that His people should be allowed to go serve Him, and that includes you and me[1118] Everyone who subscribes to genuine kingdom service always ends up a kingdom giant with amazing blessings to show for it because God is no user of men, but a rewarder.

"And ye shall serve the LORD your God, and he shall bless thy bread, and thy water; and I will take sickness away from the midst of thee. There shall nothing cast their young, nor be barren, in thy land: the number of thy days I will fulfil."[1119]

1116   1 Corinthians 9: 23-27
1117   2 Timothy 2:7
1118   Exodus 3:18; 7:16; 8:1; 9:13; 10:3
1119   Exodus 23:25-26 KJV

Service to God guarantees career breakthrough, sound health, long life, preservation and fruitfulness. However, only those who genuinely commit to serving God are entitled to those blessings. God knows all that we need and desire but He has paved a path that will lead us there. That path is the path of service, we are now left with a choice either to do it or not.

"So do not worry, saying, 'What shall we eat?' or 'What shall we drink?' or 'What shall we wear?' For the pagans run after all these things, and your heavenly Father knows that you need them. But seek first his kingdom and his righteousness, and all these things will be given to you as well."[1120]

A genuine and acceptable service in truth and reverence to God is the free ticket to a life of additions, but the moment the decisions not to serve Him is made, God moves to the next available person. He will never force anyone because we are creations of choice.

"Thus saith the Lord, stand ye in the ways, and see, and ask for the old paths, where is the good way, and walk therein, and ye shall find rest for your souls. But they said, we will not walk therein."[1121]

Like David, Apostle Paul, and other disciples of God, let us remain committed to KINGDOM SERVICE.

1120   Matthew 6:31-33
1121   Jeremiah 6:16 KJV

"I was glad when they said unto me, let us go into the house of the Lord."[1122]

"...I would rather be a doorkeeper in the house of my God than dwell in the tents of the wicked."[1123]

A wise man once said, "Kingdom service which anchors on Matthew 6:33 is the greatest jackpot of life."

Prayer: Lord, grant me the grace to be steadfast, and let the zeal of Your house consume me.

1122   Psalms 122:1
1123   Psalms 84:10

About Author

Abiodun Adetayo Olajire is a distinguished figure in both spiritual and clinical realms. As an ordained clergy at Winners Chapel International Maryland, he brings a deep commitment to pastoral care and spiritual guidance, reflecting his dedication to nurturing faith and supporting his community. His role as a board-certified clinical chaplain and pastoral counselor underscores his expertise in providing compassionate, evidence-based support to individuals navigating personal and spiritual challenges.

In addition to his pastoral work, Olajire is a skilled counselor, integrating his theological insights with psychological principles to offer holistic care. His College of Pastoral Supervision and Psychotherapy (CPSP) membership highlights his professional commitment to advanced training and ethical practice in pastoral psychotherapy.

Currently, Olajire is pursuing an advanced degree in Counseling. This study highlights his commitment to expanding his knowledge and enhancing his contributions to both spiritual and clinical areas. His work exemplifies a meaningful integration of faith and professional expertise, making him a significant asset to his community and the field of pastoral care.

Glossary

Names / Meaning / Origin

Abraham / Father of many (Nations) / Hebrew

Boaz / Swiftness/Strength / Hebrew

Cain / Acquired/Spearer Hebrew

Daniel / God is judge / Hebrew

Elijah / Jehovah is my God / Hebrew

Esther / Star / Hebrew

Festus / Joyous/Festive / Latin

Gehazi / Valley of Vision / Hebrew/Bible

Hannah / Favor/Grace / Hebrew

Isaac / One who laughs (Rejoices). / Hebrew

Joseph / He (Jehovah) will add / Hebrew

Knowledge / Knowing through observation or experience./ Greek (Gnosis)

Luke / Light (Bringer of Light / Latin/Greek

Mary / Beloved (derived from Miriam). / Hebrew

Martha / Lady/Mistress / Greek/Aramaic

Nehemiah / God comforts / Hebrew

Obededom / Servant / Hebrew

Paul / Small/Humble / Roman

Queen / Royalty, Symbol of authority / English

Ruth / Friend/Companion / Hebrew

Solomon / Peace / Hebrew

Thomas / Twin / Hebrew

Uzziah / God is my strength / Hebrew

Vashti / Goodness/Lovely Persian

Word / Expression / God/Bible

Xerxes / Hero among Heroes/king Persian/Greek

Yeshua / Deliverer/Savior/Rescue Hebrew

Zechariah God remembers / Hebrew

Made in the USA
Middletown, DE
11 September 2024